DOUBLEDAY
CELEBRATES
100 YEARS OF
EXCELLENCE

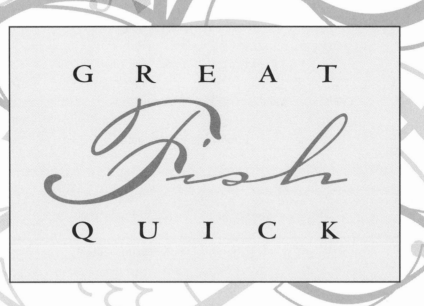

GREAT *Fish* QUICK

LESLIE REVSIN

PHOTOGRAPHS BY RICHARD BOWDITCH

DOUBLEDAY New York London Toronto Sydney Auckland

PUBLISHED BY DOUBLEDAY
a division of Bantam Doubleday Dell Publishing Group, Inc.
1540 Broadway, New York, New York 10036

DOUBLEDAY and the portrayal of an anchor with a dolphin are
trademarks of Doubleday, a division of Bantam Doubleday Dell
Publishing Group, Inc.

Book design by Bonni Leon-Berman

Library of Congress Cataloging-in-Publication Data
Revsin, Leslie.
Great fish, quick / Leslie Revsin.—1st ed.
p.   cm.
Includes index.
1. Cookery (Seafood)   2. Seafood.   I. Title.
TX747.R55   1997
641.6′92—dc21   97-3067
CIP

ISBN 0-385-48538-7

FOR RACH AND VEAL,
the lights of my life

Acknowledgments

There are so many ways one can be blessed—with encouragement, suggestions, inspiration, direction, even criticism. First, my heartfelt thanks to both Susan Ginsburg, my agent, and Judy Kern, my editor. And to my loving family, friends, and generous colleagues, who helped me keep what really matters in sight, at least some of the time!

They are Carola Mann, Carol Durst, Ruth Rosenblum, Marie Zazzi, Cecile Lamalle, Doris Tobias, Lori Longbotham, MaryAnn Zimmerman, Abby Kirsch, Pat Baird, Susan and Steve Eisenberg, Kate Johnson, Paul Fiala, Richard Troy, Joseph Piazza, Donna Cunningham, Donna and Adria Roberts, Arno Schmidt, Linda Stone, Dee and Kate Munson, Randy Feldman, Madeleine Kamman, Julia Child, and Barbara Kafka. And to Bob Musich, Laura King, and the members of my cooking class at the Rockrimmon Country Club who were among the first to help me put my "fishy" thoughts into written form.

Particular thanks to Scott Allmendinger and John Fiorillo of *Seafood Business* magazine, Lila Gault and the Alaska Seafood Marketing Institute, Marti Badila of the National Fisheries Institute, Howard Hellmer and the American Egg Board, and Jeanne Bauer. Many thanks also to Julie Schumacher and Tracy Geiger for the Catfish Institute, and, as always, to Wendy Littlefield and Don Feinberg of Vanberg & DeWulf. And thanks to Mrs. Park, who supplied me with excellent fish, and Peter Cruz, who filleted it all so beautifully. And thank you, Michael Feldman, one of my idols, of NPR's "Whaddaya Know?" who kept me agog with his wit and spontaneity every Saturday while I worked in the kitchen.

And in the "there's not enough thanks in the world department," to Sue Davis, my "official-unofficial" recipe tester, who fearlessly gave me her insightful, smart, and irritatingly (sometimes) right-on-the-mark suggestions! And to Ethan, who selflessly ate every recipe that Sue tested, all the while swearing an oath against fish!

And, of course, to my neighbors and friends: Amanda and Pen; Ruth, Marc, and Asher; Liz, David, and Annie; Claudia, Joel, Adam, and Peter; Adrienne and Matt; and Kathy, who, without complaining too much, helped keep my refrigerator from exploding cooked fish fillets far and wide throughout the neighborhood!

Contents

Introduction

When you think about it, cooking fish fillets is very much like cooking boneless chicken breasts, just as quick—sometimes quicker—and just as convenient and versatile. But seafood has something else in its favor that chicken can't deliver: Chicken breasts will always taste like "you know what" even when they're all dressed up (and I love chicken), but "chickens of the sea" taste like buttery salmon; or sweet, lightly rich red snapper; or delicate, milky cod; or juicy, meaty swordfish. And when you add quick-cooking shellfish like shrimp, crab, scallops, clams, mussels, oysters, and lobster, the dinner possibilities are just about endless. Personalities abound—meet as many as you can!

This book is divided into three simple sections—Delicate White Fleshed Fillets, Darker Fleshed Fillets with Richer Flavor, and Sea Animals with Shells and Armor—along with a short final section of recipes using a variety of "sea animals."

Look for the fillet or shellfish you want within its section—it'll be there, with buying and cooking guidelines and all its recipes.

And the recipes themselves have a range of tastes: vibratingly peppery, mild and delicate, pungent and salty, spicy and rich, tangy and tart, mellow and sensual. This is as it should be, for each of these deep-water denizens brings along its particular, and compatible, quality. My pleasure has been getting to know them, often feeling as much a sleuth as a cook, peering into their "fishy souls" to see what food matches might make them come alive!

Many of the recipes can be prepared in thirty minutes or under—you'll find those listed in the Appendix under "Quickest of the Quick." And while you're visiting the Appendix, be sure to check out the other pages: "Recipes for the Grill"—to expand your summer grilling repertoire; "Good for Parties Too"—suggestions for hors d'oeuvre, first courses, and party main dishes; "Do-All Sauces and Accompaniments"—for recipes that can be used all over the marine map; and "Techniques and Tips"—an index of the kitchen hints that are scattered, pell mell, throughout the book. And check out "Clean Air Tricks" for ways of staving off, and clearing, lingering fishy odors. But if you're looking for instruction in scaling, gutting, and filleting, don't look here, there are other good books out there for that.

I

DELICATE
WHITE FLESHED
Fillets

OCEAN BASS

FLAVOR:	Mild, sweet, and flaky
ORIGIN:	Striped Bass is farmed. Black Sea Bass is caught along the eastern Atlantic Coast
GOOD SIGNS:	Flesh is firm yet resilient. Striped Bass is translucent white to beigy pale pink. Sea Bass is a translucent pristine white. Bass has a clean ocean aroma.
BAD SIGNS:	Discolored flesh; soft or mushy muscle tone, separating segments; any hint of ammonia smell
HEALTH TIPS:	A raw 7-ounce fillet is approximately 200 calories with a medium level of both omega-3 fatty acids and protein.

It used to be that wild striped bass was one of the East Coast's great eating fish. I served it frequently in restaurant stints in the mid to late '70s. But then pollution took its toll, and striped bass became essentially unavailable. Its place has been partially filled by a farmed hybrid, a cross between a wild bass and a freshwater one. The cross has given us a mildly sweet, flaky fillet but with a flavor that can have a muddy or murky quality. Its flavor lacks the pure sweet tones of the saltwater parent. However, occasional wild ones have begun to show up again, so be on the lookout!

Black sea bass is a natural wild beauty—sweet, delicate, flaky, and flavorful at the same time. It's a small and handsome fish, no bigger than 3 pounds, covered with black and brightly contrasting white markings with super-sharp spines that can be a painful menace in its whole form. Black sea bass is most familiar in Chinese cuisine, where it's frequently steamed or fried whole. While it certainly has an affinity with Oriental seasonings and techniques, branch out and cook the fillets—sautéed, baked, broiled, grilled, or roasted—with other kinds of seasonings.

Bass with Caper Vinaigrette, Watercress, and Avocado

4 servings

PREP AND COOKING TIME 30 minutes

*P*uree some capers, lemon juice, olive oil, garlic, and mustard in a blender for a minute or so, and you get a smooth dressing with a tangy edge. Broil the bass (or sauté or bake it), put it on a bed of peppery watercress with some dead-ripe, diced, buttery avocado, and drizzle the whole thing with caper vinaigrette—it's very light, and really satisfying, and it's a perfect summer supper. Try it with swordfish, salmon, bluefish, sea trout, halibut, sole fillets, and scallops and lobster too.

> 1 teaspoon Pommery mustard (seeded mustard from France)
> 1 teaspoon Dijon mustard (or 2 teaspoons of Dijon only), preferably French
> 1 tablespoon + 2 teaspoons drained capers, preferably the tiny ones called nonpareil
> 1 tablespoon caper brine
> 1 tablespoon fresh squeezed lemon juice
> $^1/_2$ small garlic clove, roughly chopped
> $^1/_3$ cup + 1 tablespoon olive oil
> Salt and freshly ground black or white pepper to taste
> Four 7-ounce bass fillets, each $^1/_2''$–$^3/_4''$ thick
> 1 bunch watercress, 2″ of stems trimmed, washed and dried
> 1 ripe avocado, preferably Hass variety from California (the ones with pebbly skin), cut in $^1/_2''$ dice, drizzled with 1 teaspoon lemon juice to hold

TO PREPARE: Preheat the broiler, placing the rack at the top rung or 3″ below the heat source.

Place the mustards, 1 tablespoon of the capers, the brine, lemon juice, and garlic into the blender jar and blend them very well. While the machine is running, add the $^1/_3$ cup of olive oil in a steady stream until the vinaigrette thickens slightly, 1 to 2 minutes. Season the vinaigrette with salt and pepper and set it aside. Or cover and refrigerate it for up to 2 weeks, being sure to take it out of the refrigerator to come to room temperature before serving.

Dry the fillets with paper towels, season them with salt and pepper, and rub them all over with the tablespoon of olive oil. Put them in a pan under the broiler, and cook them, skin side down, without turning, until they are lightly browned and just cooked through, about 5 minutes. To check, make a slit in the thickest part of one fillet to see if it's opaque throughout. If necessary, broil for another minute or so.

TO SERVE: Scatter the watercress over the center of 4 dinner plates. Top with a bass fillet and scatter the avocado around the fish. Drizzle everything with the vinaigrette, garnish with the remaining 2 teaspoons of capers, and serve right away.

Here are 3 tips for easily squeezing a small quantity of lemon, lime, or orange juice:

1. Have the fruit at room temperature—it juices more easily when it isn't cold.
2. Right before squeezing, roll the fruit back and forth on the counter, exerting a little pressure with your palm—that breaks up the pulp inside and lets the juice flow more readily.
3. Place a small strainer over a bowl. Cut the fruit in half and insert the tines of a dinner fork into the center of one of the halves. Move the fork back and forth against the pulp while slightly twisting the fruit in your other hand to release the juice into the strainer. No strainer is needed for limes; they don't have seeds.

Broiled Bass with
Garlic-Parsley Bread Crumb Sauce

4 servings

PREP AND
COOKING
TIME
25–30
minutes

*T*his sauce is vibrant with garlic and a touch of vinegar, and we have Spain to thank for it! When first made, it's a lovely pale green liquid, thick with bread crumbs. When you gently warm the sauce for serving, it thickens to a wonderfully soft texture that is as good with sautéed monkfish, red snapper, or halibut fillets (and as a dip for grilled shrimp hors d'oeuvre), as it is with bass. If you have even a tablespoon left, make yourself a soft-scrambled-egg lunch the next day with a little dollop on top. Yum.

> $^1/_4$ cup dry bread crumbs
> 1 tablespoon red wine vinegar
> 1 large garlic clove, roughly chopped
> $^1/_4$ cup packed fresh flat-leaf or curly parsley leaves, rinsed and dried
> 1 tablespoon + 2 teaspoons olive oil
> $^1/_2$ cup chicken broth (cool or room temperature)
> Salt and freshly ground black or white pepper to taste
> Four 7-ounce bass fillets, each $^1/_2''$–$^3/_4''$ thick

TO PREPARE: Preheat the broiler with the rack at the top rung.

Put the bread crumbs in a small mixing bowl, stir in the vinegar, and set aside. Put the garlic and parsley in the bowl of a food processor and process the ingredients until they're fairly well chopped, scraping the bowl down once or twice. Add the vinegared crumbs and process until the parsley is in very small pieces, scraping the bowl down once or twice. Add the tablespoon of olive oil and, with the motor still running, gradually add the chicken broth. The sauce should be a lovely pale green and slightly liquid. If it seems very thick, add a few more drops of chicken broth. Season it with salt and pepper, to taste, and set aside. Or cover and refrigerate it for up to 3 days.

Season the bass fillets with salt and pepper. Rub them with the 2 teaspoons of olive oil, put them in a pan skin-side-down, and set under the broiler. Broil them, without turning, until lightly browned and just cooked through, about 5 minutes. To check, make a slit in the thickest part of one fillet to see if it's opaque throughout. If necessary, broil for another minute or so.

TO SERVE: Put the garlic-parsley bread crumb sauce in a small saucepan over low heat, stirring occasionally. Heat until it's just warm. While it's warming, place the fillets on warm dinner plates. Place a spoonful of thickened sauce next to each fillet and serve right away.

When considering baking or roasting times for cooking fish fillets, take into account the heft of your roasting pan—the heat of the oven does the work in conjunction with the heat transferred by the pan.

If your pan is light, like unlined stainless steel or thin aluminum, it will cook 2 to 5 minutes faster than thicker metals like iron or heavy gauge aluminum. There's one simple reason: A light pan gets hot more quickly than a heavy one. A heavy pan takes a few extra minutes to heat through before it begins transferring its heat to the fillets. And no, this isn't a recommendation for lighter pots and pans—in fact, I prefer heavier ones because they conduct heat more evenly—but it's good to know what to expect from the equipment you have. In fact, I tested these recipes using a thin roasting pan, imagining that to be the most commonly owned.

Sautéed Bass with Lime Sesame Oil

4 servings

PREP AND
COOKING
TIME
30 minutes

*D*ip the bass in frothy egg white, sauté it in a little sesame oil in a non-stick pan, and serve it with more sesame oil mixed with grated lime rind and soy sauce. The bass becomes light and crisp, with a nice lime flavor, and the delicate taste of the fish comes through. If the bass sticks because the pan isn't hot enough, "it looks like hell," as Sue Davis, recipe tester and sister-in-law "par excellence," reports, "but still tastes great." You can substitute snapper, sole, orange roughy, Arctic char, or halibut fillets; and the oil is delicious over plain grilled salmon and tuna steaks.

2 tablespoons + 2 teaspoons sesame oil
1 tablespoon soy sauce
$1^{1}/_{2}$ teaspoons grated lime zest (about 3 limes—no bitter white pith, see
  page 133)
$4^{1}/_{2}$ teaspoons lime juice (from the grated limes)
Salt and freshly ground black or white pepper to taste
Four 7-ounce skinless bass fillets, each $^{1}/_{2}''$–$^{3}/_{4}''$ thick
1 large egg white

TO PREPARE: Put the 2 tablespoons of sesame oil in a small mixing bowl and stir in the soy sauce, grated lime zest, and lime juice. Season it with salt and pepper and set it aside. Or cover and refrigerate it for 4 to 5 days.

    Lay the bass fillets on a cookie sheet or another flat pan and season them with salt and pepper. Put the egg white in a small mixing bowl and beat it with a fork until it's frothy, about 30 seconds. Pour the egg white over the fillets, turning them several times to coat both sides completely.

    Put the 2 teaspoons of sesame oil in a large nonstick sauté pan (or 2 medium) set over medium heat. When the oil is hot, place the fillets, round side down, in the pan. Begin browning the fillets, but don't move them around in the pan until the egg has set, 2 to 4 minutes. Continue sautéing the fillets for 3 or 4 minutes more, adjusting the heat if necessary, until the first side is a beautiful golden brown. Turn them over and cook them over medium heat on the second side for 3 to 5 minutes, or until the fillets are just cooked through. To check, make a small slit in the thickest part of one fillet to see if it's opaque throughout. Cook a minute or so longer if necessary.

TO SERVE: Turn the fillets over onto warm dinner plates so their round side faces up. Give the lime oil a stir, spoon some over each of the fillets, and serve right away.

If I have a choice, I much prefer to buy, cook, and eat my fresh fish fillets the same day. But when that isn't possible, I go by this rule of thumb: Fillets that are good today will still be good tomorrow, if not as perfect. So, if your fillets showed all the good signs when you bought them, you can feel comfortable refrigerating them—out of any supermarket packaging and on a clean plate covered with plastic wrap—for 2 days.

Some fillets naturally hold better than others—salmon and swordfish being 2 excellent examples. If they were fresh when you bought them, they should be fine for 3 days, providing they're kept *very* cold.

Roast Bass with Herb Pepper Rub

4 servings

PREP AND
COOKING
TIME
30 minutes

The herb pepper rub is a thin, spicy coat of fresh black pepper, cumin, and Hungarian paprika, a little sweetened by ground coriander, thyme, and oregano. Roasted in a hot oven, the bass skin gets crisp in the pan, and altogether, it's a satisfyingly earthy contrast with the juicy white meat. You can also use red snapper, Arctic char, salmon, catfish, or trout fillets.

$1/2$ teaspoon freshly ground black pepper, somewhat coarse

1 teaspoon ground cumin

1 teaspoon "sweet" Hungarian paprika or other paprika

1 teaspoon dried thyme

$1/2$ teaspoon dried oregano

1 teaspoon ground coriander seed

Salt to taste

2 teaspoons olive oil

Four 7-ounce striped or black bass fillets, each $1/2$" thick

1 tablespoon very thinly sliced scallion, white and green parts

Lemon wedges

TO PREPARE: Preheat the oven to 450° with the rack at the top.

Mix the ground pepper with the cumin, paprika, thyme, oregano, and coriander in a small bowl. Dry the fillets on paper towels and season them with salt. Sprinkle the herb-pepper mixture evenly over the top of the fillets and rub it in lightly. Drizzle the 2 teaspoons of olive oil over the fillets and pat it in lightly. Lightly salt the herb-pepper rub.

Oil the bottom of a roasting pan large enough to comfortably hold all the bass fillets. Place the fillets in the pan, skin side down, and put the pan in the oven on the top rack. Roast the fillets until they are just cooked through, 8 to 10 minutes. To check, place the end of your metal spatula or paring knife in the thickest part of one fillet and gently push or cut the flesh open slightly to see if the fillet is opaque throughout. The skin will have crisped and you can lift the fillets out with a metal spatula. (Depending on your roasting pan, the skin may stick. Heavy roasting pans stick less than thin ones. Try oiling the pan a little more heavily next time if you like crisp roast skin.)

TO SERVE: Place the fillets on warm dinner plates and sprinkle them with the scallion. Serve right away with lemon wedges on the side.

CATFISH

FLAVOR:	Mild, very sweet, flaky, and juicy
ORIGIN:	Predominantly farmed, Mississippi, Alabama, Louisiana
GOOD SIGNS:	Flesh very firm with somewhat coarse-appearing flakes even when raw; clean, creamy white to pale pink with occasional yellow streaking along top of fillets; no aroma
BAD SIGNS:	Discolored, dingy flesh color; mushy, deteriorating muscle tone, ripped or bruised; muddy flavor—sometimes in bottom feeding wild fish; any musty or strong odor
HEALTH TIPS:	A raw 7-ounce fillet is approximately 230 calories with a low level of omega-3 fatty acids but a good level of protein.

I want to say that catfish is an underrated fish, but that can't be entirely true, since it's the fifth most popular fillet in the country! And not all of those sales are in the South, as you might expect. California is a heavy contender. But regardless of regional preferences, catfish fillets are terrific. They're delicate in flavor with a satisfying chew—a little like grouper, tilefish, or monkfish fillets in that way. And they're exceptionally sweet, juicy, and mild. You can sauté, pan-fry (in cornmeal is the classic way), deep-fat fry, braise, and grill them. I tried grilling them for the first time and loved it: Their firmness makes them a breeze to handle and they take on a wonderful, smoky flavor.

But be warned, if you must buy them prewrapped in the supermarket, they don't take kindly to air deprivation and go bad quickly. Check the "sell-by" date closely and smell the package for *any* hint of ammonia. Or look for them individually-quick-frozen in packages stamped with the catfish "Certified Processors" seal of approval, meaning they've passed their industry's inspections for taste and wholesomeness.

Pan-Fried Catfish in Cornmeal

4 servings

PREP AND
COOKING
TIME
25 minutes +
20–30
minutes'
waiting time

This is one of the most satisfying ways to prepare catfish fillets. Bread them in cornmeal mixed with dried marjoram and cayenne pepper, and pan fry them in bacon fat (I'd do practically anything to be near bacon in any form!) or vegetable oil. The cornmeal brings out the naturally sweet quality of the catfish and a little hot stuff, by way of cayenne and some Tabasco, make the fillets spicier and fun to eat. This method also works well with trout and perch fillets.

Four 6–7-ounce catfish fillets, each $^1/_2''$–$^3/_4''$ thick
Salt and freshly ground black or white pepper to taste
$^1/_4$ teaspoon cayenne
2 teaspoons dried marjoram
Flour for dredging
2 eggs
1 tablespoon water
2 teaspoons vegetable oil
About 1 cup yellow cornmeal
3–4 tablespoons rendered bacon fat, *or* $^1/_4$ cup vegetable oil
Tabasco sauce to taste
Lemon wedges

TO PREPARE: If the fillets are damp, dry them with paper towels. Lay the fillets on a cookie sheet and season both sides with salt and lots of pepper. Mix the cayenne and marjoram together in a little bowl and sprinkle *half* of it over one side of the catfish, pressing the seasoning in with your hand. Turn the catfish over, sprinkle it with the rest of the seasoning, and press it in.

Set up the ingredients for breading. Place the flour on a large plate or platter. Lightly beat the eggs in a shallow bowl with the water and vegetable oil. Place the cornmeal on another large plate or platter. Now you're ready to bread the fillets. Remember to use one hand for wet ingredients and the other hand for dry, otherwise you'll have breaded hands!

Dip all the catfish fillets in the flour and pat off the excess. Then, with one hand, place one fillet in the beaten eggs and turn it over to coat thoroughly. With your wet hand, pick up the fillet and place it in the cornmeal. With your dry hand turn it over several times, pressing the cornmeal onto the fish. Continue until all the fillets are breaded. Place them on a cookie sheet or platter in one layer and refrigerate them, uncovered, for at least 20 minutes or up to an hour. (This helps the breading to adhere.)

Put the bacon fat or vegetable oil into a large, heavy skillet over medium heat. (This is why God invented black iron pans!) When the oil is hot (it will sputter when you drop in a pinch of flour) but not smoking, carefully add the catfish, round side down. Your skillet may not fit all the fillets without crowding, so do this in 2 batches or 2 skillets if necessary.

Adjust the heat so you hear the sound of gentle frying. Cook the fillets for about 5 minutes, until they're lightly golden brown on the first side. Turn them over, reduce the heat to low, and cook the second side for 8 to 10 minutes, or until brown, crusty, and flaky white inside. If you're doing this in 2 batches, place the cooked fillets on a cookie sheet covered with paper towels and keep them warm in a low oven while cooking the rest.

TO SERVE: Shake a few drops of Tabasco over each fillet, or let everyone do their own. Serve the catfish right away, with wedges of lemon.

If you think of catfish as a gross bottom-feeding fish, think that no more. Well, maybe catfish is still not as lovely as Princess Di, but it has stopped its ugly bottom feeding ways! Since most of what we get in the market now has been pond-raised, there's no chance of its having that muddy, murky flavor that sometimes shows up in wild fish. In fact, its become the Eliza Doolittle of the pond scene, having learned to pluck its food, demurely I'm sure, from the top of the water.

Grilled Catfish with
Spicy Mayonnaise

4 servings

PREP AND
COOKING
TIME
25–30
minutes

I have always loved catfish fillets with some sort of spicy, creamy mayonnaise. Generally, that sort of sauce shows up with breaded, fried fillets, which is awfully good. But I'm putting a dollop on grilled catfish, one of my favorite fillets to grill. The spiciness in this sauce doesn't start out with a bang—it sneaks up on you, but it never burns. A little oregano, thyme, and a few capers round out the taste. The mayo would also be good with perch fillets, fish and chips, chilled shrimp, lobster and crab meat, or as a dip for raw vegetables.

$^1/_2$ teaspoon dry mustard

$^1/_2$ teaspoon water

$^1/_4$ cup homemade or storebought mayonnaise

1 teaspoon fresh squeezed lemon juice

$^1/_8$ teaspoon dried oregano

$^1/_8$ teaspoon dried thyme

$^1/_4$ teaspoon cayenne, or to taste

1 teaspoon drained capers, preferably the tiny ones called nonpareil

Salt and freshly ground black or white pepper to taste

Four 7-ounce catfish fillets, each $^3/_4''$–1″ thick

4 teaspoons vegetable oil

TO PREPARE: Start a hot fire in the grill (or preheat the oven broiler). Fifteen minutes before you're going to grill the catfish fillets, put the grill grate 4″ above the glowing coals if it isn't already there. (I also like to brush the top of the grate with vegetable oil just before grilling to help prevent sticking.)

Place the dry mustard in a small mixing bowl, add the water, and stir to make a smooth mixture. Stir in the mayonnaise and the lemon juice until smooth. Stir in the oregano, thyme, cayenne, and capers. Season the mayonnaise with salt and pepper. Cover and set the mayonnaise aside while you grill the fillets, or refrigerate it for up to 2 weeks.

Season the catfish fillets with the salt and pepper and rub them on both sides with the vegetable oil. Place the catfish fillets, round side down, on the preheated rack. Grill them for 5 to 6 minutes, until they're golden brown, and turn them over with a metal spatula. Grill the second side for another 3 or 4 minutes. Depending on the intensity of the heat, the fillets should be done at this point. (If broiling, place them round side up and broil, without turning, until cooked through.) To check, slightly separate the flesh in the center of one fillet with your metal spatula—it should be white and opaque throughout.

TO SERVE: Place the catfish fillets on warm dinner plates. Place a dollop of spicy mayonnaise on top of each, and serve right away.

Grilled Catfish in
Tamari-Coriander Marinade

4 servings

PREP AND
COOKING
TIME
20–25
minutes +
optional
30–45
minutes'
marinating
time

Catfish fillets grill beautifully—they come out all juicy and smoky. And marinated in tamari sauce, lemon juice, and ground coriander seed (whose flavor, something like a soft combination of lemon and sage, really blossoms in the heat of cooking), they're delicious. It's a real quick throw-together kind of thing, with other ingredients that keep in the pantry, like dried orange peel and garlic powder. If you don't have time to marinate the catfish, brush them with a little marinade while grilling, and spoon more over them after they're cooked. The marinade is also wonderful with grilled trout fillets (the skin gets so crisp), salmon, swordfish, shark, tuna, or drizzled over pan-fried soft-shell crabs. Try roasting fish fillets marinated in it too.

2 tablespoons + 1 teaspoon tamari sauce (supermarket Oriental shelf)

2 tablespoons + 1 teaspoon fresh squeezed lemon juice

$1/8$ teaspoon garlic powder

$1^1/4$ teaspoons ground coriander seed

Generous $1/4$ teaspoon dried orange peel (supermarket herb and spice rack)

$4^1/2$ tablespoons olive oil

Salt and freshly ground black or white pepper to taste

Four 7–8-ounce catfish fillets, each $3/4''$–$1''$ thick

TO PREPARE: Start a hot fire in the grill (or preheat the oven broiler).

Mix the tamari sauce, lemon juice, garlic, coriander, and orange peel in a medium-size bowl. Gradually whisk in the olive oil using the coiled snake towel trick if your bowl doesn't have a flat base (see page 153). Use the marinade right away or refrigerate it for up to 3 weeks.

Season the catfish fillets with the salt and pepper and marinate them in about three quarters of the tamari marinade for 30 to 45 minutes, if there is time. Otherwise brush them with the marinade before and during grilling. Fifteen minutes before you're going to grill the catfish fillets, put the grill grate 4″ above the glowing coals if it isn't already there. (I also like to brush the top of the grate with vegetable oil just before grilling to help prevent sticking.)

Place the catfish fillets, round side down, on the preheated rack. Grill them (or broil round side up) for 5 to 6 minutes, until they've browned, and turn them over with a metal spatula. Grill (or broil) the second side for another 3 to 4 minutes. Depending on the intensity of the heat, the fillets should be done at this point. To check, slightly separate the flesh in the center of one fillet with your metal spatula—it should be white and opaque throughout.

TO SERVE: Place the catfish fillets on warm dinner plates, drizzle over more of the tamari-coriander marinade, and serve right away.

Remember one basic thing about cooking fish fillets: Their cooking time is determined by how thick they are at their thickest point. Here are a few guidelines to help, using a generic $3/4''$-thick fillet as the model.

BROILED: 8–9 minutes with the pan close or at the top rung of the broiler

BAKED: at 400°, 10–12 minutes, though it could be a good 5 minutes more, depending on the thickness of the baking pan, whether the fillets are covered in a thick sauce, and the density of the fish itself

GRILLED: 5–8 minutes, depending on the intensity of the fire, proximity to the charcoal or heating element, and the density of the fish itself

SAUTÉED: 8–15 minutes total cooking time if browned first on the top of the stove then finished in a 400° oven. Cooking times vary greatly here, depending on the delicacy or density of the fillets.

Always check the fillets before they're supposed to be done, because you can always cook them longer, but you can never take it back! And remember, one person's 400° oven can be someone else's 425°. Check early!

Sautéed Catfish with
Black Pepper, Basil, and Lemon

4 servings

PREP AND
COOKING
TIME
30 minutes

This is so simple, yet the flavors hit all the bases. I like it when the black pepper is somewhat coarsely ground—the little pieces make your mouth glow. Then the lemon juice refreshes your palate and the fresh basil pulls it all together. It's just right with catfish, but it would also be good with red snapper, perch, sole, halibut, or bass fillets.

Four 7-ounce catfish fillets, each $\frac{1}{2}$″ thick
Salt and freshly ground black pepper (preferably coarsely ground)
2 tablespoons fresh squeezed lemon juice
2 tablespoons vegetable oil
Flour for dredging
4 teaspoons butter
$\frac{1}{4}$ cup somewhat coarsely chopped fresh basil leaves (see page 51)

TO PREPARE: Preheat the oven to 350°.

Dry the catfish fillets on paper towels if they're damp. Season the fillets on both sides with salt and a generous amount of black pepper, lightly pressing the pepper into the fillets. Drizzle them with a tablespoon of the lemon juice, rubbing it in all over, and let the fillets sit for 5 to 10 minutes, uncovered. (The lemon flavor will permeate a little during this time.)

In 1 large or 2 smaller ovenproof skillets, heat the vegetable oil over medium heat. Dredge the catfish fillets in flour and pat off the excess. While you're flouring the fillets, raise the heat under the skillet to high, and add the butter. As soon as the butter has frothed, place the fillets in the skillet, round side down. Sauté them until they're deep golden brown on the first side, 4 to 5 minutes. Turn the fillets over and place the pan in the oven. Cook the fillets until they're opaque all the way through, 4 to 5 minutes more. To check, make a small cut into the thickest part of the fillet. If they're done, remove the skillet from the oven.

TO SERVE: Place the catfish fillets on warm dinner plates. Drizzle them with the remaining tablespoon of lemon juice, sprinkle them with the chopped basil, and serve right away.

COD

(Including Scrod, Hake, Pollack, Haddock, and Cusk)

FLAVOR: Mildly sweet, with large, moist, easily separated flakes

ORIGIN: Atlantic, Pacific, and Alaska

GOOD SIGNS: Flesh is somewhat firm; translucent white flesh; clean ocean aroma

BAD SIGNS: Discolored flesh; mushy, bruised, or ripped, or separating flakes; any strong smell or hint of ammonia

HEALTH TIPS: A raw 7-ounce fillet is approximately 180 calories, low in omega-3 fatty acids but moderately high in protein.

Our earliest settlers practically used to scoop the cod into their boats, rarely having to venture more than a few miles off our eastern shores. However, New England cod fishing went into a steep decline in the 1960s (due to unregulated overfishing, both foreign and American), and it's still struggling to recover. But there are abundant supplies of Pacific cod and scrod (scrod is a small cod) fillets, both fresh and frozen. And they are deliciously sweet, satiny-moist fillets that lend themselves to baking, frying, steaming, broiling, and sautéing. Don't try grilling them directly on a grill, however; they'll just fall into large flakes on the rack. Other less familiar fillets like orange roughy (a New Zealand product that generally arrives frozen), hake, haddock, pollack, and cusk have meat with very similar characteristics and make excellent, and less costly, substitutes.

If you ever have the opportunity to try cod cheeks and tongues, grab it—they're succulent little morsels. Lightly bread or flour them and sauté them golden brown in a little butter and oil. All they need are wedges of lemon. I was introduced to these delicacies one summer while vacationing on a tiny island off the coast of Maine. The resident fisherman pinned a small, torn, hand-scribbled sign to a board in the local store announcing his catch that day. Once it unceremoniously announced "Cod cheeks and tongues," we had to have them.

Baked Cod with Oregano, Romano, and Hot Pepper Flakes over Orzo

4 servings

PREP AND
COOKING
TIME
35–40
minutes

This is one of those serendipitous combinations that works almost effortlessly. Fun too, because these ingredients are often on hand. The flavors bring out the sweet juiciness of the fillets with a little glow from a sprinkle of hot pepper flakes. And the Romano cheese adds richness without actually tasting cheesy. I love cod with the satiny texture of tiny orzo pasta, but it's just fine on its own too. Tell the kids you're having pizza topping on fish tonight. On second thought, just tell them you're having a really good dinner! You can substitute haddock, hake, pollack, cusk, orange roughy, halibut, or sole fillets.

Four 7-ounce cod fillets, each $^3/_4''$–1$''$ thick
$^1/_4$ cup olive oil
$^1/_2$ lemon
Salt and freshly ground black or white pepper to taste
$^1/_2$ teaspoon dried oregano leaves
Scant $^1/_4$ teaspoon hot pepper flakes, or to taste
6 tablespoons freshly grated Romano cheese
1 cup orzo (supermarket pasta section)
1 tablespoon butter, at room temperature

TO PREPARE: Preheat the oven to 400°. Bring a medium-size pot of water to a boil.

Place the fillets round side up, in an ovenproof baking dish large enough to hold them comfortably in one layer. Pour the olive oil over the fillets and rub it all over them. Squeeze the lemon over the fillets and season them with the salt and pepper. Sprinkle the oregano and hot pepper flakes evenly over the top of the fillets. Lastly, sprinkle 2 tablespoons of the grated cheese evenly over the top of the fillets and place them in the oven. The fillets will be cooked through in 20 to 25 minutes. To check, insert the edge of a metal spatula or paring knife into the thickest part of one fillet to separate the flakes gently. If the fillet is milky white throughout, it's done.

While the cod bakes, prepare the orzo. Add a generous amount of salt to the boiling water and when it's boiling furiously again, add the orzo. Boil the pasta for about 8 minutes, or according to package directions. Drain it well, and pour it back into the same pot. Stir in the butter and the remaining 4 tablespoons of grated cheese and season it with salt and pepper. Cover the pot and keep the orzo warm while the fillets finish baking.

TO SERVE: Make a bed of orzo in the center of 4 warm dinner plates. Place a cod fillet on each of the beds. There should be some olive oil-y, milky juices left in the baking pan. Pour this over the fillets, if you like, and serve right away.

Cod Baked with
Tomatoes and Fresh Thyme

4 servings

PREP AND
COOKING
TIME
30–35
minutes

Cod is such a straightforward fish—it's happiest combined with simple, undemanding ingredients. "Outsiders," in the form of sophisticated flavors and textures, fight with the purity of the fish. In this dish, there are 3 elements the cod fillets can cozy up to: tomatoes, olive oil, and fresh thyme. Be sure to inhale the fragrance of the thyme as you strip its leaves from the stems! You can substitute haddock, hake, pollack, cusk, orange roughy, halibut, sole, red snapper, or bass fillets for the cod.

Four 7-ounce cod fillets, each $^3/_4''$–$1''$ thick
Salt and freshly ground black or white pepper to taste
2 tablespoons olive oil
1 bunch fresh thyme, rinsed and patted dry if it looks dusty
1 cup chopped, *well-drained* canned plum tomatoes

TO PREPARE: Preheat the oven to 425°.

Season both sides of the fillets with salt and pepper. Drizzle them with 1 tablespoon of the olive oil and place them, flat side down, in a roasting pan large enough to comfortably hold them. (If you have any thin tail pieces, fold them by tucking the tail under the wider end.) Set the pan aside while you pick the thyme leaves.

Pick up a thyme sprig, press your thumb and first finger around the top of the stem, and pull down the stem to release the leaves. Most of them will come off this way, except for the ones at the top of the stem—pinch those off. Strip and pick enough leaves to measure $^3/_4$ tablespoon. Refrigerate the remaining sprigs for another use. Lightly chop the thyme leaves, cutting through them and any tender stems 2 or 3 times to begin to release their aroma and flavor. Scatter the thyme over the top of the fillets. Spread a little of the chopped tomatoes over them and distribute the rest in the pan. Season the tomatoes with a little salt and pepper and drizzle everything with the remaining tablespoon of olive oil.

Bake the fillets in the oven until they're just cooked through and very juicy, 12 to 16 minutes. (To check, place the end of your metal spatula or a paring knife in the thickest part of one fillet and gently push or cut the flesh open slightly so you can see if the fish is milky-white and opaque throughout; if it is, it's ready.) Remove the fillets to a warm platter while you finish the tomatoes.

Pour all the baking juices and tomatoes into a saucepan (or keep them in the roasting pan) and boil them down over high heat, stirring occasionally and adding any juices that collect on the platter, until the liquid has reduced by about half and tastes rich and good, 3 to 5 minutes. It'll be a somewhat thick, chunky tomato sauce when it's ready. Adjust the seasoning with salt and pepper.

TO SERVE: Place the cod fillets on warm dinner plates, spoon the sauce over them, and serve right away.

NOTE: The fish usually continues to "weep" as it sits, which is very irritating! So, if there's extra liquid on the platter when the sauce is ready, discard it.

When you bake fish fillets and prepare sauce simultaneously in the same baking pan, a lot depends on the size of the pan. If you have a pan that allows at least an inch of space around each fillet, use it—it lets the hot oven evaporate some of the liquid as the fish bakes, and it'll take less time to boil down the sauce at the end.

Sautéed Cod with
White Wine and Capers

4 servings

PREP AND
COOKING
TIME
30 minutes

In the "olden days," there were up-scale restaurants referred to as "Continental," which meant they served a so-called French-Italian cuisine, often doing neither cuisine any great justice. One frequent menu item, Sole Francese, was the original of this recipe. It was a piece of sole dipped in beaten egg and sautéed in butter with white wine—unexciting, certainly, for restaurant fare, but it had an appealing innocence and, apparently, was immensely popular. I always thought it would make a good homey supper. So, here it is, reborn, with cod fillets. It's also good with sole, haddock, hake, pollack, cusk, orange roughy, halibut, bass, or snapper fillets.

1 egg beaten with 2 tablespoons cold water
Four 7-ounce cod fillets, each 1″ thick
Salt and freshly ground black or white pepper to taste
2 teaspoons vegetable oil
Flour for dredging
2 tablespoons butter
2 tablespoons white wine or dry vermouth
1 tablespoon drained capers, preferably the tiny ones called nonpareil

TO PREPARE: Preheat the oven to 350°.

Place the beaten egg in a shallow container large enough to dip 1 cod fillet. Season the cod fillets with the salt and pepper. Place the flour on a plate.

Place a large, ovenproof skillet over low heat and add the vegetable oil. Meanwhile, dredge both sides of each fillet in flour and pat off the excess. Place the floured fillets into the beaten egg, turning them over to coat both sides. Set them on a plate as you finish them.

Turn the heat under the skillet to medium-high and add the butter. When the butter is melted and frothing, slip the fillets into the skillet round side *down*. Sauté the fillets for 4 to 5 minutes, until they're golden on the bottom, lowering the heat if they're browning too quickly. Turn them over with a metal spatula and place the skillet in the oven. Cook the fillets until they're just cooked through, milky-white and opaque throughout, and still very moist, about 10 minutes. To check, slip the edge of your spatula into the thickest part of one fillet and gently separate part of it. Cook a moment or two longer if necessary.

Remove the cooked fillets to a platter (reserve the fish juices in the skillet) and keep them warm while you make the sauce. Pour the white wine into the skillet over high heat. Boil the juices and wine down rapidly, adding any juices that have collected on the platter and scraping up any brown bits that have stuck to the skillet (they have good flavor) until you have about 3 tablespoons. Turn off the heat, stir in the capers, and adjust the seasoning with salt and pepper.

TO SERVE: Place the cod fillets on warm dinner plates, spoon some sauce on top of each, and serve right away.

Roast Cod with
Fresh Green Herbs

4 servings

PREP AND
COOKING
TIME
25–30
minutes

*F*resh herbs are so alive—they're like little musical notes of flavor that "pop" in your mouth. This dish is nothing more than the sweet clean taste of cod with a little melted butter, herbs, and a few bread crumbs. Feel free to add other herbs to the mixture, just be careful to restrain yourself with powerful ones like rosemary, marjoram, and oregano, because they can knock the cod out of the water, so to speak! This preparation is also good with haddock, hake, pollack, cusk, orange roughy, red snapper, sole, and halibut fillets.

Four 7-ounce cod fillets, each ³/₄″–1″ thick
Salt and freshly ground black or white pepper to taste
Vegetable oil for pan
2 tablespoons butter, melted
¹/₄ cup mixed fresh chopped herbs (such as parsley, dill, tarragon, and
    chives), *or* all parsley and dill with ¹/₄ teaspoon dried tarragon
1¹/₂ tablespoons dry bread crumbs

TO PREPARE: Preheat the oven to 450° with the rack at the top.
    Season both sides of the fillets with the salt and pepper. Lightly oil a cookie sheet large enough for all the fillets with at least an inch of space between them. Drizzle the top of the fillets with 1 tablespoon of the melted butter. Sprinkle the herbs evenly over the top of each fillet and press them down lightly to adhere. Sprinkle the bread crumbs evenly over the herbs and drizzle them with the remaining tablespoon of melted butter.
    Bake the fillets, flat side down, until they're just cooked through, 12 to 15 minutes. To check, place the end of your metal spatula or a paring knife in the thickest part of one fillet and push the flesh open slightly to see if it's white and opaque throughout.

TO SERVE: Place the cod fillets on warm dinner plates and serve right away.

GROUPER

FLAVOR: Mild, slightly sweet, and very moist

ORIGIN: Temperate waters of the Mid-Atlantic through the Gulf of Mexico

GOOD SIGNS: Flesh firm and somewhat satiny in texture; translucent white to pale flushed pink; clean, ocean aroma

BAD SIGNS: Discolored flesh, bruising; fillets more than $3/4''$ to $1''$ thick; soft or mushy; any hint of ammonia smell

HEALTH TIPS: A raw 7-ounce fillet is approximately 180 calories with a low level of omega-3 fatty acids but a high level of protein.

A grouper in the wild is not a pretty thing; it has an oversized head with serious Mick Jagger lips. But the fillets are delightful and mildly sweet, with a slight satisfying chewiness to which I'm partial. Young, they're ideal for sautéing, frying, grilling, stir-frying, broiling, roasting, and baking.

The thickness of a grouper fillet matters. If you see fillets that are more than $3/4''$ in thickness, they've been cut from a very large fish, and when cooked, they usually become coarse and tough. They may be fine for a slow-braised fish dinner, but they'll turn on you if you approach them with short-cooking methods! Sautéed, grilled, or quickly broiled, they can become contrary and turn themselves into gnarled, twisted shapes, stubbornly refusing to finish cooking in a rational fashion! Don't unleash the beast in them—buy small fillets!

Grilled Grouper with Ancho Chile Butter

4 servings

PREP AND
COOKING
TIME
35–40
minutes

*A*ncho chiles are dried chiles from Mexico and they're full of deep, lusty, earthy flavor and moderate heat. Before drying, they're a fresh chile known as a poblano; when dried, they're wrinkled and deep brown, almost black. To use them, briefly soak them in hot water until they're pliable, and puree them with other ingredients for a quick sauce or as a flavoring agent. When pureed with butter, cayenne, lemon juice, and fresh cilantro, the butter turns a beautiful rusty orange. Somehow, melted over grilled grouper, the chile butter makes the fish even more luscious! Also good with shark, salmon, swordfish, shrimp, and scallops.

> 1 dried ancho chile, about 3″ × 2″ without the stem
> 1 small bunch fresh cilantro
> Four 7-ounce grouper fillets, each $^1/_2″$ thick
> Salt and freshly ground black pepper to taste
> 4 teaspoons vegetable oil
> $3^1/_2$ tablespoons butter, at room temperature (malleable but not completely soft)
> $^1/_8$ teaspoon cayenne, or to taste
> 1 tablespoon fresh squeezed lemon juice

TO PREPARE: Start a medium-hot fire in the grill (or preheat the oven broiler). Fifteen minutes before you're going to grill the grouper fillets, put the grill grate about 4″ over the hot coals if it isn't already there. (I also like to brush the top of the grate with vegetable oil just before grilling to help prevent sticking.)

If your hands are sensitive to chiles, wear thin surgical-type gloves. Lay the ancho chile on the counter and make a slit along the length of one side to open it up. Dump out the seeds (the seeds contain the most heat and are the greatest irritant) and tear or cut out the stem and discard it. Trim away any pronounced ribs. Put the chile in a bowl and cover it by at least 1″ of very hot water. Let the chile soak until it's pliable, about 15 minutes. (If the chile is very dry, it will be darker and more brittle and may break into pieces when you slit the side. No matter, clean it and soak it in pieces, if necessary.)

Pick enough cilantro leaves from the bunch to measure $^1/_4$ lightly packed cup and wash and dry them on paper towels. Refrigerate the rest for another use.

Dry the grouper fillets with paper towels, season them with salt and pepper, and rub them all over with the vegetable oil. Set them aside.

Remove the ancho chile from the water and pat it dry with paper towels. Discard the soaking water. Cut or rip the chile into rough pieces and put them in the bowl of a food processor with the butter, cayenne, lemon juice, and cilantro leaves. (Or, save the cilantro leaves as a garnish for the cooked fillets.) Pulse the ingredients, scraping the bowl frequently, until the chile is in tiny pieces and the butter has turned a rusty orange. It's a small amount, and you'll have to scrape the bowl with a rubber spatula frequently. Season it with salt and a generous amount of pepper. Remove the butter from the processor bowl and set it aside while you grill the grouper. (Refrigerate the butter if the kitchen is hot, if the butter has gotten very soft, or to hold it up to 2 weeks. It also freezes very well.) The butter should be served somewhat soft, however, so it melts on the fish.

Place the grouper fillets, skin side up, on the preheated grate over the coals (or skin side *down* in the broiler pan). Grill (or broil) them for 6 to 7 minutes, until they've browned, and turn them over with a metal spatula. (If broiling, do not turn them.) Grill the second side for another 3 to 4 minutes. Depending on the intensity of the coals, the grouper fillets should be done at this point. To check, slightly separate the flesh in the center of one fillet with your metal spatula—it should be white and opaque throughout.

TO SERVE: Place the grouper fillets on warm dinner plates, top each with a dollop of slightly soft ancho butter, and serve right away.

Sautéed Grouper with
Spicy Black Beans

4 servings

PREP AND
COOKING
TIME
35–40
minutes

*Y*ears ago I was the chef at a restaurant in New York called 1/5, and fish was a major part of my menu. One of the best dishes was the original of this, but it was more labor and time intensive because we made it with freshly cooked, dried black beans. Here, I've taken away much of the work but kept the spirit. You can sauté, broil, bake, or grill the grouper fillets, or try the recipe with shark, monkfish, or tilefish fillets.

One 19-ounce can black beans
2 teaspoons Dijon mustard, preferably French
1 large garlic clove, finely chopped
2 teaspoons red wine vinegar
3 tablespoons olive oil
$^{1}/_{3}$ cup finely diced red onion
$^{3}/_{4}$–1 teaspoon Tabasco sauce, or to taste
Salt and freshly ground black or white pepper to taste
1 tablespoon vegetable oil
Four 7-ounce grouper fillets, each $^{3}/_{4}$″ thick
Flour for dredging
Slivered scallions, white and green parts, or cilantro leaves

TO PREPARE: Preheat the oven to 400°.

Pour the black beans into a strainer and drain them until most of the liquid is gone but they're still very moist. Set them aside while you prepare their dressing.

Measure the Dijon mustard and garlic into a medium-size mixing bowl and whisk in the vinegar. Gradually whisk in the olive oil to form a thick, creamy liquid. Stir in the onion, black beans, and Tabasco sauce. Season the mixture well with salt and pepper and set it aside at room temperature while you sauté the grouper—or make it up to 4 or 5 days ahead and refrigerate it.

Over medium heat, begin heating the vegetable oil in an ovenproof skillet large enough to comfortably hold all the fillets. Meanwhile, season the fillets with salt and pepper and lightly dredge them in flour, patting off the excess. Turn the heat to high, and when the oil is hot, slip the fillets, round side down, into the skillet. Cook the fillets on one side until they're golden brown, 2 to 3 minutes. Turn them over with a metal spatula and place the skillet in the oven until they're just cooked through, 8 to 10 minutes. To check, place the end of a metal spatula in the thickest part of one fillet where the flesh is beginning to separate into flakes and push it open slightly. If it's done, that piece will move away from the rest of the fillet. Remove the fillets from the oven, turn the oven off, and place them on a platter to keep warm.

Pour the black bean mixture into the same skillet and set over low heat just long enough to heat the beans, 2 to 3 minutes. Add any accumulated juices from the platter and adjust the seasoning if necessary. (If you're serving this with grilled fish, gently heat the beans in a skillet and serve as below.)

TO SERVE: Spoon the black beans onto the center of 4 warm dinner plates to form a bed. Place a grouper fillet on top of each of the bean beds and sprinkle with the slivered scallions or cilantro leaves. Serve right away.

You probably already saw that the black bean mixture in the grouper recipe above is very similar to a bean salad—it officially becomes one as soon as you chill it! To make it less sharp and aggressive (chilling already accomplishes some of that), whisk in another spoonful of olive oil when you make the dressing and decrease the Tabasco a little if you like. Spoon the beans onto beautiful lettuce leaves—like red-leaf or red-tipped romaine— and garnish them with the scallions or cilantro. I can happily eat it as is, but when I want animal protein (which is not a rare occurrence), I love it with smoked chicken, too!

Sautéed Grouper with Tropical Fruit Salsa

4 servings

PREP AND
COOKING
TIME
40 minutes

*T*alk about a good summer dinner! Grill, broil, or sauté the grouper fillets and serve them with this slightly hot—hotter if you want it to be—salsa of mango, papaya, and pineapple. The mango makes me swoon—it's like a great, juicy, satiny peach in texture, and an apricot in intensity of flavor. (I can't remember the last time I had a fresh apricot that wasn't like eating cotton swabs, however.) The papaya is more subtle, not as sweet, with a mysterious quality all its own, and the pineapple keeps the combination grounded. To choose ripe fruit, first press it lightly, it will give like firm flesh. Then, smell—put your face down close and breathe. If it's good, you'll smell its sweet fruity fragrance. Ripe fruit can yield to pressure but still be utterly flavorless. That's where the nose comes in! This salsa is also good with sole but better with halibut fillets—the juiciness of the fruit is a nice match for the satiny flakes of the halibut.

$^{1}/_{2}$–1 pickled or fresh jalapeño pepper, or to taste
2 teaspoons distilled white vinegar
2 teaspoons fresh squeezed lime juice
1$^{1}/_{2}$ tablespoons thinly sliced red onion cut into $^{1}/_{2}$″ lengths
$^{2}/_{3}$ cup finely diced ripe mango
$^{1}/_{3}$ cup finely diced ripe papaya (or all mango)
1$^{1}/_{4}$ cups finely diced ripe pineapple
Salt and freshly ground black or white pepper to taste
2 teaspoons chopped fresh cilantro
1 tablespoon vegetable oil
Four 7-ounce grouper fillets, each $^{3}/_{4}$″ thick
Flour for dredging

TO PREPARE: Preheat the oven to 400°.

Cut off and discard the stem of the jalapeño pepper and cut it in half lengthwise. Scrape out and discard the seeds (unless you want it very hot—the seeds are the hottest part) and chop the pepper fine. (If you're sensitive to chiles, wear disposable surgical gloves.)

Put the vinegar, lime juice, jalapeño, and red onion in a mixing bowl and stir to combine. Add the diced fruit and fold gently with a rubber spatula. Season with a little salt and fresh pepper and fold in the cilantro. If it's a hot summer night, refrigerate the salsa while you cook the fillets, or to keep for up to 3 or 4 days. But be sure to serve it at room temperature.

Put the vegetable oil in an ovenproof skillet large enough to comfortably sauté all the fish, and place it over high heat. Salt and pepper the grouper fillets and lightly dredge them in flour, patting off any excess. When the oil is hot, slip the fillets, round side down, into the pan. Cook the fillets on one side until golden brown, 2 to 3 minutes. Turn them over with a metal spatula and place the skillet in the oven until they're just cooked through, 8 to 10 minutes. To check, place the end of a metal spatula in the thickest part of a fillet, where the flesh is beginning to separate into flakes, and push it open slightly. If it's done, the piece will move away from the rest of the fillet. Remove the fish from the oven.

TO SERVE: Place the grouper on dinner plates, spoon some fruit salsa next to each, and serve right away.

If you've got the time and inclination, serve the salsa *with* the Sautéed Grouper with Spicy Black Beans (see page 30)—the colors and tastes are festive and delicious. Serve the salsa in a bowl on the side and people can spoon on as much as they want.

Peeling and cutting a mango can be maddening if you don't know how they're "built." The important point is that the pit is almost as long as the fruit itself, almost as wide, and it's flat. The flat side of the pit corresponds to the flat side of the fruit. (Mangoes differ somewhat in shape, depending on their country of origin—some are a little more round and voluptuous.)

First, cut off a small slice from each end of the fruit. Stand it up on one end—it will be more steady now—and place your knife at the top, where the skin and flesh meet.

Cut down with a slight sawing motion to the base of the fruit, staying as close to the skin as you can to remove a long section of the peel. Continue doing this all the way around the mango until it's completely peeled.

Now, still standing the mango on end, and with the flatter sides at a 90° angle to you, slice the flesh off one side of the pit from top to bottom. If you're too close to the pit, you'll have difficulty and run into some ornery fibers—move your knife a little farther away from the center. Repeat on the other side of the pit. Now you have 2 oval-shape sections of flesh. There's still more to get: Slice down the *edges* of the pit to get narrow strips of flesh.

If you're a mango fanatic, you won't want to waste what remains on the pit. Pick it up and chew and slurp around it!

Broiled Grouper with
Grain Mustard–Pineapple Vinaigrette

4 servings

PREP AND
COOKING
TIME
25–30
minutes

*G*rouper fillets—with just a light coating of olive oil—turn golden brown under the broiler, and that's worth mentioning because lots of other fillets need help in the "broiler browning" department. Whole-grain mustard has a milder flavor than the Dijon, and when the two are mixed with chopped pineapple, they tame the assertiveness of the fruit, and the whole thing becomes delicately sweet and sour. The vinaigrette works with halibut, sole, and salmon fillets as well.

> Four 7-ounce grouper fillets, each ³/₄″ thick
> Salt and freshly ground black or white pepper to taste
> 2 teaspoons + 1 tablespoon olive oil
> 2 teaspoons whole-grain mustard, preferably French
> ¹/₂ teaspoon Dijon mustard, preferably French
> 1¹/₂ teaspoons cider, rice wine, or white wine vinegar
> 2 tablespoons vegetable oil
> ¹/₃ cup fresh or canned finely chopped pineapple, drained

TO PREPARE: Preheat the broiler, placing the rack at the top rung or 3″ below the heat source.

Season the fish fillets with salt and fresh pepper, rub them with 2 teaspoons of the olive oil, place them, flat side down, on a broiling pan, and set them aside while you make the vinaigrette.

Place the mustards in a small mixing bowl and whisk in the vinegar (using the coiled snake towel trick if your bowl doesn't sit steady, page 153). Gradually add the remaining tablespoon of olive oil and the vegetable oil, whisking the entire time, to make a creamy, smooth emulsion. Stir in the chopped pineapple and season the vinaigrette with salt and pepper. Set the vinaigrette aside or refrigerate it for up to several days, bringing it to room temperature before serving. Place the fillets under the broiler and broil without turning until they're just cooked through, 10 to 12 minutes. To check, place the end of a metal spatula in the thickest part of one fillet where the flesh is already beginning to separate into flakes, and push it open slightly. If it's done, the piece will move away from the rest of the fillet.

TO SERVE: Place the grouper fillets on warm dinner plates, spoon some of the vinaigrette on the side, and serve right away.

HALIBUT

FLAVOR:	Delicate, slightly sweet, with large moist flakes; Pacific fillets firmer and slightly chewier than their Atlantic relatives
ORIGIN:	Frigid waters of the northern Atlantic and Pacific
GOOD SIGNS:	Flesh firm but resilient, slightly silky in feel; translucent or pearlescent snow white in color; clean ocean aroma
BAD SIGNS:	Discolored flesh; soft, mushy, or with apparent separations between flakes; fillets thicker than 1″; any hint of staleness or ammonia
HEALTH TIPS:	A raw 7-ounce fillet is approximately 210 calories with a low level of omega-3 fatty acids and fat, and a high level of protein.

Halibut is the largest flatfish in the sea, occasionally hitting 10 feet in length and 4 feet in width. Imagine a huge one, in all its funny looking, both-eyes-on-the-top-of-its-back glory, flapping and flopping around near the bottom of the ocean! Fishermen call these humongous ones "barn doors"! Brownish green to near black on its top side, and creamy white on the belly, when it makes it to our table it's become a delicate slice of snow white, satiny-moist flakes—a pleasure to eat. Gently braise halibut fillets, sauté them, bake them, broil them, or poach them. They can be grilled too—the taste is lovely—but unless you put them between one of those fish-grill contraptions, you may have a problem with the Atlantic variety sticking and falling apart. Pacific halibut, however, is firmer and it grills beautifully without breaking up. But whatever you do, don't overcook them—halibuts dry out badly. And try to avoid buying fillets cut from one of those "barn doors"—large halibut tend to be coarse. Stick to fillets under 1″ thick.

Halibut Braised in Belgian Ale Broth

*I*f you haven't had any of the great Belgian beers, this is a nice way to introduce yourself. Belgians venerate their beers like great wines. They produce hundreds and hundreds of them, from "gin" beers to "white" beers to "red" beers to monastery beers, and each has an individual personality that can be deep and powerful or filled with extraordinary finesse. And, of course, the Belgians cook with beer—"Cuisine à la Biere" as they call it—and open restaurants with food cooked only with their beers. I've chosen a soft, golden ale for the halibut fillets and sweetened it further with some lightly caramelized onions and carrots. You use relatively little of the bottle, so be sure to drink and share the rest. Try this recipe also with red snapper, tilefish, or other delicate white fleshed fillets.

4 servings

PREP AND
COOKING
TIME
40–45
minutes

2 tablespoons butter

$1^3/_4$ cups thinly sliced onions

$^1/_2$ cup thinly sliced carrot

1 tablespoon + 1 teaspoon chopped fresh flat-leaf or curly parsley

Salt and freshly ground black or white pepper to taste

$^1/_2$ teaspoon ground coriander seed

$^1/_2$ cup Belgian Affigem Ale or another Belgian ale such as Duvel, Chimay, or Scaldis (don't include the head in the measurement)

$1^1/_2$ tablespoons fresh squeezed lemon juice

Four 7-ounce halibut fillets, each $^1/_2''$–$^3/_4''$ thick

TO PREPARE: Preheat the oven to 350°.

In a skillet large enough to hold the halibut fillets comfortably in one layer melt the butter over medium heat. Stir in the onions, carrot, and 1 tablespoon of the parsley, and season lightly with salt and pepper. Cook over low to medium heat, stirring frequently, until the vegetables are light golden and almost tender, 8 to 10 minutes. Stir in the ground coriander and cook for another few seconds. Add the ale and lemon juice and simmer for 5 minutes to allow the vegetable flavors to infuse the ale. (If your skillet isn't large enough for all the veggies and fillets, prepare the recipe to this point and pour the ale broth and veggies into a larger baking dish or roasting pan before proceeding.)

(continued)

Season the fillets with salt and pepper and place them, skin side up, in the broth. Raise the heat to bring the liquid to a simmer, and cover the skillet (if you're using a roasting pan, cover it with foil) and place it in the oven. Bake until the fish is just cooked through, 10 to 15 minutes. To check, peel back the skin from the thickest fillet by lifting it from one end and peeling it toward the other end. It will come off very easily, unless it's undercooked. If the fillets are done, move them, skin side up, to a platter. Peel off and discard all the skin. Taste the broth for seasoning and adjust it with salt and pepper if necessary.

TO SERVE: Place each halibut fillet, round side up, in a warm, shallow, soup plate. Spoon some onions and carrot over each with a small ladle of broth. Sprinkle them with the remaining 1 teaspoon of chopped parsley and serve right away.

Frequently fillet skin gets stuck to the bottom of a broiling or baking pan if the pan hasn't been oiled sufficiently, or at all, or if there's no added liquid. This can make for frustration and/or mangled fillets when you try to remove them, but it's easily remedied.

Do this: Slide a wide metal spatula between the skin and the bottom of the cooked fillet and gingerly maneuver it from side to side as you push it all the way under—it will pass right through if the fillet is completely cooked. Now you can lift the fillet away from the skin, which remains stuck to the pan, and onto a plate. This works because the underside of the fillet, immediately next to the skin, has a thin layer of fat, which softens and partially melts in cooking, enabling you to pass the spatula through easily.

Broiled Halibut with Curried Veggies

I chose carrots, turnips, potatoes, red peppers, and celery for this curry because that's what I had in my vegetable drawer—and they were begging to be used! But you could choose others as well, like mushrooms, zucchini, cabbage, and string beans. Whatever you use, keep in mind that watery vegetables, like mushrooms and zucchini, throw off extra liquid which may need to be concentrated at the end. And if you'd rather, the halibut fillets can be sautéed, roasted, or slow-poached on top of the stove. Other good choices to serve with these veggies are salmon, bass, snapper, tilefish, or sole fillets, and swordfish or shark steaks.

4 servings

PREP AND
COOKING
TIME
40–60
minutes

1½ tablespoons + 2 teaspoons vegetable oil
½ cup thinly sliced onion
1 cup sliced carrots, about ¼″ thick (halved first if large)
¾ cup sliced peeled turnip, about ¼″ thick (quartered first if large)
½ cup peeled, sliced new potatoes, about ¼″ thick (quartered first if large)
½ cup thinly sliced celery, about ¼″ thick
¼ cup diced red bell pepper, about ½″ square
1 teaspoon curry powder
⅓ cup crushed canned plum tomatoes
⅓ cup plain yogurt
Salt and freshly ground black or white pepper to taste
Four 7-ounce halibut fillets, each ¾″–1″ thick; *or* four 8-ounce halibut steaks
1 tablespoon fresh squeezed lemon juice

TO PREPARE: Preheat the broiler with the rack at the top.

Place 1½ tablespoons of the vegetable oil in a large skillet over medium-high heat. When the oil is hot, stir in the onion, carrots, turnip, potatoes, celery, and red pepper. Season with salt and pepper and sauté them, stirring frequently, for 4 or 5 minutes. Reduce the heat to low, stir in the curry powder, and cook the mixture for 15 to 20 seconds to take the rawness off the curry. Stir in the tomatoes and yogurt, reduce the heat to low, cover the skillet, and simmer, stirring occasionally, until the vegetables are tender, about 20 minutes. Turn off the heat and set the skillet aside while you broil the fish. Or cover and refrigerate for up to 3 days.

Rub the fish on both sides with the remaining 2 teaspoons of vegetable oil, season with salt and pepper, and place in a pan under the broiler. Broil (skin side down for fillets) until the fish is lightly browned and just cooked through, 6 to 8 minutes. To check, place the end of your metal spatula or a paring knife in the thickest part of one piece and gently push or cut the flesh open slightly to see if it's white and opaque throughout.

Gently reheat the veggies, adjust the seasoning, and stir in the lemon juice.

TO SERVE: Make a bed of curried veggies on warm dinner plates, top them with the fillets, and serve right away.

Sautéed Halibut with Orange Butter Sauce

4 servings

PREP AND
COOKING
TIME
30–35
minutes

I think of this as a quintessential spring dish. My favorite time to make it is in early April when the first asparagus arrives in New York, and I can serve the halibut fillets, orange butter sauce, and asparagus together. (I refuse to buy imported asparagus during the winter—its flavor isn't very good, and, somehow, it just doesn't feel right. I mean, it's practically light-years until their pointy little heads push up out of the ground in my neck of the woods!) But when the elements come together, the taste of the orange connects it all in a subtle way. And of course you can serve the halibut fillets without asparagus, if you must (fresh spinach would be good)! The fillets would also be good sautéed, poached, or broiled. And you can substitute sole, tilefish, or any delicate white fleshed fillets for the halibut.

1–2 large oranges

$^1/_3$ cup dry white wine or dry vermouth

6 tablespoons *cold* butter, cut into small pieces

Salt and freshly ground white pepper to taste

1 tablespoon butter or vegetable oil

Four 7-ounce halibut fillets, each $^1/_2''$–$^3/_4''$ thick

Flour for dredging

Optional: 1 pound medium or large asparagus, peeled and boiled (see Notes)

Optional: 1 teaspoon fresh thyme leaves, *or* 1 tablespoon snipped fresh chives

TO PREPARE: Preheat the oven to 400°.

Rinse and dry 1 orange. Remove all its peel with a vegetable peeler, making sure not to go into the bitter white part. (If you do get some of the white part, lay the peel flat with the white part facing up and "shave" it off with a knife.) Cut the orange in half and squeeze the juice to get $^1/_2$ cup. Squeeze the other orange if necessary to get the full measure.

Place the orange peel, juice, and white wine in a small, preferably nonaluminum, saucepan over high heat and bring it to a boil. Boil until the *liquid* is reduced to approximately $1^1/_2$ tablespoons. To measure, pull the pan off the heat briefly to let the bubbles subside. If there's too much liquid, return the pan to high heat. Otherwise, put the pan back over high heat and dump in all the cold butter at once, grabbing the pan by the handle and swirling the liquid energetically. Keep the pan over high heat, swirling the entire time—the butter will begin to be absorbed as the liquid comes back to a boil. (If the butter is soft, it will melt before it has a chance to be absorbed, making it greasy instead of lightly creamy.) When the boil is reached, most of the butter will have been absorbed into the liquid to create a lightly thickened sauce. Turn off the heat and swirl the pan a few seconds longer until you can no longer see any pieces of butter.

Season the sauce with salt and white pepper. Strain it, pressing on the rinds, into a small bowl. Cover the bowl and keep it warm. It will hold well for at least an hour, as long as it doesn't get either too cold (it will start to solidify) or too hot (the butter will break out of it). I keep it at the back of my stove where it's somewhat close to the hot oven vent, but not too close. Find your equivalent spot.

Put the tablespoon of butter or vegetable oil into a skillet large enough to hold the fillets comfortably in one layer, and place the skillet over medium heat. Season the fillets with salt and freshly ground white pepper and lightly dredge them in flour, patting off the excess. When the butter has frothed up or the oil is hot, turn the heat to high and slip the fillets, flesh side down, into the skillet. Lightly brown the fillets on one side, 2 to 3 minutes. Turn them over with a spatula and place the skillet in the hot oven until the fish is just cooked through, about 5 minutes. To check, place the end of your metal spatula or paring knife in the thickest part of one fillet and gently push or cut the flesh open slightly to see if it is opaque throughout.

TO SERVE: Place the halibut fillets on warm dinner plates. Drizzle the orange butter sauce over them (see Notes), and garnish with the asparagus spears. Sprinkle everything with herbs if desired, and serve right away.

NOTES: Make sure the asparagus is well drained—paper towels are good—because excess water will dilute the sauce.

Any leftover butter sauce can be refrigerated for about a week, or frozen, and melted over vegetables or other fillets at another time.

Halibut Baked with Rosemary and Preserved Lemon

4 servings

PREP AND
COOKING
TIME
25–30
minutes

One freezing winter day, I shoveled snow from two sidewalks and a driveway, struggled with a flickering overhead kitchen light (I lost), and went shopping for dinner—only to find myself in my car sliding down a steep, icy hill straight into an intersection. When I got home, I wasn't much in the mood for making dinner. Thank heavens for the rosemary plant on the window sill and the preserved lemons in the refrigerator. This is what I made. Substitute sole, snapper, bass, Arctic char, sea trout, salmon fillets, swordfish, shark, or tuna steaks for the halibut.

2 generous teaspoons finely chopped fresh rosemary, *or* 1 teaspoon dried

4 generous teaspoons finely chopped preserved lemon (see Pantry, to Make)

$^1/_2$ teaspoon ground cumin

2 teaspoons + 2 tablespoons olive oil

Four 7-ounce halibut fillets, *or* four 8-ounce steaks, each $^3/_4''$–$1''$ thick

Salt and freshly ground black or white pepper to taste

$^1/_4$ cup dry white vermouth or white wine

$^1/_4$ cup of the *juices* from canned tomatoes (refrigerate the tomatoes for another use, such as Cod Baked with Tomatoes and Fresh Thyme, page 22)

TO PREPARE: Preheat the oven to 375°. Mix the rosemary, lemon, and cumin together in a little bowl and set aside.

Oil a baking pan, large enough to hold the halibut fillets comfortably in one layer, with the 2 teaspoons of olive oil. Place the fillets in the pan and turn them over once to coat both sides lightly with oil. Season the fish with salt and pepper. Spread the rosemary-lemon mixture evenly over the fillets. Drizzle them with the vermouth and the tomato juice. Then drizzle everything with the remaining 2 tablespoons of olive oil.

Place the pan in the hot oven, uncovered (skin side down for fillets), until the fish is just cooked through, 15 to 18 minutes. To check, place the end of your metal spatula or a paring knife in the thickest part of one fillet and gently push or cut open the flesh slightly to see if it's opaque throughout. Remove the pan from the oven and place the fillets on a warm platter.

Put the baking pan directly over medium heat (or pour all the juices into a small saucepan) and boil down the juices a minute or two to concentrate the flavor. Meanwhile, the fillets will have exuded juices onto the platter—add these to the pan. When the juices have a bit of body and are becoming syrupy, they're done. Taste them for seasoning and adjust them if necessary with salt and pepper.

TO SERVE: Place the halibut fillets on warm dinner plates, drizzle them with the pan juices, and serve right away.

Displaying fish on ice in the market is an important part of keeping the catch fresh. However, avoid fish fillets and steaks that you see sitting *directly* on ice, because the ice can "burn" the flesh and puddles of melting ice can waterlog it. The best way for the market to preserve and protect fillets and steaks is to hold them on trays *over* ice in a refrigerated case. Whole fish have skin and scales to protect them, so they can safely lie on ice. And when you get your vulnerable fillets home, place them on a clean plate, cover them with plastic wrap, and keep them in the coldest part (usually the lowest part) of your refrigerator until you're ready to use them.

Halibut Fillets with Roasted Tomato Vinaigrette

4 servings

PREP AND
COOKING
TIME
40 minutes

*A*alibut is one of my favorite fish because of its mild, sweet flavor and big, white, satiny flakes. I like to dip the fillets lightly in bread crumbs before sautéing them, so their tops and bottoms come out pale gold with a pebbly, crunchy texture. The tomatoes are roasted in a very hot oven until their skins blister, which intensifies their flavor and adds a slight smokiness. (It's a basic technique in Mexican cooking.) Then they're pureed, skin and all, with olive oil, a touch of mustard, balsamic vinegar (for roundness), and red wine vinegar (for sharpness) until they turn into a creamy, pumpkin-colored vinaigrette. The vinaigrette is also good with snapper, bass, or sole fillets; tuna or swordfish steaks; and scallops, shrimp, or crab meat. Not to mention roast or grilled vegetables, or spooned over steaming rice or grains!

$1/2$ pound ripe plum tomatoes (about 3 medium)
1 garlic clove, sliced
1 teaspoon Dijon mustard, preferably French
$1^1/2$ teaspoons balsamic vinegar
2 teaspoons red wine vinegar (or $3^1/2$ teaspoons vinegar of one type)
$1/4$ cup olive oil
Salt and freshly ground black or white pepper to taste
3–4 tablespoons dry bread crumbs
Four 7-ounce halibut fillets, each $3/4''$–$1''$ thick
1 tablespoon butter or olive oil
Optional Garnish: $1/2$ teaspoon fresh thyme leaves

TO PREPARE: Preheat the oven to 500° with the rack at the top for the tomatoes. (You can also use a toaster oven for this.)

Rinse and dry the tomatoes and cut them in half lengthwise. Place them, cut side down, on a baking sheet or pan with a couple of inches between them. Roast the tomatoes until the skins are blistered and popping off, and the flesh is soft when pressed, about 15 minutes. If the skins have blackened a little, all the better—it adds a good smoky flavor. Remove the pan from the oven and place the tomatoes on a plate to cool for 5 minutes. Lower the oven temperature to 400°.

Place the tomatoes, blistered skins and all, in the jar of a blender (or processor, but the blender makes it smoother) with the garlic, mustard, balsamic and red wine vinegars, and puree them until the mixture is well amalgamated, about 1 minute. While continuing to puree, gradually add the $1/4$ cup olive oil until the mixture has become creamy and smooth, 2 to 3 minutes. Season the vinaigrette with salt and pepper and set it aside. (It can be refrigerated for a week, but take it out an hour before serving to remove the chill.)

Place the bread crumbs on a plate. Season both sides of the fillets with salt and pepper and lightly press each side into the bread crumbs. Place a large ovenproof skillet (or 2 medium ones) over medium-high heat with the butter or olive oil ($1^1/_2$ teaspoons per pan, if using 2). When the butter has frothed and subsided (or the olive oil is hot), place the fillets in the skillet, round side down, and sauté until they're pale gold, 3 to 4 minutes. Turn them over with a metal spatula and put the skillet in the oven until the fillets are just cooked through, 4 to 6 minutes. To check, place the end of your metal spatula or a paring knife between the flakes of the thickest part of one fillet and gently push the flesh open to see if it is white and opaque throughout; it's ready if it is.

TO SERVE: Place the halibut fillets on warm dinner plates, spoon some of the room-temperature tomato vinaigrette next to each, and sprinkle everything with the thyme, if using it. Serve right away.

MONKFISH

(Also known as anglerfish, bellyfish, and goosefish)

FLAVOR:	Mild and sweet, with a firm, solid texture
ORIGIN:	The Atlantic, European waters, and the western Pacific
GOOD SIGNS:	Flesh very firm and dense, but resilient; creamy white in color; clean aroma
BAD SIGNS:	Discolored flesh, particularly around its edges; soft, mushy, or ripped flesh; any hint of fishiness
HEALTH TIPS:	A raw 7-ounce fillet is approximately 160 calories, with low fat and low protein content.

This fish is practically unimaginably hideous. If you saw Julia (Child) in one of her early TV shows lifting this monstrosity by the tail before the eyes of America, you'll never forget it. To describe it is a poor second. The head and body—seemingly bloated out of all proportion to the rest—are covered with a thin, mottled brown-gray, scaleless membrane (skin!) that slides and slips over the body, with two flapping winglike fins that end in a graceless, long tapering tail (the tail is the only edible part except for the liver, which is, in fact, a delicacy). And if that weren't enough, it has a huge, wide mouth (think a demonic Carol Channing) filled with nasty teeth, which it employs indiscriminately on items such as fish, eels, ducks, lobsters, lobster buoys, bathers' feet, et cetera. For charm, it has several silly antennae that wave around on the top of its head. Yes, a real looker! Hungry yet?

Okay, so here's a case where you truly cannot judge a book by its proverbial cover. The tail meat, when boned (cooking it on the bone keeps it moist, if you ever have the opportunity) and cleaned of outer skin and slippery inner pinkish-gray membrane, is sweet and succulent, pleasingly firm, and very tender. Its texture is almost sea scallop–like, though not its flavor. And you can do almost anything to it and it'll keep its integrity, although it does shrink more in cooking than other fillets. It has tremendous versatility, accommodating itself equally well to delicate and assertive seasonings. Grill it, fry it, stir-fry it, sauté it, braise it, broil it, roast it, stew it, or poach it. A "Goodfella" in the water, it's a good guy in the kitchen.

Sautéed Monkfish Medallions with Lemon-Shrimp (or Lobster) Oil

4 servings

PREP AND
COOKING
TIME
20–25
minutes with
shrimp or
lobster oil on
hand

*T*his is exceptionally quick if you have shrimp or lobster oil on hand (from leftover shells; see Pantry, to Make). The monkfish fillets are cut into thick medallions, then floured and sautéed. When they're all brown, crusty, and tender, drizzle them with a stirred-together-mixture of lemon juice, shrimp or lobster oil, and dried herbs. If you want, scatter some diced fresh tomato and dill on top when they're served. The lemon-shellfish oil is also good spooned over halibut, sole, red snapper, bass, grouper, trout, or Arctic char fillets, or scallops.

3 tablespoons shrimp or lobster oil (see Pantry, to Make), at room temperature

2 tablespoons fresh squeezed lemon juice

$^1/_4$ teaspoon dried *herbes de Provence* or a mixture of dried herbs such as tarragon, oregano, thyme, and rosemary

Salt and freshly ground black or white pepper to taste

2 pounds cleaned and trimmed monkfish fillets

$1^1/_2$–2 tablespoons olive oil

Flour for dredging

Optional: $^1/_2$ cup diced fresh tomato

Optional: 1 teaspoon chopped fresh dill

TO PREPARE: Place the shrimp or lobster oil in a small mixing bowl and whisk, or stir, in the lemon juice just long enough to emulsify the mixture lightly. Add the dried herbs and season the oil with salt and pepper. Set the mixture aside while you sauté the medallions. Or refrigerate it for up to 1 week, being sure to let it come to room temperature before using it. At some point the oil will separate; whisk it again before you serve it, but don't worry if it doesn't reemulsify; it won't adversely affect the flavor.

Make sure the fillets are completely clean of slippery gray membrane (see page 55) and cut them crosswise into 1″-thick medallions. Dry them well on paper towels.

Place a large nonstick skillet* (or use 2 medium ones) over medium heat with 1¹/₂ tablespoons of the olive oil (or split this amount if using 2 pans). While the skillet is heating, season the medallions with salt and pepper and lightly dredge them in flour, patting off the excess. Turn the heat to high, and, as soon as the oil is beginning to smoke, brown the medallions on one side, 2 to 3 minutes. (The medallions will shrink as they brown, enabling you to push the browned ones toward the back of the skillet; or remove them, making room for others. Add a little more olive oil if necessary—keeping in mind they need the oil to crust nicely.) Turn them over, turn the heat to medium, and continue to cook the medallions, uncovered, about 5 more minutes, adjusting the heat as necessary. They're done when they're completely white and opaque throughout. Make a slit in the center of one with a paring knife to check, or use the wooden skewer trick—see page 53.

TO SERVE: Divide the medallions among 4 warm dinner plates. Stir the lemon-shellfish oil and spoon it over the medallions. Scatter the diced tomato and chopped dill, if using, over the top and serve right away.

*It's easiest to get good browned surfaces on the medallions in a nonstick pan, but you can also use a regular, preferably heavy, skillet with more olive oil. Just be sure not to crowd the skillet and keep the heat high as you're browning them.

Monkfish Baked with Roasted Red Peppers, Marsala, Black Olives, and Basil

4 servings

PREP AND COOKING TIME
35 minutes + 20 minutes if you roast the pepper yourself

The monkfish fillets are baked in a pan with roasted peppers and Marsala, so their flavors mingle and penetrate deeply. But the ripe olives and fresh basil aren't added until the last minute, so those tastes remain distinct and individual. If you feel organized, roast and peel the red bell pepper today and make the dish tomorrow—or you can always use bottled roasted red peppers. Swordfish, salmon fillets, or sea scallops would be good in this dish too.

1 large red bell pepper, *or* 6 tablespoons finely chopped, bottled roasted red peppers
1 teaspoon vegetable oil
$^1/_3$ cup Marsala
3 tablespoons fresh squeezed lemon juice
Salt and freshly ground black or white pepper to taste
$1^3/_4$ pounds cleaned and trimmed monkfish fillets
2 tablespoons olive oil
$^1/_4$ cup chopped fresh basil
6–8 pitted Mediterranean-style ripe olives (such as niçoise, kalamata, or Gaeta), cut into strips

TO PREPARE: Preheat the broiler, putting the rack at the top. (Skip this step if you're using bottled roasted peppers.) Cut the pepper in half lengthwise and remove and discard the seeds and ribs. Place the pepper halves on the counter, cut side down. Flatten each half by pressing down with your palm. Rub a broiler pan with the vegetable oil and place the peppers, skin side up, on the pan. Broil them until the skins blister and blacken, about 8 minutes. Transfer the peppers to a paper bag or a covered bowl to steam until cool enough to handle. Turn the oven to 350°.

When the peppers are cool, peel away the blackened skin and discard it. Chop them finely by hand or in a food processor. Mix the Marsala, lemon juice, and chopped peppers in a small bowl with a little salt and pepper, and set it aside.

Make sure the fillets are trimmed of all membrane and fat. Cut them crosswise into 2″-thick sections and dry them well on paper towels.

Heat the olive oil in a large ovenproof skillet over high heat. (Or use an ovenproof nonstick pan with just a few drops of oil.) Season the cut fillets with salt and pepper, and, when the oil is hot, add them to the skillet without crowding. Turn them around on all sides to brown slightly. Do this in several batches, putting the finished fillets on a plate while you complete the rest. When all the fillets are done, turn off the heat, place them back in the skillet, and pour the Marsala mixture over them. Return the heat to high and bring the liquid to a good simmer. Then place the skillet in the oven until the fillets are just cooked through, about 8 minutes. To check, make a small slice in the center of one piece to see if it's white and opaque throughout, or use the wooden skewer trick (see page 53).

When the fillets are cooked, transfer them to a warm platter. Place the skillet over high heat to boil down and concentrate the sauce, adding any juices that collect on the platter. Let it boil, stirring occasionally, until it's no longer watery and has thickened nicely, 3 to 6 minutes. Turn off the heat, adjust the seasoning, and return the fillets to the pan (discarding any remaining platter juices). Stir gently to coat the fillets and add *half* the basil and all of the olives.

TO SERVE: Place the monkfish fillets and sauce on warm dinner plates, sprinkle each serving with some of the remaining basil, and serve right away.

This is the best way to wash and cut large leafy herbs such as basil, sage, and mint: Pick the leaves from the stems and put them in a *large* bowl of cold water. With your hand, push them gently up and down. Repeat this several times. Then let the leaves remain undisturbed for a minute or two, long enough to let any sand or grit settle on the bottom. Remove the leaves by scooping them out without stirring up any sediment on the bottom of the bowl. Dry the leaves in a salad spinner or roll them in paper towels.

Stack 3 or 4 leaves on top of one another. Slice through them the long way with a sharp knife—and yes, it does have to be sharp—into thin strips. Turn the strips 180° and cut across the strips to make tiny pieces. Repeat with the remaining leaves. By cutting the herbs this way, you don't mash them into a blackening mess. Most important, they retain their full potency.

Monkfish Grilled with
Rosemary-Garlic-Lemon Oil

4 servings
with 2 extra
recipes
rosemary oil

PREP AND
COOKING
TIME
25–30
minutes +
optional 30
minutes'
marinating
time

*M*onkfish grills very well—its natural slight chewiness is enhanced by grilling, and its little edges get so crisp! This is one of the great all-purpose marinades. I keep a jar of it in my refrigerator at all times. It's full of rosemary and garlic flavor, so even if you don't have time for marinating, a spoonful over the monkfish after grilling will do the job. It's also good with cod, grouper, trout, swordfish, tuna, shark, and salmon fillets, as well as lobster and soft-shell crabs. And if that's not enough, use it with pasta, chicken, veal, and to marinate goat cheese! This recipe makes enough oil for 3 grilled monkfish recipes.

2 tablespoons lightly packed fresh rosemary *leaves* (see Note)

1 large garlic clove, unpeeled

1 1/2 teaspoons grated lemon zest (no white pith, see page 133)

1 cup olive oil

Salt and freshly ground black or white pepper to taste

1 3/4 pounds cleaned and trimmed monkfish fillets

TO PREPARE: Start a medium-hot fire (or preheat the oven broiler). Fifteen minutes before you're going to grill the monkfish fillets, put the grill grate about 4″ from the glowing coals if it isn't already there. (I also like to brush the top of the grate with vegetable oil just before grilling to help prevent sticking.)

Roughly chop the rosemary and put it in the food processor. (This helps the processor chop it better.) Crush the garlic clove with the side of a large knife, peel it, and put it in the food processor with the lemon zest. Process the ingredients to break them up and combine their flavors, about 1 minute. Add the olive oil and process everything until the solids are chopped into tiny pieces, about 2 minutes. Season the oil with salt and pepper. The oil can be used immediately, or covered and refrigerated for several weeks. (The flavor continues to develop—if at any point it becomes strong for you, add a little more olive oil.)

Make sure the monkfish fillets are trimmed of all membrane and fat (see page 000). Cut the fillets into 2″-thick cross-sections and dry them well with paper towels. Put them in a bowl, season them with salt and pepper, and pour 1/4 cup of the rosemary-garlic oil over them, stirring to coat them thoroughly. Marinate them, covered, for 30 to 60 minutes if possible at room temperature (unless the kitchen is very hot), or grill them right away.

Place the cut fillets on the preheated grill rack. Grill them until the first side is brown, about 5 minutes. Turn them over and grill them until they're cooked through and still very moist, about 5 minutes more. To check, make a small slice in the center of one piece to see if it's white and opaque all the way through, or use the wooden skewer trick (see page 53).

TO SERVE: Place the cut fillets on warm dinner plates and drizzle them with more room-temperature rosemary-garlic-lemon oil (refrigerating the rest for another use). Serve right away.

NOTE: If the rosemary *stems* are very young, they're tender and pliable—don't worry about some of them getting into the mix. They'll become chopped up fine as you process everything, and they are perfectly edible. More mature stems, however, are woody and indigestible.

Another way to check for doneness in dense types of fillets, like monkfish and swordfish, is to use a common wooden skewer. When you think the fillets are almost cooked, insert the skewer slowly, going all the way through the thickest part of one fillet. If the skewer hits a raw spot, you'll feel some resistance. When the fillet is cooked through, the skewer will penetrate smoothly and evenly. (This method won't help if the fillets are already over-cooked.) I don't suggest a metal skewer because the slickness of the metal glides through more easily and isn't as reliable.

Keep trying until you get the hang of it, it's no big deal if the fillets have a few tiny holes! And get in the habit of checking before you know they're done, so you can begin to feel the difference between the two stages.

Sautéed Monkfish Medallions with Roasted Garlic and Sherry Vinegar

4 servings

PREP AND
COOKING
TIME
35–40
minutes if
you have
roasted garlic
on hand

Roasted garlic lovers can revel in this dish. The sauce is packed with roughly chopped—to give you something more to get your teeth into—roasted cloves of garlic mixed with slightly sweet, aged Spanish sherry vinegar and olive oil. The nutty, earthy intensity of the sauce complements the meaty pieces of monkfish, but it's kept from being too sweet by the vinegar edge. It's also good with bass fillets, swordfish or tuna steaks, and shrimp.

1½ tablespoons roughly chopped roasted garlic (see Pantry, to Make)

1½ tablespoons aged sherry vinegar, *or* ½ tablespoon balsamic vinegar cut with 1 tablespoon cider vinegar or white or red wine vinegar

6–6½ tablespoons olive oil

Salt and freshly ground black or white pepper to taste

2 pounds cleaned and trimmed monkfish fillets

Flour for dredging

2 teaspoons chopped fresh flat-leaf or curly parsley

TO PREPARE: Place the roasted garlic in a small mixing bowl and stir in the sherry vinegar (use the coiled snake towel trick, see page 153, if your bowl doesn't sit steady). Gradually whisk in 4½ tablespoons of the olive oil, and season the mixture well with salt and pepper. Set it aside at room temperature or refrigerate it for up to 2 weeks, but be sure to serve it at room temperature.

Make sure the fillets are completely clean of slippery gray membrane (see page 55) and cut them crosswise into 1″-thick medallions. Dry them well on paper towels.

Heat 1½ tablespoons of the olive oil in a large nonstick skillet* (or use 2 medium ones, dividing the oil between them) over medium heat. While the skillet is heating, season the medallions with salt and pepper and dredge them lightly in flour, patting off the excess. Turn the heat to high, and as soon as the oil is beginning to smoke, brown the medallions on one side, 2 to 3 minutes. (The medallions will

---

*It's easiest to get good browned surfaces on the medallions in a nonstick pan, but you can also use a regular, preferably heavy, skillet with more olive oil. Just be sure not to crowd the skillet and keep the heat high as you're browning the fish.

shrink as they brown, enabling you to push the browned ones toward the back of the skillet, or remove them, making room for others. Adding a little more olive oil if necessary—keeping in mind they need the oil to crust nicely.) Turn them over, turn the heat to medium, and continue to cook the medallions, uncovered, adjusting the heat as necessary, about 5 minutes more. They're done when they're completely white and opaque throughout. Make a slit in the center of one with a paring knife to check, or use the wooden skewer trick (see page 53).

TO SERVE: Stir the chopped parsley into the roasted garlic sauce and adjust the seasoning if necessary. Place the medallions on warm dinner plates and spoon some of the sauce over each. Serve right away.

I've never seen monkfish tails that still had their tough, dark outer gray skin, but I have seen them poorly trimmed. Being poorly trimmed means that some of the membrane that lies under the skin hasn't been completely removed. It can be easily cut away.

If you see any ugly grayish membrane covering the fillets, slip your knife (a narrow one, 4″ to 5″ long would be ideal, but any sharp knife will do) under it where it's attached to the fillet and cut horizontally with a slight sawing motion to remove it.

You may also see some dark fatty sections—trim them off in the same fashion. What you now have is a length of clean white meat that's ready to cut into pieces. (There will still be a dark red, narrow fat strip that runs the length of the tail—you can trim it out if you want, but it isn't crucial.)

Grilled Monkfish with
Walnut–Herb–Olive Oil Sauce

4 servings

PREP AND
COOKING
TIME
30 minutes

*T*his is a deliciously thick sauce of walnuts that have been ground with fresh tarragon, sage, garlic, and olive oil, reminiscent of a Turkish sauce called *tarator*. It's a wonderful accompaniment for monkfish fillets snatched from the grill and pulsating with smoky taste! It's also good with bass, snapper, tuna, swordfish, shark, and trout fillets.

6 tablespoons walnut pieces

1 small garlic clove, roughly chopped

2 teaspoons roughly chopped fresh sage leaves

2 teaspoons fresh tarragon leaves

2$^1/_2$ teaspoons fresh squeezed lemon juice

$^1/_4$ cup + 4 teaspoons olive oil

Salt and freshly ground black or white pepper to taste

1$^3/_4$ pounds cleaned and trimmed monkfish tails

TO PREPARE: Start a hot fire (or preheat the oven broiler). Fifteen minutes before you're going to grill the monkfish tails, put the grill grate about 4″ above the glowing coals if it isn't already there. (I also like to brush the top of the grate with vegetable oil just before grilling to help prevent sticking.)

Place the walnuts, garlic, sage, and tarragon leaves in the bowl of a food processor. Process the ingredients, scraping the bowl down occasionally, while adding the lemon juice and then gradually adding the $^1/_4$ cup of olive oil, until you have a thick, slightly creamy sauce that softly mounds in a spoon. Season the sauce with salt and pepper and set it aside. It can be covered and refrigerated for up to 2 weeks.

Make sure the monkfish tails are trimmed of all membranes and fat (see page 55). Cut the tails crosswise into 2″ sections and dry them well with paper towels. Rub them with the 4 teaspoons of olive oil and season them with salt and pepper. Place the monkfish pieces on the preheated grill rack. Grill them until the first side is brown, about 5 minutes. Turn the pieces over and grill them for an additional 5 minutes, until they're cooked through but still very moist. To check, make a small slice in the center of one piece to see if it's white and opaque all the way through, or use the wooden skewer trick (see page 53).

TO SERVE: Place a large dollop of walnut sauce on each of 4 warm dinner plates, spreading the sauce around slightly with the back of a spoon. Place the grilled monkfish pieces on top of the sauce and serve right away.

OCEAN PERCH

(Pacific perch is frequently called rockfish.)

FLAVOR:	Mild, sweet, and tender
ORIGIN:	Atlantic and Pacific oceans, Alaskan waters
GOOD SIGNS:	Flesh slightly firm and creamy, white to beigy-pink in color; skin bright orange-red or brown-black; clean ocean aroma
BAD SIGNS:	Discolored, yellowing flesh; soft, mushy, or separating flesh segments; any hint of ammonia
HEALTH TIPS:	A raw 7-ounce fillet is approximately 200 calories, low in omega-3 fatty acids but with good protein content.

To me as a kid, perch was something that arrived rock solid in a frozen rectangular box. I have vivid memories of my mother thawing them out on a kitchen counter (now, of course, you would only thaw them inside the refrigerator) and watching her pry apart those little fillets when the ice block began to give way. I can still hear the soft crunching of the deteriorating ice crystals as she pried. Those fillets looked like a weird kind of family, all nestled together in a wormy little way! When I first saw fresh perch fillets in a supermarket on some business trip to the Midwest, I was shocked. I didn't recognize them at all; they looked like exotic, vividly red-skinned something-elses. I honestly couldn't imagine, even then, that perch existed outside those boxes. And in my deepest food memories, they only came to life on a Formica counter in my mother's hands.

In reality, perch fillets *are* sweet little things—flaky, tender, and unsophisticated. They're good for frying, pan-frying, baking, sautéing, broiling, grilling, and steaming. Pacific perch are sometimes referred to as red snappers, but not only are they *not* the red snapper from the Gulf of Mexico, they can't hold a candle to the true red snapper's fine bearing and generosity of taste! And be warned—prewrapped supermarket perch fillets turn bad fast! Watch that "sell-by" date and inspect the fillets closely.

Perch "Adrienne," Baked with Garlic, Lemon, and Herbs

4 servings

PREP AND
COOKING
TIME
25–30
minutes

Adrienne is my across-the-street neighbor in the pale blue house. She tells me, as I hand her plates of fish recipe tests, that she cooks all fish one tried-and-true way: with garlic and lemon juice, period. (But hastens to add, she's delighted to try anything new.) I decided to do what she does, but add a little . . . well, something (I couldn't help it!). And when she gave me her reaction to the recipe I named for her, she said, "It was okay, but it needed more garlic." So, be true to Adrienne and add as much as you like! Substitute sole, halibut, catfish, shark, or salmon fillets, and tuna or swordfish steaks, or anything!

Four 7-ounce fresh or frozen perch fillets, each ½″–¾″ thick; *or* eight
  small ones (if frozen, defrost in the refrigerator overnight)
Salt and freshly ground black or white pepper to taste
1 tablespoon garlic, very finely chopped, almost pureed (see page 59)
3 tablespoons fresh squeezed lemon juice
2½ tablespoons olive oil
1 teaspoon mixed dried oregano, basil, and savory or crumbled sage
  leaves
Optional: 2 tablespoons thinly sliced scallion, white and green parts

TO PREPARE: Preheat the oven to 400°.

Season the fillets with salt and pepper and place them in a baking pan large enough to hold them comfortably in one layer.

In a small mixing bowl, mix the garlic, lemon juice, olive oil, and dried herbs and season the mixture with salt and pepper. Spoon the mixture evenly over the top of the fillets, lightly rubbing it into the flesh with the back of a spoon.

Place the fillets in the oven, skin side down, and bake them until they're cooked through but still juicy, 12 to 15 minutes. To check, gently open the flesh at a natural separation in the thickest part of one fillet to see if it's opaque throughout. Bake for a minute or two longer if necessary.

TO SERVE: Place the perch fillets on warm dinner plates, pour the pan juices over them, and sprinkle them with the scallions, if desired. Serve them right away.

When I rub fillets with garlic, I like the garlic so finely chopped it's almost pureed. Sometimes, it's too small an amount for the food processor—which does a great job of finely chopping garlic, by the way, unlike the job it does on shallots or onions. (For the shallot story, see page 161.) Here's a way to chop fine without machinery.

First, slice the garlic somewhat thin. Then, with a large knife, begin chopping it into small pieces. When it's been fairly well chopped, hold your knife so that the edge of the blade makes a small angle with the counter—almost flat. Pull the blade toward you, retaining the same angle and pressing down, to smear out the garlic. Keep doing this until the garlic has been smeared almost to a puree. Sprinkling the garlic with salt, particularly a coarse salt like kosher salt, makes the job even easier and faster. But if you do this, remember that you've already added salt, before you season the dish further.

Pan-Fried Perch with
Celery Salt and Thyme

4 servings

PREP AND
COOKING
TIME
25 minutes +
15 minutes'
waiting time

Tastes that mean something to you never die, they just attach themselves to new recipes! When I was a kid in Chicago, our corner hot dog vendor served hot dogs with thin wedges of fresh tomato shoved into the bun, and sprinkled it all with a good dose of celery salt. I never got over those dogs, or that combination—it may have been my first sophisticated, albeit subtle, taste experience. Together, the slightly bitter, light anise flavor of the celery salt, the dripping juice of the ripe tomato, the sweet meat of the hot dog, and the snap of its casing excited me. Try celery salt and thyme with catfish and sole fillets, too.

1 pound fresh or frozen ocean perch fillets (if frozen, defrost in the
   refrigerator overnight)
Salt and freshly ground black or white pepper to taste
$^1/_2$ teaspoon dried thyme leaves
1 egg beaten with 1 tablespoon water + a few drops of Tabasco sauce
Flour for dredging
Approximately $^3/_4$ cup dry bread crumbs
$^1/_4$ cup vegetable oil
$^1/_4$ teaspoon celery salt
Lemon wedges

TO PREPARE: Dry the fillets on paper towels. If you're using frozen fillets, separate the block of defrosted fillets first before drying. Season both sides of the fillets with a little salt and pepper. Sprinkle the flesh of the fillets, not the skin, with the thyme, pressing it in to adhere. Set them aside while preparing the breading ingredients.

Pour the beaten egg-Tabasco mixture into a shallow bowl. Place the flour in a shallow bowl or on a plate big enough to hold several fillets. Place the bread crumbs in another shallow bowl or on a plate. Now you're ready to bread the fillets. Remember to use one hand for wet ingredients and the other for dry, otherwise you'll have breaded hands!

Dip all the perch fillets in the flour and pat off the excess. Then, with one hand, place several perch fillets at a time in the beaten egg, turning them over to coat thoroughly. With your *wet* hand, move them over to the bread crumbs. With your *dry* hand, press the crumbs into the fillets, turning them over several times. Continue until all the fillets are breaded. Place them, skin side down, on a cookie sheet or platter in one layer and refrigerate them, uncovered, for at least 15 minutes or up to 1 hour. (This helps the breading to adhere.)

Pour the vegetable oil into a large, preferably heavy skillet set over medium heat. When the oil is hot (it will froth when you drop in a pinch of flour) but not smoking, carefully add the fillets, flesh side down. (The flesh side is the rounder side.) Most likely your skillet won't fit all the fillets without crowding, so do this in 2 batches, keeping the first batch in a 250° oven on a cookie sheet lined with paper towels.

Adjust the heat so you hear the sound of gentle frying. Cook the fillets for 3 to 4 minutes, until they're nicely browned on the first side. Turn them over with a metal spatula, and cook the second side for 3 to 4 minutes, until it's brown and crusty too. To check for doneness, make a small cut through a fillet at its thickest point to see it it's opaque throughout.

TO SERVE: Put all the perch on a warm platter and sprinkle them with the celery salt. Serve right away with wedges of lemon. My husband wants tartar sauce too, and you may as well. The recipe's below.

Tartar Sauce

$^1/_2$ cup homemade or storebought mayonnaise

2 teaspoons Dijon mustard, preferably French

1 tablespoon chopped sour pickles (such as French cornichons) or sweet
   pickles, or hot dog relish (how appropriate!)

1 teaspoon drained capers, slightly chopped

Optional: 1 tablespoon chopped fresh flat-leaf or curly parsley

Salt and freshly ground black or white pepper to taste

Mix the mustard into the mayonnaise until it's smooth, and stir in the remaining ingredients. Season the sauce with salt and pepper if needed. Cover and refrigerate for up to 2 weeks.

Sautéed Perch with
Buttery-Lemon Pecans

4 servings

PREP AND
COOKING
TIME
25–30
minutes

Sauté perch fillets 'til they're golden, and top them with a small spoonful of pecans briefly toasted in the same skillet with butter and lemon juice. The pecans would also be good with halibut, sole, trout, snapper, catfish, or bass fillets.

Four 7- or 8-ounce fresh or frozen ocean perch fillets, each ½″–¾″ thick
    (if frozen, defrost in the refrigerator overnight)
Salt and freshly ground black or white pepper to taste
Flour for dredging
3 tablespoons vegetable oil
¼ cup coarsely chopped pecans
3 tablespoons fresh squeezed lemon juice
2 tablespoons butter, in small pieces
Optional: 1 tablespoon finely cut fresh chives

TO PREPARE: Dry the fillets on paper towels and season them with salt and pepper. Place the flour on a large plate or platter. Place a very large skillet (or 2 medium) over low heat with the vegetable oil. (If using 2 pans, divide the oil between them.) While the oil is heating, dredge the fillets in the flour, patting off the excess. Turn the heat to medium-high and, when the oil is hot, place the fillets in the skillet, skin side up, without crowding the pan.

Sauté the fillets on the first side until they're golden brown, about 5 minutes. Turn, reduce the heat to medium, and continue cooking the fillets for 3 to 4 minutes more, until they're completely cooked through but still juicy. (The edges will curl once they've been turned over; let 'em!) To check, make a small slit in the thickest part of one fillet to see if it's opaque throughout. Cook them a minute or so longer if necessary. Remove the skillet from the heat, place the fillets on a warm platter or on dinner plates, and add the pecans to the same skillet. (Use 1 skillet for the pecans if you've sautéed the fillets in 2.)

Toast the pecans over low heat, stirring continuously until they're very lightly browned and you can smell them toasting, 30 to 60 seconds. Add the lemon juice and the butter and let them sizzle together with the pecans, stirring once or twice. Turn off the heat and season the pecans with salt and pepper.

TO SERVE: Top the perch fillets with the buttery-lemon pecans, sprinkle them with the chives, if desired, and serve right away.

RED SNAPPER

FLAVOR: Mild, flavorful, sweet, and tender, with moist flakes

ORIGIN: Gulf of Mexico

GOOD SIGNS: Flesh slightly firm, creamy pale pink in color, and feels moist but not wet to the touch; skin lustrous red-pink; clean ocean aroma

BAD SIGNS: Discolored, yellowing flesh; soft, mushy, or separating flesh segments; blood blotches, although these don't necessarily mean fillets have gone bad; fillets thicker than $^{3}/_{4}$"; any hint of ammonia

HEALTH TIPS: A raw 7-ounce fillet is approximately 200 calories, low in omega-3 fatty acids but high in protein.

Red snapper is one of the greats. Its delicate flavor is full of character—elegant but sweet, and noble but friendly. It takes to just about any seasoning or accompaniment without losing itself in the process. (Unless maybe you've baked it in a jar of sticky-thick-sweet, fake-smoke barbecue sauce or a can of Spaghetti-O's in tomato-ketchup sauce!) Stick to thinner fillets, no more than $^{3}/_{4}$", because thicker ones are likely to be coarse.

There are a number of snappers, apparently, in addition to Ms. Red herself, worthy of the name. (Pacific ocean perch, sometimes called Pacific red snapper, is not one, however. But when POP, as it's known in the trade, isn't being proferred as something it isn't, it's a mild, sweet-tasting fish in its own right. See Ocean Perch, page 57.) I've tasted and served a snapper called silk, which looks like a red, but has yellow eyes instead of red ones. It's very close in flavor and texture to Ms. Red, but not quite as sweet or as full of nuance, to my taste. I understand that mutton snapper (muttonfish) is another worthy contender, but I've never tasted it. If you see either, snap it up. All snapper fillets can be sautéed, baked, broiled, grilled, pan-fried, poached, steamed, and roasted. They hold fairly well prewrapped in supermarket plastic—inspect them and their "sell-by" date closely.

Red Snapper Baked with
Slivers of Carrot and Fennel

4 servings

PREP AND
COOKING
TIME
35–45
minutes

$\mathcal{S}$napper fillets baked with lightly sautéed carrots and fennel bulb, dried tarragon, a pinch of Chinese five-spice powder—and a tiny amount of light cream that mixes with the natural juices—make a dish that expresses the snappers' elegant *and* homey spirit. I would serve this at any dinner party any time or for a lovely meal with my family. Try it with bass, tilefish, sole, Arctic char, trout, or halibut fillets too.

Four 7-ounce red snapper fillets, each about $^1/_2''$ thick

Salt and freshly ground white pepper to taste

1 generous teaspoon dried tarragon

1 small fennel bulb

2 tablespoons butter

1 cup diagonally sliced, peeled carrots, about $^1/_8''$ thick (see Note)

Scant $^1/_4$ teaspoon Chinese five-spice powder

$^1/_4$ cup white wine or dry vermouth

$^1/_4$ cup light cream (if unavailable, use half heavy cream and half milk)

Optional: 2 tablespoons whole cilantro leaves, washed and dried

TO PREPARE: Preheat the oven to 400°.

Place the fillets, skin side down, in a baking pan large enough to hold them comfortably. Season them with salt and pepper and sprinkle them with the tarragon. Set them aside while you prepare the vegetables.

Cut the stalks off the fennel bulb and discard them. Cut the fennel bulb in half through the root end, and cut out, and discard, the core from each half, following its natural **V** shape. Separate the bulb into layers, and cut enough layers into very thin strips about $1^1/_2''$ long to make 1 cup.

Melt the butter over medium heat in a medium-size skillet and add the carrots and fennel. Season them with salt and pepper and cook them, stirring occasionally, 8 to 10 minutes, until they are firm-tender and a little bit brown. Stir in the five-spice powder and the white wine, letting it boil for about a minute, or until it's half evaporated. Stir in the cream, adjust the vegetables for seasoning, and remove the skillet from the heat. Use the vegetable mixture right away or cover and refrigerate it for up to 2 days, being sure to reheat it gently before proceeding with the recipe.

Distribute the vegetables and juices on top of, and around, the fillets, and place the pan in the oven until the fillets are just cooked through, 15 to 18 minutes. (To check, place the end of your metal spatula or a paring knife in the thickest part of one fillet and gently push or cut the flesh open slightly to see if it's white and opaque throughout.

TO SERVE: Place the snapper fillets and vegetables on warm dinner plates and pour any pan juices over them. Scatter a few cilantro leaves around the plate if you like, and serve right away.

NOTE: Cutting the carrots is fast and easy if you have one of those plastic man-dolines that are so good for slicing. Or cut them in a food processor with the slicing disc and pretend they're cut on the diagonal!

Red Snapper Baked with
Black Olive Paste and Orange

4 servings

PREP AND
COOKING
TIME
30–35
minutes

love the slightly bitter, astringent richness of olives, particularly the black or purple Mediterranean ones. When you turn them into a paste with capers, garlic, a little anchovy, lemon juice, and olive oil, it's known as tapenade. (It was created in Marseille in the nineteenth century and originally served mixed with cooked tuna as part of an *hors d'oeuvre varies*.) These days, it's still frequently served as an hors d'oeuvre, without the tuna. But do something else with it: Try mixing it with some grated orange zest, just enough to perfume and flavor it, and spread it thinly over snapper fillets before baking them. It's an addition that also works with bass or salmon fillets, and swordfish or tuna steaks—either as a spread before baking or as a dollop on top after grilling or sautéing. But whatever you do, don't use black California olives, they don't have the right flavor, texture, or character!

$^{1}/_{3}$ cup pitted ripe mediterranean olives (such as provençal, kalamata, Gaeta, or Alphonso)

$^{1}/_{2}$ teaspoon anchovy paste or chopped anchovy fillets

2 teaspoons drained capers

1 small garlic clove, coarsely chopped

$^{1}/_{4}$ cup fresh flat-leaf or curly parsley leaves, washed and dried, + 4 (flat-leaf) parsley sprigs

Optional: $^{1}/_{4}$ teaspoon *herbes de Provence*

1–2 teaspoons fresh squeezed lemon juice

1 tablespoon + 1 teaspoon olive oil

$^{1}/_{2}$ teaspoon grated orange zest (no white pith, see page 133)

Salt and freshly ground black or white pepper to taste

Four 7-ounce red snapper fillets, each about $^{1}/_{2}''$ thick

2 tablespoons fresh squeezed orange juice (see Note)

1 tablespoon white wine

TO PREPARE: Preheat the oven to 375°.

Place the olives, anchovy paste, capers, garlic, parsley leaves, and *herbes de*

Provence, if using, in the bowl of a food processor. Process, scraping down the bowl several times with a rubber spatula. Add 1 teaspoon of lemon juice and the 1 tablespoon of olive oil and continue to process until the mixture is a paste of very small pieces, about 2 minutes. (Cover and refrigerate the olive paste for up to 2 weeks if you're not using it today. The orange zest becomes too powerful if you add it now.) Add the grated orange zest, pulsing, just to incorporate it. Taste the paste and add the remaining teaspoon of lemon juice if it seems too sweet. Season the paste with salt, if necessary, and pepper. Remove it from the processor bowl and set it aside while you season the red snapper fillets.

Oil a baking pan large enough to hold all the red snapper fillets comfortably in one layer with the teaspoon of olive oil. Season the snapper fillets with salt and pepper. Cover the top of each fillet with a quarter of the olive paste, spreading it in a thin layer with the back of a spoon. Grind some more fresh pepper over the olive paste covering the fillets. Lift the snapper fillets with your hands or a metal spatula and place them in the baking pan, olive side up. Drizzle the orange juice and white wine around the fillets and put the pan in the oven.

Bake the snapper fillets until they're just cooked through, 10 to 12 minutes (it may be a few minutes longer if your baking pan is a heavy one). To check, slightly separate a section of the flesh of one fillet with the corner of your metal spatula at the thickest part to see if it's white and opaque throughout. Bake a minute or two longer if necessary.

TO SERVE: Place the snapper fillets on warm dinner plates, drizzle them with any baking juices, garnish with the parsley sprigs, and serve right away.

NOTE: Two average oranges yield approximately $\frac{1}{2}$ teaspoon of grated rind, but you need only 1 orange for juice. Wrap the unjuiced orange tightly in plastic wrap and refrigerate it. The plastic acts as a surrogate skin and keeps the inside of the orange juicy. If you toss the orange into the refrigerator bin without a new "coat," you'll find a dry orange ball in a couple of days!

Pitting ripe olives is no big deal—their flesh is usually yielding. Place the olives on your counter and press the flat side of a large knife or the bottom of a small skillet on top of each one, exerting a little pressure. The olive will split open and you can pull the pit out with no problem. Or you can buy pitted olives; I have seen good ones in the supermarket.

Sautéed Red Snapper with Roasted Tomatoes

4 servings

PREP AND
COOKING
TIME
35–40
minutes

*E*ven lackluster winter tomatoes take on good flavor when you roast them until they're soft and blistered, making them more intense and slightly smoky in taste. Adding chopped garlic, a little soy sauce, dried oregano, basil, and lemon juice turns them into a simple, refreshing, and slightly rich accompaniment for snapper—or bass, sole, grilled catfish, salmon, shark, monkfish, or trout—fillets. And you can fold the tomatoes into leftover pieces of cooked fish, room temperature or chilled, for a good first course or lunch. (Or dollop it onto open-faced melted cheddar cheese and sourdough sandwiches for lunch!)

3 ripe tomatoes, about $2^1/_2''$ in diameter; *or* 5–6 large plum tomatoes
Salt and freshly ground black or white pepper to taste
$^1/_2$ teaspoon dried oregano
$^1/_2$ teaspoon dried basil
2 teaspoons soy sauce
1 medium garlic clove, finely chopped
$1^1/_2$ tablespoons fresh squeezed lemon juice
Four 7-ounce snapper fillets, each $^1/_2''$ thick
1 tablespoon vegetable oil, plus additional for roasting the tomatoes
Flour for dredging

TO PREPARE: Preheat the oven to 550° with the rack at the top.

Rinse and dry the tomatoes, cut out and discard the core, and cut each regular tomato into 4 to 6 wedges. If using plum tomatoes, cut them in half lengthwise. Put the tomatoes in a mixing bowl and season them with salt, pepper, the oregano, and the basil. Lightly oil a large roasting pan and immediately pour the tomatoes with any juices into it, or place the plum tomatoes cut side down with any juices. Roast the tomatoes on the top rack until they're soft and squishy and the skins are blistered, 10 to 15 minutes. If the skins haven't blistered by the time the tomatoes are soft, remove them from the oven anyway, reduce the oven temperature to 400°, and lower the rack to the middle.

Scrape the tomatoes out of the roasting pan onto a cutting board and chop them into medium-size pieces—you should have about 1 cup. (Some tomato skins are tough; if they haven't tenderized in the roasting, pick them out and discard them.) Put the chopped tomatoes into a mixing bowl. Pour the soy sauce into the roasting pan (if the pan hasn't burned) and scrape up any brown bits. Add the soy sauce and brown bits to the chopped tomatoes along with the garlic and lemon juice. Season the mixture well with salt and pepper and set it aside. (This can be made up to 3 days ahead and refrigerated.)*

Season the snapper fillets with salt and pepper. Place 1 or 2 large skillets over high heat with the vegetable oil. (If using 2 pans, divide the oil equally between them.) Meanwhile, dredge the fillets lightly in flour and pat off the excess. When the oil is hot, place the fillets in the skillet(s), skin side up, for about 3 minutes, or until light golden brown. Turn the fillets over and place the skillet(s) in the oven.

Roast the snapper fillets until they are just cooked through and still very juicy, about 5 minutes. To check, place the end of your metal spatula or a paring knife in the thickest part of one fillet and gently push or cut the flesh open slightly to see if the fillet is white and opaque throughout.

TO SERVE: Place the snapper fillets on warm dinner plates and spoon some of the room temperature roasted tomatoes next to each. Serve right away.

---

*Some tomatoes are juicier than others, so the sauce may be wetter or drier, depending on the tomatoes.

Red Snapper Sautéed with
Rosemary–Brown Butter and Avocado

4 servings

PREP AND
COOKING
TIME
25–30
minutes

*M*y favorite way to eat sautéed snapper fillets is glistening with brown butter and lemon juice. But sometimes I like to push it a bit by adding rosemary sprigs to the butter as it's browning, and then pouring this piney, nutty butter over the fillets, which I've just covered with thin slices of perfectly ripe avocado. You can substitute halibut, bass, grouper, or sole fillets.

1 ripe avocado, preferably Hass variety from California (the ones with
   pebbly skin)
5 teaspoons fresh squeezed lemon juice
Salt and freshly ground black or white pepper to taste
Four 7-ounce snapper fillets, each $1/2''$ thick
2 teaspoons vegetable oil
4 teaspoons + 3 tablespoons butter
Flour for dredging
$1^1/2$ teaspoons dried rosemary, *or* eight $3''$ sprigs fresh rosemary, rinsed
   and dried

TO PREPARE: Preheat the oven to 400°.

Cut the avocado in half lengthwise and twist the halves to separate them. Remove and discard the pit (see page 71). Cut each half into 8 long slices and peel off their skin. Place them on a plate, sprinkle them with a teaspoon of lemon juice, and season them with salt and pepper. Cover them and set them aside while you sauté the fillets.

Dry the fillets on paper towels and season them with salt and pepper. Place 1 large skillet (or 2 medium ones) over medium-high heat with 2 teaspoons of vegetable oil and 4 teaspoons of butter. (The oil keeps the butter from burning and the butter adds flavor. If using 2 pans, divide the oil and butter equally between them.) Dredge the fillets lightly in flour and pat off the excess. When the butter has frothed and subsided, place the fillets in the skillet, skin side up. Sauté the first side until light golden brown, about 3 minutes. Turn the fillets over and place the skillet in the oven.

While the fillets cook, start the rosemary brown butter: If using fresh rosemary, bruise it slightly with the back of a wooden spoon or the side of a large knife, to release more flavor. Place the dried or fresh rosemary in a small pan with the remaining 3 tablespoons of butter over *low* heat and cook for 1 minute. The butter shouldn't brown at this point; the purpose is to release some of the rosemary flavor into the butter before you brown it later. Set the pan aside while the fillets finish cooking.

Roast the fillets until they are just cooked through, about 5 minutes. To check, place the end of your metal spatula or a paring knife in the thickest part of one fillet and gently push or cut the flesh open slightly to see if the fillet is opaque throughout. If it is, remove the skillet from the oven and place the fillets on warm dinner plates. Lay 4 of the reserved slices of avocado diagonally over each fillet, and set them aside to keep warm while you finish the butter.

Place the rosemary butter over medium-high heat, swirling the pan—the butter will begin to turn brown rapidly, in about 30 seconds. When the butter has turned a golden nut brown, turn off the heat, add the 4 teaspoons of lemon juice, and season it with salt and pepper.

TO SERVE: If you've used dried rosemary, pour the brown butter through a small strainer onto the avocado-dressed fillets and discard the rosemary. If you've used fresh rosemary, spoon the brown butter over the fillets with the sprigs and serve the fillets right away. (You don't eat the fresh rosemary either, but it looks nice.)

To remove an avocado pit cleanly, place an avocado half on the counter with the pit facing up. With a large sharp knife, make one quick chopping motion into the center of the pit, keeping your other hand a safe distance away. The knife will become imbedded in the pit, and you can pull the pit out by pulling up on the knife while you hold the avocado half down with your other hand.

To remove the pit from the knife, do one of two things:

1. Drape a clean kitchen towel (for protection) over the hand that's going to hold the pit and pull the knife away from the pit. You may have to rock the knife, gently back and forth to loosen it. *Or,*

2. Place the knife, with the pit still attached, flat against the top edge of a metal garbage can or other metal container so that the pit gets stuck against the edge. Pull back on the knife so the resistance of the edge will free the knife and drop the pit into the container.

Grilled Red Snapper with Tomatillo Salsa

4 servings

PREP AND
COOKING
TIME
25–30
minutes

*D*iana Kennedy, the great writer of Mexican cookbooks, serves a tomatillo salsa with whole baked pompano. Tomatillos are small, light green fruit with papery husks that aren't related to our common tomato, but to the gooseberry. Fresh ones need to be simmered in water until they're soft, but they're available in cans as well. I've adapted her recipe to go with red snapper fillets which I first rub with ground cumin and then grill. The salsa, with its mild acidity, little bit of chile pepper heat, fresh cilantro, and parsley, brings a freshness and a high, almost musical, note to the delicate fillets. The salsa is also good with halibut, sole, grouper, or pompano fillets, soft-shell crabs, and hot or cold lobster or crab meat.

Four 7-ounce red snapper fillets, each $^1/_2$" thick
1 tablespoon ground cumin
Salt and freshly ground black or white pepper to taste
2–2$^1/_2$ tablespoons vegetable oil
$^1/_2$ cup drained canned tomatillos (available in some supermarkets or in specialty stores or by mail order)
1 garlic clove, sliced
$^1/_2$–1 small pickled serrano or jalapeño chile pepper (available in supermarkets)
$^1/_4$ cup lightly packed cilantro leaves, washed and dried
$^1/_4$ cup lightly packed fresh (flat-leaf or curly) parsley leaves, washed and dried
$^1/_2$ tablespoon distilled white vinegar
Several teaspoons cool water, if needed
Lime wedges

TO PREPARE: Start a hot fire in the grill (or preheat the oven broiler). Fifteen minutes before you're going to grill the snapper fillets, put the grill grate about 5" above the glowing coals if it isn't already there. (I also like to brush the top of the grate with vegetable oil just before grilling to help prevent sticking.)

Rub the flesh side of the snapper fillets with ground cumin and season them with salt and pepper. Finally, rub both sides generously with vegetable oil. Set the fillets aside while you prepare the salsa.

Place the tomatillos, garlic, chile pepper, cilantro, parsley, and vinegar in a blender jar or a food processor. Blend the ingredients until they're pureed into a thick, somewhat smooth, sauce, adding a little water if the mixture is too thick. The salsa should be fluid but have nice body. Season it with salt and pepper and set it aside, or cover and refrigerate it for up to 1 week.

Place the snapper fillets, skin side down, on the grill or broiler pan. (If you grill them skin side up first, they'll curl when you turn them over, making them difficult to get off the grill.) Grill the skin side until it's slightly crisp, 2 to 3 minutes. Turn the fillets over and grill the flesh side for 3 to 4 minutes more, until they're golden brown and the flesh is white and opaque throughout. (Broil the fillets without turning.) To check, insert a paring knife or fork in the thickest part of one fillet and gently push the flesh open slightly to see.

TO SERVE: Place the snapper fillets on warm dinner plates with a spoonful of tomatillo salsa next to each one. Garnish the plates with lime wedges and serve right away.

Roasted Red Snapper with Eggplant and Dill

4 servings

PREP AND
COOKING
TIME

25 minutes +
25–40
minutes'
eggplant
roasting and
cooling time

Roasting an eggplant in a hot oven, scooping out the pulp, and then sautéing it in olive oil, makes it satiny in texture and even more eggplant-y in taste. A bit of tarragon vinegar and Chinese oyster sauce add a little sexy mystery, just enough to complement the delicacy of the snapper fillets. Or serve the eggplant with bass, sole, halibut, Arctic char, or trout fillets.

Two ³/₄-pound eggplants to cook more quickly, *or* 1 large

Four 7-ounce snapper fillets, each ¹/₂″ thick

2 teaspoons + 1 tablespoon olive oil

1 tablespoon white wine or dry vermouth

Salt and freshly ground white pepper to taste

¹/₄ teaspoon dried thyme

1 tablespoon tarragon vinegar

1 tablespoon bottled Chinese oyster sauce (supermarket Oriental shelf)

2 teaspoons chopped fresh dill

TO PREPARE: Preheat the oven to 450°.

Pierce the eggplants several times with a sharp fork and place them on a baking pan in the oven until they are squishy when squeezed, 20 to 35 minutes, depending on the size. Cut them in half lengthwise and let them cool long enough to handle. Meanwhile, prepare the fillets for roasting.

Place the fillets in a roasting pan large enough to hold them comfortably. Drizzle them with 2 teaspoons of the olive oil and the white wine. Season them with salt and pepper and set them aside while you chop the eggplant.

Pour off any liquid that has drained from the eggplants and scrape out the pulp with a spoon, discarding the skin and stem. Chop the pulp into small pieces—you'll have about 1¹/₂ cups. Place the fillets in the oven while you sauté the eggplant.

In a medium-size skillet, heat the remaining tablespoon of olive oil over high heat. Stir in the eggplant and thyme and cook, stirring frequently, until the eggplant is moist but not drippy and forms a soft mound in a spoon, 3 to 5 minutes. (If the mixture sticks somewhat and begins to brown, adjust the heat so it doesn't burn, but keep in mind that a little browning adds good flavor.) Stir in the vinegar and cook for another 30 seconds, scraping up any little brown bits that may be on the bottom of the skillet. Turn off the heat and stir in the oyster sauce. Adjust the seasoning with salt and pepper, and keep the mixture warm while the fillets finish roasting.

Remove the fillets when they're just cooked through, 12 to 15 minutes. To check, slip the edge of a metal spatula or a paring knife into a natural separation in the thickest part of one fillet to open it slightly and see if it's white and opaque throughout.

TO SERVE: Place the fillets on warm dinner plates, nestle mounds of eggplant next to them, and sprinkle everything with fresh dill. Serve right away.

SOLE/FLOUNDER

FLAVOR: Mild, sweet, and very lean, with fine flakes

ORIGIN: Atlantic, Pacific, and Alaskan waters

GOOD SIGNS: Flesh, depending on type, somewhat soft to firm; translucent white to creamy gray or beige-white flesh; clean ocean aroma

BAD SIGNS: Dull or discolored flesh; mushy, bruised, or with separations; any strong smell, hint of ammonia, or chemical smell

HEALTH TIPS: A raw 7-ounce fillet is approximately 180 calories, low in omega-3 fatty acids but high in protein.

The only true sole, depending on who you believe, comes from European and Mediterranean waters and it's a beaut. It is, of course, Dover sole, with its thin, extraordinarily firm, elegant fillets. And you should certainly try it any chance you get, simply flouring and sautéing it in butter and lemon—it's pristine, perfect, and utterly satisfying. But I haven't focused on it in this book because its fillets aren't commonly found in most markets.

Here's the news about the rest of the soles we do see: They aren't sole, they're really flounders! To keep their perceived value high, they're marketed under more up-scale names: Hence, blackback flounder becomes lemon sole (blackback is fun to say, but maybe too challenging), witch flounder becomes gray sole (I *can* understand Archibald Leach being renamed Cary Grant and Frances Ethel Gumm becoming Judy Garland, but witch flounder sounds like a star to me!), dab flounder becomes sand dab (the "namers" have a point here), rock flounder becomes rock sole (shouldn't that be Rock *Soul?*), and on it goes. But can you tell me why, then, some nameless flounder is being sold as just "flounder"? Were the "namers" worn out by that point?

In the sea they're all flatfish, with whitish bellies, brownish topsides, and both their eyes on top. And their fillets all look very similar: white, somewhat thin, and with relatively fine flakes. All are very mild, moist, sweet, and tender when cooked. For me, gray sole is the top of the line of this group. Its snow-white fillets have fine, firm flakes and are elegant and sweet. The other sole are softer in texture, creamier in color, and somewhat coarser. But each is worthy and good, and they can be substituted interchangeably. Sole fillets are called the perfect fillets for fish eaters and "nonfish eaters" alike, because they are so mild, available, and versatile. They can be broiled, baked, sautéed, and poached, but bear in mind they're easily overwhelmed by powerful accompaniments. They hold fairly well prewrapped in supermarket plastic, but inspect them closely and watch the "sell-by" date.

I'm sorry to report that certain fish processors soak their fillets in chemical preservatives before shipping them to our markets. Gray sole, lemon sole, yellowtail flounder, and orange roughy are fillets that are known to receive this treatment at times. While it is a law that these fillets be labeled as such, if they are laid out in a refrigerated case, you won't know by looking at them, so do ask. Wanting to avoid sulfites and sodium tripolyphosphates isn't only a question of health but a question of flavor and quality as well. It's apparent, as you eat, that something is amiss. There's an unidentifiable—until you realize what it is—iodine-like, or just plain chemical strangeness to the flavor, which interferes with the anticipated, but then undeliverable, pure sweetness of the fish. This treatment is called "brining"—ask your fish seller if the fillets you're buying are "brined." If he doesn't know, ask him to read the label on the box the fillets were packed in, if they weren't filleted in the store.

Sautéed Sole with
Balsamic Brown Butter

4 servings

PREP AND
COOKING
TIME
25–30
minutes

*Q*uickly sauté the sole fillets until they're golden, put a few nuggets of butter in a small skillet, and cook the butter to a nutty brown—it takes less than a minute—and add a splash of balsamic vinegar. Pour the balsamic brown butter over the fillets and sprinkle them with fresh herbs such as chives, tarragon, and thyme. (I particularly like tarragon with the buttery, vinegar-y sole.) But if you don't have fresh herbs, don't let that stop you from making this dish, it's delicious without them. It's also good with flounder, snapper, bass, monkfish, swordfish, salmon, and Arctic char fillets and tuna steaks.

> 3 tablespoons vegetable or olive oil
> Four 7-ounce sole fillets
> Salt and freshly ground black or white pepper to taste
> Flour for dredging
> 5 teaspoons butter
> 5 teaspoons balsamic vinegar
> Mixed:
>> 1½ tablespoons snipped fresh chives or thinly sliced scallion, green
>> part only
>> 1 teaspoon roughly chopped fresh tarragon
>> 1 teaspoon fresh thyme leaves

TO PREPARE: Put the vegetable or olive oil in a very large skillet (or 2 medium) set over low heat while you prepare the fillets. (If using 2 pans, divide the oil between them.)

Season both sides of the fillets with salt and pepper. Fold the narrow tails of the fillets under their wide ends, keeping the flat side of the fillet inside, to form a triangle. This gives the fillet double thickness and makes it easier to sauté.

Raise the temperature under the skillet to high. While it's getting very hot, dredge both sides of the folded fillets in the flour and pat off the excess. When the oil is beginning to smoke, slip the fillets into the skillet, wide side down. (Be careful not to crowd them, they need at least an inch of space around them.)

Sauté them until the first side is light gold in color and almost cooked through, 3 to 5 minutes (the cooked side will be opaque, the tail section facing up will still be translucent). Turn the fillets over and sauté the second side until they're just done and completely opaque, 2 to 3 minutes. To check, lift the top side and look inside. Cook a minute or two more if necessary. Immediately remove the skillet from the heat and transfer the sole to warm dinner plates with a metal spatula while you make the balsamic brown butter.

Place the butter in a small skillet over medium-high heat. The butter will froth up and then subside within a minute. When the butter begins to subside, swirl the pan by the handle—the butter will begin to turn brown as it subsides. When the butter has turned a golden nut brown in a matter of seconds, turn off the heat and pour in the balsamic vinegar—it will bubble up furiously in the pan. Season the butter with salt and pepper.

TO SERVE: Spoon the balsamic brown butter over the sole fillets. Sprinkle them with the mixed fresh herbs, and serve right away.

Sole Baked with Mushrooms and Mint

4 servings

PREP AND
COOKING
TIME
40–45
minutes

Finely chopped mushrooms cooked in a little butter and shallots develop their natural flavor when all the liquid is evaporated and they start to fry in the pan. In fact, you can hear the sound change from a gurgling liquid to the start of a crackling sauté. That's also your clue that the mushrooms are almost ready and you need to stir them! Adding mint provides a freshness that goes well with halibut, bass, and snapper fillets too.

¹/₂ pound mushrooms

1 large shallot, thinly sliced; *or* 2 tablespoons sliced scallion, white part only

1 medium garlic clove, sliced

2 tablespoons butter

Salt and freshly ground black or white pepper to taste

2 tablespoons chopped fresh mint, *or* 1 teaspoon dried; *or* 1¹/₂ tablespoons fresh dill; *or* 2 tablespoons chives

1 teaspoon vegetable oil

Four 7-ounce sole fillets

4 teaspoons dry bread crumbs

TO PREPARE: Preheat the oven to 425°.

Rinse the mushrooms quickly in cool water—don't let them soak, they'll get waterlogged—and dry them on paper towels. Quarter the mushrooms if they're large, and cut them in half if they're small. Place the mushrooms, shallot or scallion, and garlic in the processor bowl. Pulse everything until the mushrooms are in tiny pieces, about 30 seconds.

Heat the butter in a medium-size skillet over high heat. When the butter is melted and sizzling, add the mushroom mixture and season it lightly with salt and pepper. As the mushrooms cook, they will first appear dry. Very quickly, however, their water will start to come out—stir them occasionally at this point. Within 4 to 5 minutes most of the water will have evaporated and the mushrooms will begin to sizzle in the pan. Just as they're beginning to brown, turn off the heat. Adjust the seasoning with salt and pepper and stir in the mint. Let the mixture cool briefly while you season the fish.

With the vegetable oil, grease a baking pan large enough to hold the fillets comfortably in one layer. Place the fillets in the oiled pan and season them well with salt and pepper. Fold each fillet in half to form a triangle by tucking the narrow end underneath the wide end with the round side of the fillet up. Divide the mushroom mixture over the folded fillets, spreading it evenly on top. Sprinkle each with 1 teaspoon of bread crumbs and place the pan in the hot oven for 8 to 10 minutes, until the fillets are just cooked through. To check, cut through a small part of the thick folded end of one fillet with the edge of your spatula to see if the flesh is white and opaque throughout.

TO SERVE: Transfer the fillets to warm dinner plates and serve right away.

Broiled Sole with
Red Onion–Herb Vinaigrette

4 servings

PREP AND
COOKING
TIME
25–30
minutes

Lots of diced, sweet red onion lightly sautéed in olive oil and mixed with a little rice wine vinegar and a handful of fresh herbs—like chives, dill, basil, and tarragon—makes a perfect, and pretty, light summer accompaniment for sole fillets. And if you have any leftover vinaigrette, you'll find that the herbs permeate it overnight, deepening its character. Serve the vinaigrette warm or at room temperature, or toss it with pieces of cooked fish, shrimp, crab, or lobster for a chilled salad. It would also be good with halibut, bass, snapper, shark, monk, cod, or salmon fillets.

5 tablespoons olive oil

1 cup finely diced red onion

Salt and freshly ground black or white pepper to taste

2 tablespoons rice wine vinegar

1 teaspoon fresh squeezed lemon juice

Four 7-ounce sole fillets

2 teaspoons vegetable oil

2 teaspoons fresh snipped chives or thinly sliced scallion, green part only

2 teaspoons chopped fresh dill

1 tablespoon chopped fresh basil

1½ teaspoons roughly chopped fresh tarragon

TO PREPARE: Preheat the broiler with the rack at the top or 3″ below the heat source.

Put 2 tablespoons of the olive oil into a medium-size skillet over high heat. Add the onion, season it lightly with salt and pepper, and cook, stirring frequently, until lightly browned but only half cooked and still a little crisp, 3 to 5 minutes. Adjust the heat if the onion is browning too rapidly.

Scrape it into a small mixing bowl, stir in the rice wine vinegar and lemon juice, and gradually whisk in the remaining 3 tablespoons of olive oil (using the coiled snake towel trick if your bowl doesn't sit steady, see page 153). Season the vinaigrette with salt and pepper, and set it aside while you broil the sole fillets.

Season the fillets on both sides with salt and pepper. Fold each fillet in half to form a triangle by tucking its narrow tail underneath its wide end, keeping the round side of the fillet up. Using vegetable oil, lightly grease a broiling pan large enough to hold all the fillets comfortably and place them in the pan, wide side up. Rub the 2 teaspoons of vegetable oil over the top of the folded fillets and slide the pan under the broiler. Broil the fillets until they are lightly browned and cooked through, 4 to 5 minutes. To check, make a slit through the thickest section of the folded part to see if it's completely white and opaque.

TO SERVE: Stir the fresh herbs into the vinaigrette, place the sole fillets on warm dinner plates, and spoon some of the onion vinaigrette on top of the fillets. Serve right away.

Gray Sole Sautéed with Tomatoes, Sage, and Lemon

4 servings

PREP AND
COOKING
TIME
25–30
minutes

This dish has an utterly simple charm that I love. Start by crisping the sole fillets in olive oil. Then add bits of fresh sage and slices of red, vine-ripe tomatoes. (Make this when you have tomatoes that are the real McCoy.) The tomatoes are cooked for the briefest amount of time, just to warm them, so their final "collapse" happens in your mouth, creating a lovely, melting foil for the fine, slightly resilient, texture of the gray sole. But don't worry if you cook them too long, the delicious flavors will all still be there. And use small tomatoes if you can, they're easier to deal with. This recipe is also good with halibut, bass, snapper, catfish, and trout fillets.

Four 6–7-ounce gray or other sole fillets
Salt and freshly ground black or white pepper to taste
3–4 small ripe tomatoes
$^1/_4$ cup olive oil
Whole-wheat or white flour for dredging (see Note)
2 tablespoons chopped fresh sage leaves, *or* 1$^1/_2$ teaspoons dried
3 tablespoons fresh squeezed lemon juice

TO PREPARE: Season both sides of the fillets with salt and pepper. Fold the tails under the wide ends to form triangles, keeping the flat side of the fillets inside. This doubles the thickness of the fillets to $^3/_4''$ to 1$''$ and makes it easier to handle them while sautéing.

Rinse and dry the tomatoes and slice them into $^1/_4''$-thick rounds. There should be 3 or 4 slices per person. Place a very large skillet (or 2 medium ones) over medium heat with the olive oil. (If using 2 pans, divide the oil between them.) While the oil is heating, dredge both sides of the folded fillets in the flour and pat off the excess. Turn the heat to high, and when the oil begins to smoke, slip the fillets into the skillet, wide side down. Be careful not to crowd them, they need at least an inch of space to keep them from steaming and to make handling easier.

Brown the first side until it's golden and about three quarters cooked, 3 to 4 minutes (the cooked side will be opaque and most of the tail section, facing up, will still be translucent). Turn the fillets over and sauté the second side until they're just cooked through and completely opaque, 2 to 4 minutes. Immediately remove the skillet from the heat and transfer the sole to warm dinner plates with a metal spatula while you cook the tomatoes.

Place the skillet back over medium heat and add the sage (it may brown and crisp—that's good), immediately followed by the tomatoes. Quickly turn the tomatoes over with a metal spatula and add the lemon juice. With the spatula, scrape up any brown bits under the tomatoes, and cook until the tomatoes begin to wilt, 15 to 30 seconds. Turn off the heat and season the tomatoes with salt and pepper.

TO SERVE: Tilt the skillet and spoon the tomatoes and juices on top and around the fillets. Serve right away.

NOTE: The whole-wheat flour helps the sole to brown and adds a subtle nutty flavor. Use it if you have it, but don't buy any if you have no other plans for it. You can, of course, use twice as many small fillets if large ones aren't available. Be sure, however, to sauté them in several batches—they'll cook quickly and be trickier to handle.

Baked Sole with
Vegetable–Bread Crumb Stuffing

4 servings

PREP AND
COOKING
TIME
40–45
minutes

*T*he first time I made this stuffing, I put my basic pantry vegetables and a few forsaken Portobello mushroom stems in it, and I liked it. If you've got sweet peppers dying to be used, or some summer squash, or a little bit of cabbage, or scallions, or herbs, or . . . use them. You can play around with this stuffing and clean out your vegetable crisper at the same time! Just remember, if you use watery veggies (like mushrooms or summer squash), cook off their excess liquid during the initial sauté to keep the stuffing from becoming too soggy. I like it best with *gray* sole—the fillets are pure white with a slight firmness that is particularly satisfying with the softness of the golden-colored stuffing. The stuffing is also good between very thin slices of salmon or crumbled over crab meat or scallops that have been seasoned, moistened with olive oil, and put in a casserole to bake.

$^3/_4$ cup thinly sliced carrot

$^1/_2$ cup thinly sliced onion

$^3/_4$ cup thinly sliced celery

1 cup sliced mushrooms

2 tablespoons + 2 teaspoons butter

$^1/_2$ teaspoon dried thyme

$^1/_2$ teaspoon dried dill

$^1/_2$ teaspoon grated lemon rind (see page 133), *or* $^1/_4$ teaspoon dried lemon
  peel

Approximately $^1/_2$ cup dry bread crumbs

2 tablespoons chicken broth + a little more if necessary

Salt and freshly ground black or white pepper to taste

Four 5- or 6-ounce gray or other sole fillets, *or* eight 3-ounce fillets

Optional: 2 teaspoons chopped fresh flat-leaf or curly parsley

TO PREPARE: Preheat the oven to 425°.

Place the vegetables in the bowl of a food processor and chop them fine, 20 to 30 seconds. Melt the 2 tablespoons of butter in a medium-size skillet over medium heat and add the chopped veggies. Season them with salt and pepper and sauté them, stirring occasionally, until they are crisp-tender and any excess mushroom liquid has evaporated, about 5 minutes. Lower the heat at any point if the veggies are starting to stick in the pan. (They can be made ahead to this point. But don't chop them without cooking them—the food processor makes the onion begin to smell and taste like "gasoline," but immediate cooking prevents that.) Turn off the heat, stir in the thyme, dill, and lemon rind and scrape the vegetables into a medium-size mixing bowl.

Lightly stir in the bread crumbs until well combined. The stuffing should be moist and hold together. If it's too dry, drizzle a little broth over it. If it seems wet, add another teaspoon or so of crumbs. Season the stuffing with salt and pepper and let it cool while you prepare the fillets. (Or you can make the stuffing 2 to 3 days ahead and refrigerate it, the flavor will improve.*)

Pat the fillets dry with paper towels and lightly season both sides with salt and fresh pepper. Lay the fillets out flat on the counter with their round side down. Evenly spread a quarter of the stuffing over each flat side, patting it on with dampened fingers. Fold the tails over the wide ends of the fillets to make 4 triangular-shape packets, each about 1″ thick. Or divide the stuffing into 8 portions and prepare the small fillets in the same manner.

Turn the fillets over and place them, round side up, in a baking pan that's large enough to hold them in one layer with at least ½″ of space around each fillet. Drizzle them with the 2 tablespoons of chicken broth and dot them with the 2 teaspoons of butter broken into little pieces. Bake the fillets until they're white and opaque throughout, 10 to 12 minutes (several minutes less if you're using small fillets). To check, make a slit in the thickest part of one folded edge. Remove the fillets to warm dinner plates, allowing 2 per person if they're small, and pour the pan juices into a small skillet. Boil the juices down over high heat for 1 to 2 minutes, or until they've thickened slightly and taste good.

TO SERVE: Drizzle the fillets with the juices, sprinkle them with the chopped parsley, if using, and serve right away.

*You can stuff the fillets while the stuffing is still slightly warm if you bake them immediately. If you plan to refrigerate them, allow the stuffing to cool completely before using it.

Sole Broiled with
Olive Oil, Mustard, and Dill

4 servings

PREP AND
COOKING
TIME
20–25
minutes

*S*tir some Dijon mustard, olive oil, and dill together and spread the mixture over the tops of folded sole fillets before broiling them. They come out speckly brown and very moist, with a pleasantly mellowed mustard-dill flavor. Try it on halibut, grouper, snapper, bass, trout, and salmon fillets too.

Four 7-ounce sole fillets or flounder or fluke fillets

¹/₄ large lemon

Salt and freshly ground black or white pepper to taste

3 tablespoons Dijon mustard, preferably French

¹/₄ cup olive oil

2 tablespoons chopped fresh dill, *or* 1 teaspoon dried

TO PREPARE: Preheat the broiler with the rack as close to the top as possible.

Lightly coat with olive oil a broiling pan large enough to hold all the fillets comfortably. Place the fillets in the pan, squeeze the lemon juice over them, and season them well with salt and pepper. Turn them over so their flat sides are face up. Fold each in half to form a broad triangle by flipping the narrow end of each fillet onto its wide end. Turn the folded fillets over so the wide side of the triangle faces up and set them aside while you mix the topping. (They'll be ¹/₂″ to ³/₄″ thick when folded.)

Place the mustard in a small mixing bowl and (using the coiled snake towel trick if your bowl doesn't sit steady, see page 153) gradually whisk in the olive oil in a steady stream to make a thick, smooth emulsion. Stir in the dill and season the mixture well with salt and pepper.

Spread the mustard mixture evenly over the tops of the folded fillets with a small rubber spatula or the back of a spoon. Place the fillets under the broiler until they're cooked through and their tops are speckly brown, 6 to 10 minutes, depending on their thickness. To check for doneness, make a slit with a paring knife or the edge of your metal spatula through the thickest part of one folded edge—it should be completely white and opaque.

TO SERVE: Place the fillets on warm dinner plates (with a spoonful of any pan juices, if desired) and serve right away.

DARKER FLESHED

Fillets

WITH RICHER FLAVOR

BLUEFISH

FLAVOR:	Richly delicate when fresh and young, strong and oily when more mature or not fresh
ORIGIN:	Eastern Atlantic from the coast of Florida to Maine, but also found off South America, Australia, and Africa
GOOD SIGNS:	Flesh firm but giving when raw; translucent blue-gray flesh tones; shiny-bright battleship gray-blue skin; clean briney aroma
BAD SIGNS:	Unattractive brown and dingy colored flesh; soft or mushy muscle tone; any hint of ammonia smell
HEALTH TIPS:	A raw 7-ounce fillet is approximately 250 calories with a good level of both omega-3 fatty acids and protein.

I'll only eat bluefish if I know it's freshly caught or if it's from a fish seller I trust. If it isn't beautifully fresh, it tastes strongly fishy and oily. Avoid buying it prewrapped in those supermarket plastic "coffins"—it turns bad very quickly in there. If you must buy it prewrapped, check the "sell-by" date closely and buy it only if the date is several days ahead and the fish looks very fresh. Otherwise, choose other fillets. The bluefish fillets I prefer are cut from a whole fish no larger than three pounds.

Apparently, bluefish of any age and size have a vicious personality, savagely plowing through schools of fish with their razorlike teeth, leaving behind a wake of bloody destruction! Makes you want to think twice about even eating them at all! Be that as it may, bluefish fillets can be lovely and delicate (a proper revenge!). It's best to prepare them with absolute simplicity, using a little added wine or other acid such as lemon, lime juice, or tomatoes to balance their richness. The cooked flesh becomes soft and a little hard to handle, so I find it easiest to sauté, bake, or broil them.

Bluefish Baked with
Lemon Pulp and White Wine

4 servings

PREP AND
COOKING
TIME
25–30
minutes

I ate scary bluefish in a restaurant once long ago. So, of course, I completely avoided them for years, horrified at the thought of their oily fishiness. Now I see that young, small fish are actually surprisingly refined (in taste, not in personality or sense of style!), and this preparation makes the most of their delicacy. Chop and scatter pieces of peeled, segmented lemon over the fillets with a splash of white wine before you bake them—the little bits of pulp are nice to come upon as you're eating. If you want, sprinkle the fillets with ripe, diced tomato after they've cooked to add another refreshing note. Try this also with trout, mahimahi, pompano, salmon, sea trout, snapper, bass, or just about any other fillet.

> 1 large lemon, *or* 1¹/₂ tablespoons fresh squeezed juice
> Four 7–8-ounce young bluefish fillets, each ¹/₂″ thick (see Note)
> Salt and freshly ground black or white pepper to taste
> 3 tablespoons white wine or dry vermouth
> 4 teaspoons butter
> ¹/₄ cup diced ripe tomato
> Optional: 1 tablespoon coarsely chopped fresh flat-leaf or curly parsley, *or* other fresh herbs

TO PREPARE: Preheat the oven to 400°.

If you're using lemon juice rather than lemon segments, skip this step and go to the next paragraph. To use segments, slice off both ends of the lemon deeply enough to see the flesh, and discard them. Stand the lemon on one end and place your knife at the point where the rind and flesh meet. Cut down, with a slight sawing motion, to the bottom, staying close to the flesh, to remove a long section of peel. Continue doing this all the way around the lemon until it's completely peeled. Hold the lemon in one hand and, with the other, cut right next to each side of the enclosing white membranes (as you would a grapefruit segment) to liberate them. Discard the seeds from the segments and roughly chop the pulp. You should have about 1¹/₂ tablespoons pulp and its juice; place them in a small bowl.

Season the fillets with salt and pepper and place them in a baking pan large enough to hold them comfortably in one layer. Spoon the chopped lemon pulp with its juice, or just the squeezed juice, over the top of the fillets. Pour the white wine over them and dot them with the butter, broken into little pieces. Bake the fillets in the hot oven until they're just cooked through and opaque, 10 to 12 minutes. To check, slip your knife or the edge of your metal spatula between the flakes of one fillet at the thickest part and open it slightly. Cook the fillets a minute or so longer if necessary. Place the fillets on a warm platter (they will be very soft and will break easily—lifting with 2 spatulas helps) while you reduce the pan juices.

You'll have about ¼ cup of pan juices. Pour them, adding any collected juices from the platter, into a small skillet set over high heat. Boil them down until they've reduced by about half and have thickened slightly, 2 to 3 minutes. Taste, and season them with salt and pepper if necessary.

TO SERVE: Place the fillets on warm dinner plates and drizzle them with the reduced pan juices. Scatter the diced tomato over them and sprinkle them with the parsley or herbs, if desired. Serve right away.

NOTE: Young whole bluefish weigh between 2 and 3 pounds, so the fillets you want to buy are an entire side of a small fish. If you see sections cut from a much larger fillet, avoid them; they may be too oily and strong.

"The bluefish has been likened to an animated chopping-machine, the business of which is to cut to pieces and otherwise destroy as many fish as possible in a given space of time. Going in large schools, in pursuit of fish not much inferior to themselves in size, they move along like a hungry pack of wolves, destroying everything before them. Their trail is marked by fragments of fish and by the stain of blood in the sea, as, where the fish is too large to be swallowed entire, the hinder portion will be bitten off and the anterior part allowed to float away or sink. It is even maintained, with great earnestness, that such is a gluttony of the fish, that when the stomach becomes full the contents are disgorged and then again filled. It is certain that it kills more fish than it requires for its own support."

—Professor Spencer F. Baird, *Report to the United States Fish Commission,* 1874

Broiled Bluefish with
Mustard-Tarragon Vinaigrette

4 servings

PREP AND
COOKING
TIME
20–25
minutes

Young bluefish fillets are best accompanied by a simple sauce with a little sharpness to brighten up their flavor. Some Dijon mustard, tarragon vinegar, fresh lemon juice, olive oil, and a little chopped fresh tarragon and parsley do the job. Here, I've broiled the fillets, but sautéing them is a good choice as well (use a nonstick pan with a few drops of oil) because a little bit of seared crust enhances their qualities. This vinaigrette would be good with almost any fillet, light or dark, such as swordfish, tuna, salmon, shark, trout, grouper, snapper, or sole (with really delicate fish, use less vinaigrette), or with shellfish such as lobster, shrimp, and sea scallops.

2 teaspoons fresh squeezed lemon juice
1 tablespoon tarragon vinegar
1 teaspoon Dijon mustard, preferably French
$^1/_4$ cup olive oil
2 teaspoons chopped fresh (flat-leaf or curly) parsley
$^3/_4$ teaspoon roughly chopped fresh tarragon
Salt and freshly ground black or white pepper to taste
Four 7–8-ounce bluefish fillets, each $^1/_2''$ thick (see Notes)

TO PREPARE: Preheat the broiler with the rack at the top or 3″ below the heat source.

Place the lemon juice and tarragon vinegar in a small mixing bowl and stir in the mustard until the mixture is smooth. Whisk in the olive oil, using the coiled snake towel trick if your bowl doesn't sit steady (see page 153), stir in the herbs, and season the vinaigrette with salt and pepper.

Lightly season the tops of the bluefish fillets with salt and pepper and coat each of them with a teaspoon of vinaigrette. Place them, skin side down, on a broiling pan under the broiler. Broil them, without turning, until they're just cooked through, 4 to 5 minutes. To check, place the end of your metal spatula, or a paring knife, in the thickest part of one fillet where you see a separation, and open it slightly. (They probably won't brown, but if they do, be pleased—you have a great broiler!)

TO SERVE: Place the bluefish fillets on warm dinner plates (see Notes), drizzle them with more mustard-tarragon vinaigrette, and serve right away.

NOTES: Young whole bluefish weigh between 2 and 3 pounds, so the fillets you want to buy are an entire side of a small fish. If you see sections cut from a much larger fillet, avoid them; they may be too oily and strong.

If the skin sticks in the pan, which it most likely will, slip your metal spatula between the flesh and the skin and lift the fillet out of the pan. See page 38.

MAHIMAHI OR DOLPHIN FISH

FLAVOR: Mild, faintly rich, sweet

ORIGIN: All tropical and subtropical waters

GOOD SIGNS: Flesh quite firm but resilient; deep beige with rose or mauve flesh tones; clean smell

BAD SIGNS: Unattractive brown and dingy-colored flesh; flaccid muscle tone; mushy or soft; any ammonia smell

HEALTH TIPS: A raw 7-ounce fillet is approximately 180 calories with a good level of protein but a lower level of omega-3 fatty acids. Mahi is high in potassium and iron.

No, it's not a dolphin, the mammal. It's a dolphin *fish,* called mahimahi in Hawaii, and while it's only become popular and trendy on the mainland in recent years, it's been popular in Hawaii for many more. And it's a beautiful medium-size fish, albeit with a strange, very blunt head and an extremely high forehead, which, interestingly, is strongly contrasted by an elegant and deeply forked tail! In between, its body is long and streamlined and covered by skin of blue, green, and gold iridescence.

The fillets we buy, however, are always skinned, because though striking, the skin is thick and tough. The meat itself is mild and sweet, and it can be sautéed, grilled, broiled, fried, or baked. However, I've found that cooking mahimahi over (or under) high temperature causes the flesh to tighten up and dry out, even though you'll swear you haven't overcooked it. So, sauté the fillets over medium heat; broil them a distance away from the direct heat; and grill them over a low to medium fire. Then the fillets will be full of juice, mild, and pleasingly silky in texture.

Mahi is low in calories compared to some of its popular darker fleshed comrades. If a serving weighs in at 7 raw ounces, mahi packs about 180 calories; swordfish about 240; tuna, depending on its type, anywhere from 215 to 345; and salmon, depending on which kind, around 300 to 400.

Mahimahi Sautéed with Butter and Lime

4 servings

PREP AND
COOKING
TIME
15–20
minutes

*G*ently sauté the mahi fillets in butter until their tops are pale gold, and finish cooking them in the oven. Remove them, and pour fresh lime juice into the still-hot skillet—where the butter's turned golden brown. Then pour this simple sauce over the fillets. The butter and lime mingle with the cooked juices and let the mahi's personality shine through. This preparation would also be good with halibut, sole, bass, snapper, perch, catfish, grouper, Arctic char, pompano, salmon, or almost any fillet you can think of.

Four 7-ounce mahimahi fillets, each 1″ thick
Salt and freshly ground black or white pepper to taste
Flour for dredging
2 tablespoons butter
2 tablespoons fresh squeezed lime juice
Optional: 1 teaspoon chopped fresh (flat-leaf or curly) parsley

TO PREPARE: Preheat the oven to 350°.

Season the fillets on both sides with salt and pepper. Lightly dredge them in flour and pat off any excess. Melt the butter in a large ovenproof skillet over medium-high heat, and place the fillets in the skillet, round side down. Brown the fillets just until they're *very* pale gold (regulate the heat, if necessary, to keep the butter from browning at this point), 2 to 3 minutes. Turn the fillets over with a metal spatula and place the skillet in the oven for 5 to 7 minutes. When they're done, the butter should be golden brown and the fillets just cooked through and opaque. To check, make a small slit in the thickest part of one fillet.

Place the fillets on warm dinner plates (or a warm platter) and set them aside briefly to keep warm. Immediately pour the lime juice into the hot pan and stir to pick up any good little pieces stuck to the bottom of the skillet. Season the butter-lime sauce with salt and pepper.

TO SERVE: Spoon some of the sauce over each of the fillets, sprinkle each with a pinch of parsley, if desired, and serve right away.

Mahimahi Simmered in Tamari-Sesame Sauce

4 servings

PREP AND
COOKING
TIME
20 minutes

*T*amari is a fermented soybean sauce very much like the soy sauce we all know, but with a more complex, richer flavor. Stir it with sesame oil and a little mirin, the Japanese sweet rice seasoning liquid (the best ones have no added sugar), and sauté-steam the fillets in this mixture to infuse them lightly with its flavor. The fillets take on a beautiful satiny texture in the process, and there's just enough tamari to heighten their natural taste. The sauce is very versatile: Use it with other fillets such as sea bass or grouper; as a delicious marinade for grilled salmon, swordfish steaks, and shrimp; or as a seasoning base for a chicken or vegetable stir-fry. Skewered, marinated shrimp or cubed swordfish make good hors d'oeuvre.

1³/₄ teaspoons toasted sesame oil (see Great Fish Pantry) or regular sesame oil

1 tablespoon tamari sauce (supermarket Oriental shelf or health food market—see Note)

1 tablespoon mirin (supermarket Oriental shelf or health food market)

2 teaspoons brown rice vinegar (see Great Fish Pantry) or regular rice vinegar

Four 7-ounce mahimahi fillets, each ¹/₂″–³/₄″ thick

Freshly ground black or white pepper to taste

1¹/₂ tablespoons thinly sliced scallion, white and green parts, + extra for garnish

TO PREPARE: In a small bowl, stir together 1¹/₂ teaspoons of the sesame oil, the tamari, mirin, and rice vinegar, and set aside.

Place the remaining ¹/₄ teaspoon of sesame oil in a nonstick skillet large enough to hold all the fillets comfortably, and set it over medium heat. Pat the fillets dry with paper towels and pepper both sides. Place the fillets in the pan, round side down, and lightly brown the bottom for 1 to 2 minutes. Turn the fillets over, reduce the heat to low, and briefly brown the second side. Pour the sauce over the fillets and cover the pan.

Steam the fillets over very low heat for 4 to 5 minutes. Turn them over, cover the pan, and cook them for 2 to 3 minutes more, or until they're just cooked through. To check, place the end of your metal spatula or a paring knife in the thickest part of one fillet and gently push or cut the flesh open slightly to see if the fish is opaque throughout. Remove the fillets to a platter and keep them warm while finishing the sauce.

Increase the heat under the pan to medium and boil the sauce down for 1 minute, adding any juices that have collected on the platter, until the sauce is reduced to about 1 tablespoon. Be careful not to scorch it. Turn off the heat and stir in the scallion.

TO SERVE: Place the mahi fillets on warm dinner plates. Drizzle the tamari-sesame sauce over the top of each and serve right away.

NOTE: Some tamari sauces are made entirely without wheat, a good thing to know if you're wheat sensitive, but make sure you read the label, because some do use a small amount of wheat in processing. Traditional soy sauce is brewed from half wheat and half soybeans.

Grilled Mahimahi with
Wilted Escarole, Spinach, and Basil

4 servings

PREP AND
COOKING
TIME
45–50
minutes

If you can be in the kitchen wilting the greens while a designated-someone is on the patio grilling the mahi, it's an ideal division of labor! But if there's no one around to help, you can sauté or broil the mahi just as well. Be sure to cook the mahi over low to moderate heat—high heat tends to tighten and dry it out, even when you swear you haven't overcooked it. Try these greens with salmon, swordfish, grouper, catfish, or sea trout fillets too.

2 small bunches spinach, *or* one 10-ounce bag fresh spinach

1 bunch fresh basil

1 small head escarole

Four 7-ounce mahimahi fillets, each $3/4''$–$1''$ thick

Salt and freshly ground black or white pepper to taste

5 tablespoons olive oil, preferably extra-virgin

1 tablespoon finely chopped garlic

Lemon wedges

TO PREPARE: Start a low fire in the grill. Fifteen minutes before you're going to grill the mahi fillets, put the grill grate 6″ or 7″ above the glowing coals if it isn't already there. (I also like to brush the top of the grate with vegetable oil just before grilling to help prevent sticking.)

Cut or break the spinach leaves from their stems and discard the stems. Measure 4 cups, somewhat packed, and save the remainder for another preparation. Fill a *very* large bowl (or your sink) with cold water and put the spinach leaves in it. Pick the basil leaves from their stems and measure 1 cup, somewhat packed. Add the basil leaves to the spinach. Wash the leaves by pushing them up and down in the water several times. Then let the leaves remain undisturbed for a minute or two, long enough to let any sand that got stirred up settle on the bottom. Scoop the leaves out without stirring up the sediment. If there's a good amount of sand in the bottom of the bowl, empty the water and repeat the process until the water has no sand. Dry the leaves very well in a salad spinner or roll them between layers of paper towels and set them aside. You can do this up to a day ahead and refrigerate them.

Snap off the leaves of escarole and wash and dry them if they're dirty (sometimes, when fortune smiles, the ribs only need to be wiped clean with a damp paper towel—but check the green of the leaves carefully). Cut enough of the leaves crosswise into 1″ pieces to measure 3½ cups, and set them aside separate from the spinach-basil, or refrigerate them for up to 2 days. Reserve the rest for another use.

Season the fillets with salt and pepper and rub them all over with a tablespoon of the olive oil. Place them, round side down, over the coals and grill them, turning once, until they're lightly browned and just cooked through, 7 to 10 minutes. To check, make a cut in the thickest part of one fillet to see if it's opaque all the way through. When they're done, remove the fillets from the grill and keep them warm briefly while you wilt the greens. (If you're comfortable with the timing, and you have a "designated-someone," you can start the greens 2 minutes before the fillets are done.)

Place 3 tablespoons of the olive oil in a wok, or a very large skillet set over high heat. When the oil is very hot and just *starting* to smoke, add the escarole and stir-fry it for 1 to 2 minutes, until the green of their leaves has wilted. Add the spinach-basil mixture and the garlic and stir-fry them until the spinach starts to wilt, about 30 seconds. Turn off the heat—the retained heat of the wok will continue wilting the greens. At this point, all the greens should be collapsed but still quite crunchy. Adjust the seasoning with salt and pepper.

TO SERVE: Distribute the greens over warm dinner plates, place a fillet on top, and drizzle the fish with the remaining tablespoon of olive oil. Garnish the plates with lemon wedges and serve right away.

POMPANO

FLAVOR: Full, rich, sweet, and delicate at the same time

ORIGIN: Predominantly the Gulf of Mexico

GOOD SIGNS: Flesh firm and tightly grained; pearly, pink-beige color; clean smell

BAD SIGNS: Unattractive brown and dingy-colored flesh; flaccid muscle tone; mushy or soft; any hint of ammonia

HEALTH TIPS: A raw 7-ounce fillet is approximately 328 calories with a moderate amount of omega-3 fatty acids and protein. Pompano is very high in potassium.

Pompano is one of the great fish of the world but, unfortunately, not one of the most available. It's a small, flat, silver-gray-blue-skinned fish that generally weighs about 2 pounds. The fillets are thin and very firm, usually with the skin still attached. Try asking for them at up-scale markets where they'll be familiar with the fish—and charge you a pretty penny; or find a market that does a brisk ethnic trade—at better prices; or ask your regular fish man if he can order it. It's worth it, even if for only the occasional treat—like a perfect, simple dinner with friends who know, or want to know, what's good!

The inherent qualities of pompano are so high, little, if anything, need be done to show them off. Grilled, sautéed, broiled, or baked, its fine, firm, elegant richness will shine.

Grilled Pompano with
Mexican Chile Oil and Lime

4 servings

PREP AND
COOKING
TIME
20 minutes

Grilled pompano fillets are the best—the slight charring seems to focus and highlight their lush, elegant flavor. Pompano is caught in the Gulf of Mexico and, appropriately, Mexican flavors suit it. Chop pickled jalapeño or serrano peppers to a paste and stir in ground cumin and a little vegetable oil. Rub this oil over the beautiful, golden-charred flesh when the fillets come to the table, and serve them with lime wedges—utterly simple and ideal. The chile oil would also work on mahimahi, swordfish, tuna, grouper, or broiled red snapper or bass fillets.

> 1 pickled jalapeño or serrano chile pepper (Mexican ingredients,
>   supermarket shelf)
> $1/2$ teaspoon ground cumin
> 4 tablespoons vegetable oil
> Salt and freshly ground black or white pepper to taste
> Four 7-ounce pompano fillets, each $1/2''$ thick
> Lime wedges

TO PREPARE: Start a hot fire in the grill. Fifteen minutes before you're going to grill the pompano fillets, put the grill grate 4″ to 5″ above the glowing coals if it isn't already there. (I also like to brush the top of the grate with vegetable oil just before grilling to help prevent sticking.)

Trim off and discard the chile pepper stem. Chop the chile very fine, smearing it to a paste with the side of your knife, and put it in a small mixing bowl. Stir in the cumin and 2 tablespoons of the vegetable oil. Season the oil with salt and pepper and set it aside while you grill the fillets. Or cover and refrigerate the oil almost indefinitely, making sure to let it come to room temperature before serving.

Rub both sides of the fillets with the remaining 2 tablespoons of vegetable oil and season them with salt and pepper. Place the fillets on the grill, skin side up, and cook them until they're a beautiful gold, about 3 minutes. Turn the fillets over and grill the second side until they're just cooked through, 2 to 3 minutes. To check, make a small slit in the thickest part of one fillet to see if it's opaque throughout.

TO SERVE: Place the pompano fillets on warm dinner plates. Give the chile oil a stir and coat the tops of the fillets, rubbing the oil in lightly with the back of a small spoon. Serve right away.

Grilled Pompano with
Indonesian Coconut-Lime Sauce

4 servings

PREP AND
COOKING
TIME
30–35
minutes

The pompano gets so golden and crisp on the grill—while it's cooking, you can practically see its juices bubbling in the flesh! The creamy coconut and lime combo—with gentle heat from fresh green chiles—is a light, refreshing, Indonesian-inspired, counterpoint. This coconut sauce would also be delicious with grilled tuna, mahi, and grouper, or with broiled red snapper and halibut fillets. And it would make a terrific dip for grilled shrimp as a party hors d'oeuvre.

$3^1/_2$ tablespoons vegetable oil

$^1/_2$ cup thinly sliced onion

1 small garlic clove, sliced

$1^1/_2$ tablespoons thinly sliced hot green chile pepper, seeds and ribs removed

$1^1/_2$ teaspoons finely grated fresh ginger (see page 214)

$^1/_4$ cup canned coconut milk (see page 105)

1–2 tablespoons fresh squeezed lime juice

Salt and freshly ground black or white pepper to taste

Four 7-ounce pompano fillets, each $^1/_2''$ thick

TO PREPARE: Start a hot fire in the grill. Fifteen minutes before you're going to grill the fillets, put the grill grate 4″ or 5″ above the glowing coals if it isn't already there. (I also like to brush the top of the grate with vegetable oil just before grilling to help prevent sticking.)

Place $1^1/_2$ tablespoons of the vegetable oil in a medium skillet set over low heat, and add the onion, garlic, and chile. Cook the vegetables without browning them, stirring occasionally, until the onion is translucent and tender, 8 to 10 minutes. Stir in the ginger to heat through, and remove the skillet from the fire. Let the vegetables cool slightly, about 5 minutes.

Place the coconut milk and cooked vegetables in a blender jar and puree them until the mixture is smooth, 1 to 2 minutes. Add 1 tablespoon of the lime juice and season the sauce with salt and pepper. Add up to 1 more tablespoon of lime juice if the mixture seems thick or you'd like more lime flavor. Set the sauce aside while you grill the fillets. Or refrigerate it, covered, for up to 4 days, being sure to let it come to room temperature before serving.

Rub both sides of the fillets with the remaining 2 tablespoons of vegetable oil and season them with salt and pepper. Place the fillets on the grill, skin side up, and cook them until they're a beautiful gold, about 3 minutes. Turn the fillets over and grill the second side until they're just cooked through, 2 to 3 minutes. To check, make a small slit in the thickest part of one fillet to see if it's opaque throughout.

TO SERVE: Place the pompano fillets on warm dinner plates with a spoonful of the coconut-lime sauce next to them, and serve right away.

Not all that long ago, I thought coconut milk was the clear liquid that you found when you cracked open a juice-filled coconut—remember shaking them next to your ear to listen for liquid? Does anybody still do that? In fact, I rarely see fresh coconuts in the supermarket anymore, which is too bad.

But coconut milk is a whole other thing, and not so easily arrived at, except in cans! Turns out, the clear liquid is coconut *water*, which makes sense. Coconut *milk* is made by scraping the white coconut meat against a sharp grating instrument and mixing those hard-won fibers with water. When you squeeze this mixture, you get coconut milk. By mixing less water with the coconut fibers, you get coconut cream. A perfectly acceptable version of coconut milk is found in cans, generally from Thailand.

As a small aside, in the South Pacific Islands, the coconut palm grove is practically their local dairy farm. There, the coconut is used in many of the ways that we use our cow milk, cream, and butter, but they don't stop there. One form of coconut or another—meat, milk, and oil—finds its way into various parts of each meal, from soups to curries to beverages and desserts.

SALMON

FLAVOR:	Farmed fish are mildly rich; wild fish range from delicate to deep and rich
ORIGIN:	Atlantic salmon farms in Canada, Norway, the United States, the United Kingdom, and Chile; wild salmon, generally Pacific Ocean fish, live along the California coast and northward into Alaska waters
GOOD SIGNS:	Flesh moist, silky-firm, and resilient; somewhat translucent light pink to deep orange-red color in certain wild fish; clean to faintly oceany aroma
BAD SIGNS:	Unattractive discolored and dingy flesh; flaccid muscle tone and separating sections; mushy or soft; any hint of staleness or ammonia
HEALTH TIPS:	There are 6 major kinds of salmon, each with its own nutrient characteristics, which fluctuate throughout the year. A raw 7-ounce serving can range, approximately, from a caloric low of about 280 calories in wild pink salmon to 400 calories for wild king. Farmed Atlantic salmon has about 300 calories. All salmon are high in omega-3 fatty acids, protein, and vitamins A, D, B_6, and B_{12}.

To talk about salmon is to speak of something almost mythical: a worshiped, sleekly beautiful, silver-bodied being that breathed its soul deep into the life of ancient cultures as long as 25,000 years ago. Salmon is part of our lives now, too, but perhaps we take it for granted—we who don't fish for it, we who merely pick up a fillet or two at the market on our way home from work. I try to remind myself how splendid it is in nature, and how much it has meant to people I could never know.

On the practical side, salmon isn't just salmon. Each kind of salmon has its own individuality, which includes differences in flavor, fatness or leanness, and softness or firmness. The five wild Alaskan salmon—and all Alaskan salmon are wild—have a fascinating diversity worth seeking out (if your local market restricts itself to farmed salmon) to experience their different cooking and eating characteristics.

Alaska king (also known as chinook) and sockeye, plus Atlantic farmed salmon are rich in fat and are the best ones to grill or broil, although they are ideal for any other treatment as well. Alaska chum, coho (also known as silver), and pink salmon have the lowest fat content, and are better poached, sautéed, or baked, being careful not to dry them out. You won't find fillets of wild Alaskan pink salmon too often, however, for it generally ends its life in a can! It's good to know that prewrapped supermarket salmon fillets stay fresher longer than any other fillet trapped in that airless environment.

Accompaniment and seasoning possibilities for salmon fillets are limitless. But, with that said, think: The simpler the better!

"When swimming upstream to spawn, salmon leap up to 10 feet in the air to avoid cascading waterfalls. The name salmon comes from the Latin *salmo,* which means "to leap" (Alaska Seafood Marketing Institute).

And because they're absolute dynamos, they need plenty of oxygen—hence their chosen habitat: up near the surface of the ocean and cold, swiftly moving streams. They return, time after time, to spawn in the exact stream bed where they were born years before, traveling hundreds of miles to get there, but we still don't fully know how they can be so precise and on time! A little salmon mystery could be good for our souls!

Salmon, across the board, contains a high level of omega-3 fatty acids. Omega-3s are beneficial polyunsaturated fatty acids that are practically exclusive to fish and shellfish, and particularly concentrated in "darker fleshed fillets with richer flavor." It's been shown that an adequate amount of these fatty acids can help protect us against heart disease throughout our entire life. Having 2 or 3 fish dinners a week will do the job. These guidelines are for everyone: pregnant and nursing mothers, newborns, and the rest of us already-borns of recent and less recent vintage! Get out your jars of swordfish puree!

Poached Salmon with Purple Cabbage, Mushrooms, and Scallions

4 servings

PREP AND COOKING TIME
35 minutes

One of the most satisfying ways to cook is to use what's in the house. Of course, what's most fun about that is not having to run to the store, not to mention feeling virtuous and creative! I had some mushrooms that were on the old side, the ones I prefer for cooking because a little bit of age develops their flavor. (Look for darkened, but not sticky to the touch, caps whose gills have opened. But stick to white mushrooms if they're wrapped in plastic because you can't tell if they're sticky.) I keep purple cabbage around for salads and soups, and there are usually scallions hanging around in my vegetable drawer. They're common ingredients, but together they're flavorful yet surprisingly delicate with the fillets. And the pink of the salmon against the purple of the cabbage and green of the scallion is beautiful. Try grilling the fillets too. You can substitute bass, halibut, or monkfish fillets, or sea scallops.

2 tablespoons olive oil

3 cups thinly sliced purple cabbage

3 cups thinly sliced, darkening white mushrooms or white ones or creminis (about $\frac{1}{2}$ pound)

Salt and freshly ground black or white pepper to taste

Approximately 4 cups water

2 tablespoons distilled white vinegar or other vinegar

1 bay leaf

1 lemon slice

Four 7-ounce salmon fillets, each $1\frac{1}{4}$″ thick at the thickest part

2 large garlic cloves, finely chopped

1 tablespoon red wine vinegar or other vinegar

$\frac{1}{2}$ cup thinly sliced scallions, white and green parts

TO PREPARE: Place the olive oil in a large skillet set over medium heat. When the oil is hot, stir in the cabbage and mushrooms. Season them with salt and a generous amount of pepper. Cook the mixture, stirring occasionally, for 7 or 8 minutes, or until the cabbage is tender but still slightly chewy. While the cabbage is cooking, start poaching the fillets.

Place a skillet large enough to hold all the fillets in one layer over high heat. Add the water, white vinegar, bay leaf, lemon, and salt to taste. Bring to a boil, lower the heat, and let the water simmer for 4 or 5 minutes to allow the ingredients to infuse it with flavor.

Slip the fillets, skin side up, into the simmering liquid. The water should just cover the skin of the fish—add a little more *hot* water if it doesn't. Adjust the heat so a few gentle bubbles come to the surface, and poach the fillets for 8 to 10 minutes until they're slightly undercooked, so they'll be very moist. Or poach them for 1 or 2 minutes longer for well done. Remove the fillets, skin side up, to a platter, and keep them warm while putting the finishing touches on the cabbage.

When the cabbage is tender-firm, add the garlic and cook it, stirring occasionally, about 1 minute. Add the red wine vinegar and stir it in thoroughly. (At this point the cabbage can be refrigerated for up to 4 days.) Stir in all but 2 tablespoons of the scallions and just heat them through. Adjust the seasoning with salt and pepper and turn off the heat. The scallions will still be bright green. (If the cabbage has been refrigerated, place it over low heat until it's hot, and stir in the scallions just before serving.)

Remove the skin from the fillets by lifting one edge from a narrow end and peeling the skin to the opposite end. It will come off easily unless the fish is very undercooked.

TO SERVE: Place a large spoonful of cabbage on each of 4 warm plates. Turn the fillets over on top of the cabbage, sprinkle them with the remaining scallions, and serve right away.

Poached Salmon with
Basil Bread Crumbs

4 servings

PREP AND
COOKING
TIME
30–35
minutes

*W*hat a blessing to have meals that can be relatively effortless and homemade at the same time! Gently poached, these salmon fillets feel moist and silky in your mouth, contrasting with crunchy bread crumbs that are full of basil, green pepper, and sun-dried tomatoes. To make life easier, you can prepare the crumbs several days ahead and refrigerate them—just be sure to heat them slightly before sprinkling them over the fillets. Also serve these flavorful, homey crumbs over sole, halibut, and cod fillets and shark, tuna, and swordfish steaks.

> Approximately 4 cups water
> 2 tablespoons distilled white vinegar or other vinegar
> 1 bay leaf
> 1 thin lemon slice
> Salt and freshly ground black or white pepper to taste
> Four 7-ounce salmon fillets, each $1^{1}/_{4}''$ thick at the thickest part
> 1 tablespoon butter
> $^{1}/_{3}$ cup finely diced green bell pepper
> 1 tablespoon drained, finely chopped sun-dried tomatoes
> $^{1}/_{3}$ cup dry bread crumbs
> 3 tablespoons chopped fresh basil

TO PREPARE: Place the water, vinegar, bay leaf, lemon, and salt to taste in a skillet large enough to hold all the fillets comfortably in one layer, and set it over high heat. Bring it to a boil and then lower the heat so the water simmers for about 5 minutes to let the flavors come through.

Slip the fillets, skin side up, into the simmering poaching liquid. The water should just cover the skin of the fillets. Adjust the heat so that only a few gentle bubbles come to the surface. While the fish poaches, make the bread crumbs.

In a small skillet, melt the butter over medium heat and add the green pepper; cook it, stirring occasionally, until it is almost tender, 4 to 5 minutes. Stir in the sun-dried tomatoes and add the bread crumbs. Cook the crumbs, stirring frequently, for 1 to 2 minutes, or until they take on a little toasty color. Stir in the basil, season the crumbs with salt and pepper, and set the mixture aside where it will keep warm for a few minutes. Or, cover and refrigerate the crumbs for up to 4 days, being sure to warm them gently before serving.

When the fillets are ready, in 8 to 10 minutes, they will be very moist and ever so slightly underdone. For well done, poach them for 1 to 2 minutes longer. Remove the fillets, skin side up, to a platter. Remove and discard the skin from the fillets by lifting it from one narrow end and peeling it toward the other end. It comes off very easily unless the fillets are very undercooked.

TO SERVE: Turn the salmon fillets over onto warm dinner plates, sprinkle the tops with a generous spoonful of basil bread crumbs, and serve right away.

Interestingly, the nutrient content of seafood fluctuates. Depending on the time of year, its age, and its habitat, fish and shellfish will vary in protein, fat, carbohydrate, sodium, and calorie content. So, approach each one's stated nutritional figures as an intelligent guideline.

Sautéed Salmon with
Spicy Ginger Mushrooms

4 servings

PREP AND
COOKING
TIME
40 minutes

Lots of fresh ginger, some tangy-sweet Chinese hoisin sauce, and a little white wine add yummy flavor to the thickly sliced, sautéed mushrooms that are spooned over these salmon fillets. Ginger adds spicy heat, white wine cools it out a bit, and hoisin sauce pulls it all together in a slightly exotic way. And it doesn't hurt that a jar of hoisin sauce can stay in the refrigerator practically forever! Serve the mushrooms over grilled, broiled, or poached salmon or other fillets such as mahimahi, tuna, swordfish, and bass.

$3/4$ pound white mushrooms

$1^1/4$ tablespoons finely chopped fresh ginger (see page 214)

3 tablespoons Chinese hoisin sauce (supermarket Oriental section—see Note)

$1/4$ cup white wine or dry vermouth

2 tablespoons vegetable oil

Four 7-ounce salmon fillets, each $3/4''$–$1''$ thick at the thickest part

Salt and freshly ground black or white pepper to taste

Flour for dredging

TO PREPARE: Preheat the oven to 400°.

Briefly rinse the mushrooms under cool running water and dry them with paper towels. Cut them into $1/3''$-thick slices and set them aside. (You'll have about $4^1/2$ cups.) Put the ginger in a small mixing bowl and stir in the hoisin sauce and the wine or vermouth. Set the mixture aside.

On a large skillet set over medium heat, add 1 tablespoon of the vegetable oil. When the oil is hot, add the mushrooms and sauté them, stirring occasionally, just until their juices start to flow, 3 to 5 minutes. Stir in the ginger-hoisin mixture, and continue cooking them for 1 to 2 minutes more, stirring occasionally. Set them aside in the skillet while you cook the fillets. Or put them in a bowl, cover, and refrigerate them for up to 3 days.

Season the fillets with salt and pepper. Put the remaining tablespoon of oil in a large (or 2 medium) ovenproof skillet set over medium heat. (If using 2 skillets, divide the oil equally between them.) While the oil is heating, dredge the fillets in flour and pat off the excess. Turn the heat under the skillet to high and add the fillets, round side down. Sauté them until they're medium gold in color, 2 to 3 minutes. Turn the fillets over and put the skillet in the oven until they're almost cooked through, 6 or 7 minutes—or 1 to 2 minutes more for well done. To check, place the end of your metal spatula or a paring knife in the thickest part of one fillet and push the flesh open slightly—the flesh will be slightly translucent when underdone and completely opaque when well done.

Place the skillet with the mushrooms back over medium to high heat and reduce the liquid, stirring frequently, to 2 or 3 tablespoons of intense juices. The mushrooms should be lightly coated with the juices. If the mushrooms have been refrigerated, place them over low heat for 1 to 2 minutes to heat through before you start to reduce the juices. Season them with salt and pepper to taste.

TO SERVE: Place the salmon fillets on warm dinner plates, spoon the mushrooms on top of them, and serve right away.

NOTE: Hoisin sauces can vary in sweetness from brand to brand. Taste your brand before cooking with it—and drop the recipe amount by $1/2$ to 1 tablespoon if it seems much more sweet than tangy.

Much of any strong, fishy cooking odor comes from the dark, fatty sections of the fish. If the odor bothers you, and you don't like to eat that part of the fillet, you can trim it out before cooking.

For most fillets, this fatty section is located on the flat side, the skin side—obviously only reachable if your fillets are skinless. Turn the fillet so that its flat side faces you, and trim off any visible dark, fatty sections. On some fillets, such as salmon, you'll be able to trim off a good amount (depending on how much was left when the entire side was filleted in the first place). In addition, you can trim out the shallow V of fat that runs down the center. Delicate white fleshed fish have considerably less fat.

Poached Salmon
over Green Hummus

4 servings

PREP AND
COOKING
TIME
35–40
minutes

Hummus is terrific, down to earth, satisfying and all that, but when it's paired with salmon fillets, something unexpected happens: refinement! Lightened slightly, the hummus does a whole other dance with its new partner. And when you taste them together, I wonder if you'd have guessed what the creamy, lemony, pale green stuff was, if you hadn't made it yourself. I couldn't decide if I liked the salmon better grilled or poached, or the hummus with parsley or basil—it works both ways.

3 tablespoons tahini (supermarket International section)

$^3/_4$ cup drained canned chick-peas, but *save* the liquid

1 medium garlic clove, coarsely chopped

2 tablespoons fresh squeezed lemon juice

2–3 teaspoons olive oil

Salt and freshly ground black or white pepper to taste

3 tablespoons packed fresh (flat-leaf or curly) parsley leaves, washed and
dried, *or* basil leaves

Approximately 4 cups water

2 tablespoons white wine vinegar

1 bay leaf

1 lemon slice

Four 7-ounce salmon fillets, each $1^1/_4''$ thick at the thickest part

TO PREPARE: If the tahini has separated, and that's not unusual, scrape all of it into the bowl of a food processor, and process it briefly to amalgamate it again. With a rubber spatula, scrape the tahini back into its original container and measure 3 tablespoons back into the processor bowl.

Place the chick-peas, garlic, lemon juice, and 2 teaspoons of the olive oil in the processor bowl with the tahini. Process the ingredients, adding 2 or 3 tablespoons of the chick-pea liquid and scraping down the sides a few times, until the mixture is very smooth and light, 2 or 3 minutes. The hummus should be soft and very spreadable, but not runny. If it seems too heavy and thick, add a little more chick-pea liquid and another teaspoon of olive oil if you like. Season it well with salt and pepper. Add the parsley or basil leaves to the mixture and process until the leaves are chopped in tiny pieces and the hummus is tinted pale green. Set the hummus aside, covered, at room temperature while you poach (or grill) the fillets. Or refrigerate it for up to a week, being sure to bring it to room temperature before serving. (Or make a double batch and use the other half for somebody's lunch or for hors d'oeuvre on another night.)

Place the water, vinegar, bay leaf, lemon, and salt to taste in a skillet large enough to hold all the fillets comfortably in one layer, and set it over high heat. Bring it to a boil, and then lower the heat to a simmer for 4 to 5 minutes to let the flavors come through.

Slip the fillets, skin side up, into the simmering liquid. The water should just cover the skin of the fillets. Adjust the heat so that a few gentle bubbles come to the surface. Poach the fillets for 8 to 10 minutes, or until they're barely cooked through—they'll be very moist and ever so slightly underdone. Or poach them a minute or two longer for well done. Remove the fillets, skin side up, to a platter. Remove and discard their skin by lifting it at the edge of a narrow end and peeling it toward the opposite end. It will come off easily unless the fillets are very undercooked.

TO SERVE: Spread $1/4$ cup of the hummus in a rough circle in the center of 4 warm dinner plates. Pick up each fillet with a spatula, turn it over on top of the hummus, and serve right away.

Grilled Salmon
with Basil Vinaigrette

4 servings

PREP AND COOKING TIME 30–35 minutes

Lighter and fresher tasting than pesto, and bursting with the same kind of flavor, this vinaigrette is a dream accessory. It's made with handfuls of basil and parsley leaves pureed with garlic, a few capers, some lemon juice, and olive oil, and it's delicious over golden, crisp-grilled salmon fillets as well as all kinds of fish fillets, shellfish, chicken, lamb, vegetables, and grains. In fact, I'm still looking for something it *wouldn't* be good with. I serve it for family dinner, with grilled shrimp at a cookout, and for fancier dinners too—I just keep serving it! And if you stir some mayo or plain yogurt into it, it's a dip.

$^1/_2$ cup packed fresh (flat-leaf or curly) parsley leaves, washed and dried

$1^1/_2$ cups packed basil leaves, washed and dried (or eliminate the parsley and use 2 cups basil)

1 garlic clove, roughly chopped

$^1/_2$ teaspoon drained capers

2 tablespoons fresh squeezed lemon juice

$^1/_2$ cup + 4 teaspoons olive oil

Salt and freshly ground black or white pepper to taste

Four 7-ounce salmon fillets, each 1″ thick at the thickest part

Optional: 4 small basil sprigs for garnish

TO PREPARE: Start a medium fire in the grill (or preheat the oven broiler). Fifteen minutes before you're going to grill the fillets, put the grill grate 4″ to 5″ above the glowing coals if it isn't already there. With salmon fillets, I definitely brush the top of the grate with vegetable oil just before grilling to help prevent sticking.

Place the parsley, basil, garlic, capers, lemon juice, and $^1/_2$ cup of the olive oil in a blender jar or the bowl of a food processor. (The blender gives a smoother result, but it's good either way—a matter of preference.) Puree the ingredients until they're very smooth, scraping down the jar or bowl several times with a rubber spatula. Season the vinaigrette with salt and pepper and set it aside. It can be refrigerated for a day or two, but the color is bright green and beautiful when it's freshly made and turns khaki not too long after.

Dry the fillets with paper towels, season them with salt and pepper, and rub them all over with the remaining 4 teaspoons of olive oil. Place the fillets, skin side up, on the grill (or broiler pan) and cook them until they've formed a golden brown crust, 5 to 6 minutes. (If you try to move them before they've crusted, they may stick to the grill.) Turn them over and grill or broil the second side for an additional 3 or 4 minutes. To check for doneness, insert a paring knife or a fork in the thickest part of one fillet and gently push the flesh open slightly to see how completely it's cooked. It should be ever so slightly underdone in the center. I like salmon fillets cooked to this point, because they come out super-moist. Cook them to your taste, of course.

TO SERVE: Place the salmon fillets on warm dinner plates. Spoon some basil vinaigrette over them, garnish with a basil sprig, if desired, and serve right away.

If you have leftover basil vinaigrette, spread a tablespoon of it over the top of seasoned fillets of sole that have been folded in half, and sprinkle each one with a teaspoon of fresh or dry bread crumbs. Then broil the fillets. Cooking the vinaigrette mellows its taste and keeps it from overwhelming the sole. After the vinaigrette has been in the refrigerator for several days, it's lost some of its sparkle anyway.

Roasted Salmon with
Honey Mustard Sauce

4 servings

PREP AND
COOKING
TIME
30 minutes

Most of the ingredients for this can be sitting around in your pantry for months—*and* it's a snap to make. The honey mustard sauce is also good with scallops and shrimp, not to mention chicken, if I dare speak of a nonswimmer!

6 tablespoons prepared Honeycup mustard (supermarket mustard shelf)

1 tablespoon balsamic vinegar

1^1/$_2$ tablespoons soy sauce

1^1/$_2$ teaspoons finely chopped fresh ginger (see page 214)

1 medium garlic clove, finely chopped

Four 7-ounce salmon fillets, each 1^1/$_4$″ thick at the thickest part

Salt and freshly ground black or white pepper to taste

Optional: fresh cilantro leaves, green and white parts of slivered scallions, *or* other fresh herbs

TO PREPARE: Preheat the oven to 425°.

Place the mustard in a small mixing bowl and whisk in the vinegar, soy sauce, ginger, and garlic. Set the sauce aside, or cover and refrigerate it for up to a month. (Yes, really!)

Lightly oil the bottom of a baking pan large enough to hold all the fillets comfortably. (This helps to prevent any dripping sauce from burning onto the bottom of the pan.) Place the fillets in the pan and season them lightly with salt and more heavily with pepper. Spoon a tablespoon of sauce over the top of each fillet. Roast the fillets until their sides are slightly springy when pressed, 10 to 12 minutes—they will be slightly underdone at this point. Or roast another minute or two for well done.

TO SERVE: Place the fillets on warm dinner plates. (If the skin sticks to the pan, slide a metal spatula between the skin stuck to the pan and the bottom of the fillet to lift it out, leaving the skin in the pan.) Spoon a little more sauce over each fillet, or serve it on the side, and sprinkle each fillet with cilantro leaves, scallions, or other fresh herbs, if desired. Serve right away.

SHAD AND SHAD ROE

FLAVOR:	The fillets are sweet and rich. The roe is rich and considered a delicacy.
ORIGIN:	Important rivers such as the Hudson, the Connecticut, the Delaware, and the Potomac on the East Coast, and the Columbia on the West Coast
GOOD SIGNS:	Flesh of fillets firm; roe sacs intact; fillets pinky-pale to deep beige in color; roe light to dark salmon or burgundy colored; clean smell
BAD SIGNS:	Unattractive brown and dingy-colored flesh; ripped roe sacs; flaccid muscle tone; bones in the fillets; mushy or soft; any hint of ammonia
HEALTH TIPS:	A raw 6-ounce shad fillet is approximately 335 calories with a good level of protein and a high level of iron. A raw 6-ounce portion of roe (nutrition tables list roe generically) is approximately 240 calories with a higher level of protein and a lower fat content than the fish itself.

Shad is very much a seasonal fish, generally in good supply throughout the spring in the East and somewhat later on the West Coast. Shad needs to be expertly filleted, because it is composed of many tiny bones. After it's filleted, it's a thin piece of meat with two flaps that open up like book covers. Its flavor is somewhat similar to swordfish and mahimahi, but deeper and sweeter than either. Its flesh has no obvious flakes and is very tender and moist when cooked. For me, its dark, fatty areas have a deeper flavor that is reminiscent of its roe. Sometimes these fatty areas also have a slightly muddy or metallic flavor, which isn't to everyone's taste, including my own! Grill, broil, bake, or sauté the fillets.

The roe is comprised of two connected sacs of eggs, usually 4 to 6 inches in length, held together by a thin membrane. The sac membranes are traced with delicate red veining, with one large central back vein, all edible. The membranes are easily ripped when they're handled, so be sure they're intact when you buy the roe, and handle them gently during preparation. A brief initial blanching in simmering water will firm them slightly so you can handle them more easily. Simmer, sauté, bake, or broil the roe.

Broiled Shad Stuffed with
Fresh Herbs

4 servings

PREP AND
COOKING
TIME
30 minutes

Buying shad fillets completely boneless is the only way to go—otherwise they're filled with endless tiny bones. When they're properly boned—and reputable fish stores and supermarkets only sell them that way—they have flaps that open like book covers, making them the perfect vehicle for simple stuffings and seasonings. Lift open the flaps and coat the inside with vibrant herbs. Because the fish is sweet and rich, it takes well to broiling without further ado. I like to spoon a little brown butter over it when it comes out of the broiler—but you can pass on that if you choose! No other fish has built-in "book" flaps to protect the herbs from the intense heat of the broiler, but you can rub these herbs over any fish fillet, drizzle with a little lemon and butter or oil, and bake them.

2 teaspoons fresh thyme leaves

1 tablespoon somewhat coarsely chopped fresh flat-leaf or curly parsley

1 tablespoon snipped fresh chives, *or* 1 1/2 tablespoons thinly sliced scallion, green part only

1 tablespoon chopped fresh dill

Four 6-ounce shad fillets, each 1/2″ thick

1/4 large lemon

Salt and freshly ground black or white pepper to taste

Optional brown butter: 1 1/2 tablespoons butter + 2 teaspoons fresh squeezed lemon juice

Lemon wedges

TO PREPARE: Preheat the broiler with the rack at the top or 3″ below the heat source.

Cut through the thyme leaves once or twice with a large sharp knife to encourage them to release their flavor. Place them in a small mixing bowl with the parsley, chives or scallion, and the dill, and mix them thoroughly. Open up the flaps of the fillets and squeeze the lemon over the insides to moisten them. Season the insides with salt and pepper, and sprinkle the herbs evenly over the inside part that's lying flat. Fold the flaps back over to cover the herbs.

Lightly oil a broiling pan with vegetable oil and lay in the fillets, flap side up. Season their tops with salt and pepper and place them under the broiler. Broil them for 4 to 5 minutes without turning, until they're lightly browned and just cooked through. It's easy to tell if they're cooked—unfold one side of a flap and look for any pink rawness. Cook a minute or two longer if necessary. (The fillets have a good deal of brownish fat, don't confuse it with pink undercooked flesh.)

To prepare the optional brown butter, place the butter in a small skillet over medium-high heat. It will froth up and then subside. When the butter begins to subside, swirl the pan by the handle—the butter will begin to turn brown as it subsides. When the butter has turned nut brown, in a matter of seconds, turn off the heat and add the lemon juice. Season the brown butter with salt and pepper.

TO SERVE: Place the fillets on warm dinner plates. Spoon the brown butter over them, if using it, garnish the plates with lemon wedges, and serve right away.

Shad with Ginger Curry

4 servings

PREP AND
COOKING
TIME
40–45
minutes

*T*his recipe is adapted from a fish curry recipe in the Time-Life "The Good Cook" series, which called for marinating a whole fish in vinegar before poaching it in water with onions, ginger, and chiles. Don't worry, this recipe's faster, easier, and just as good! Cook chopped scallion, ginger, garlic, and fresh green chiles with a little curry powder. Let the mixture cool, and rub it over the shad fillets—it adds an Indian fragrance and some heat. When you first rub it on, you'll think it doesn't look like much, and if looks were everything, you'd be right! But that little bit of ginger-chile mixture has lots of flavor. Try rubbing it over mahimahi, pompano, or salmon fillets too.

10 thin slices peeled fresh ginger, each slice about 1″ diameter (see page 214)

4 tablespoons thinly sliced scallion, white part only

2 garlic cloves, sliced

1 large fresh jalapeño pepper (or other fresh green chile, or pickled jalapeño), seeded and sliced

1 tablespoon vegetable oil

1 teaspoon curry powder

Salt and freshly ground black or white pepper to taste

1 lemon

Four 6-ounce shad fillets, each $^1/_2$″–$^3/_4$″ thick

Optional: plain yogurt and cilantro leaves

TO PREPARE: Preheat the oven to 425°.

Chop the ginger coarsely on a chopping board. Push it together in a low mound and cover it with the scallion, garlic, and jalapeño, and chop everything together into very tiny pieces. In a small skillet, heat the vegetable oil over medium-low heat, and add the chopped vegetables. Cook the mixture, stirring frequently, for 1 minute, or until the scallion has just wilted. Turn off the heat and stir in the curry powder—the retained heat of the skillet will cook the curry powder. Season the mixture with salt and pepper and scrape it onto a plate to cool for 5 minutes.

Cut the lemon in half. Open the flaps of the fillets and squeeze the lemon juice all over the fillets, inside and out, rubbing it in gently. Season the fillets all over with salt and pepper. Divide the cooled ginger-chile mixture into 4 parts—each fillet gets one quarter. Open the flaps of one fillet and smear the inside, using the back of a teaspoon, with half of its ginger-chile allotment. Close the flaps and smear the top of the fillet with the remaining half. The fillet will look tinted with curry on its smeared surfaces even though there aren't enough vegetables to cover—that's okay, because the oil has lots of flavor to impart. Repeat this process with the other fillets.

Oil a baking pan large enough to hold all the fillets comfortably in one layer, and lay in the fillets, flap side up. Place the pan in the oven and bake for 12 to 15 minutes, or until the fillets are just cooked through. It's easy to tell if they're cooked—unfold one side of a flap and look for any pink rawness. Cook a minute or two longer if necessary. (The fillets have a good deal of brownish fat, don't confuse it with pink undercooked flesh.)

TO SERVE: Place the fillets on warm dinner plates. Top each with a dollop of plain yogurt and a scattering of cilantro leaves, if desired, and serve right away.

Shad Roe with
Vinegar-Bacon Meunière

4 servings

PREP AND
COOKING
TIME
30–35
minutes

*S*had roe needs only a shot of sharpness to cut its surprising earthiness, and a crunch of contrasting texture. With that in mind, a brown butter meunière with lemon, red wine vinegar, and a scattering of crisp bacon pieces is just right. I must warn you that shad roe can be rather explosive when sautéed—and I'm not talking about taste! The eggs can pop out of their thin membrane and fly around the kitchen. After the first recipe test, I wiped down a few walls, so I decided to suggest two things: First, blanch the roe very briefly in simmering water to firm it slightly, and second, cover the pan while sautéing. If you love shad roe, the little bit of trouble is worth it for the short period it's available in the spring. There is no substitute for shad roe, but the meunière is delicious on any other kind of fillet, with or without the bacon.

4 thin slices bacon, *or* $1^1/_2$ tablespoons vegetable oil
Salt and freshly ground black or white pepper to taste
Two pair shad roe, each pair 6–8 ounces
Flour for dredging
$1^1/_2$ tablespoons butter
1 tablespoon fresh squeezed lemon juice
2 teaspoons red wine vinegar or other vinegar
Optional: 1 tablespoon snipped fresh chives

TO PREPARE: Cut the bacon, if you're using it, into $^1/_2''$ strips and place it over low heat in a skillet that will be large enough to hold all the roe in one layer. (Or use 2 skillets later for the roe.) Cook it, stirring frequently, until crisp and brown. Remove it from the skillet with a slotted spoon and set it aside to drain on paper towels. Reserve $1^1/_2$ tablespoons of the fat in the skillet, saving or discarding the rest, and set the skillet aside. Or, place the vegetable oil in the skillet and set it aside.

Place a deep skillet or saucepan (with enough water to cover the roe) over high heat with salt and bring it to a boil. Separate each pair of roe by cutting the membrane between the lobes. Trim and discard this center membrane, trying not to puncture the roe. Don't worry if the roe is punctured, however.

Slip the roe into the water and *simmer* them, turning them once, just long enough to turn the outside raw color to brown, 10 to 20 seconds. Remove them to dry on paper towels.

Place the reserved skillet with the bacon fat or vegetable oil over medium heat. Season the roe with salt and pepper, and dredge them lightly in flour, patting off the excess. When the fat is hot, place the roe in the skillet with room around each one. Cover the pan, and brown one side of the roe for 3 to 4 minutes. Remove the cover (stand back—I use the cover as a shield!) and turn the roe over with tongs. Cover the skillet and cook the second side for 2 to 3 minutes. The inside of the roe at this point will be creamy and slightly underdone. If you like it more well done, sauté each side a minute or two longer. Remove the roe to a platter and keep them warm while you make the meunière.

In a small saucepan, melt the butter over medium-high heat—the butter will froth up and then subside. When it begins to subside, gently swirl the pan—you'll see and smell the butter begin to turn brown within a few seconds. When the butter has become nut brown, immediately add the lemon juice and vinegar and turn off the heat—the addition of the cool acid makes the butter boil briefly and stops it from browning further. Swirl or stir the mixture together and season it with salt and pepper. (You can make the meunière just before cooking the roe, if you prefer—it won't have the same immediacy of flavor but it'll still be good.)

TO SERVE: Place the shad roe on warm dinner plates, spoon the meunière over them, and sprinkle with the reserved bacon and chives, if using. Serve right away.

Smothered Shad Roe à la James Beard

4 servings

PREP AND
COOKING
TIME
30–35
minutes

*J*im Beard had an unfailing sense of purity and balance—and never, never added an ingredient unless he believed it had a real connection to the origins and taste of the dish. His classic smothered shad roe can't be much improved on, but I've taken the liberty of lightening it by using less butter, and adding tarragon for a higher note. "Smothering" the roe, incidentally, refers to cooking it slowly in butter in a covered pan to keep it creamy and tender. He suggested simple boiled potatoes and crisp bacon strips as an accompaniment. I'd include grilled or broiled tomatoes as well.

Two pair shad roe, each pair 6–8 ounces
3 tablespoons butter
Salt and freshly ground black or white pepper to taste
2 tablespoons fresh squeezed lemon juice
2 teaspoons chopped fresh (flat-leaf or curly) parsley
1 teaspoon coarsely chopped fresh tarragon, *or* $^1/_2$ teaspoon dried
Lemon wedges

TO PREPARE: Preheat the oven to 350°.

Separate each pair of roe by cutting through the membrane between the lobes. Trim and discard this center membrane, trying not to puncture the roe. But don't worry if the roe is punctured, the recipe will still work.

In a skillet large enough to hold all the roe comfortably, melt the butter over low heat. Pat the roe dry with paper towels and season them with salt and pepper. Place them in the warm, not hot, butter just long enough to turn their exterior brown, 5 to 10 seconds. Roll them over to the other side, cover the pan, and put it in the oven. Bake the roe for 10 to 14 minutes, or until they're almost cooked through but still slightly underdone in the center—make a cut in the middle of one to see. Cook them a minute or two longer if you want them well done. Remove the pan from the oven and place the roe on a platter to keep warm.

Stir the lemon juice into the buttery juices in the pan, adjust the seasoning with salt and pepper, and stir in the parsley and tarragon.

TO SERVE: Place the roe on warm dinner plates, spoon the herb butter juices over them, and serve right away, with lemon wedges on the side.

SHARK

FLAVOR: Between mild and medium, not as sweet or rich as swordfish

ORIGIN: Pacific and Atlantic oceans

GOOD SIGNS: Flesh firm but resilient; fresh white or pinkish color; clean smell (although a faint ammonia odor can be present even when fresh because of the initial cleaning process)

BAD SIGNS: Dingy or discolored; flaccid muscle tone or separating flakes; mushy or soft; strong ammonia smell

HEALTH TIPS: A raw 7-ounce steak is approximately 250 calories and contains a moderate amount of omega-3 fatty acids. Shark is fat-free (because it stores its fat in its liver) and high in protein.

Considering our fear of, and fascination with, sharks, somehow it seems only fitting that we eat them, although many people still find that thought too creepy for words! But a good shark steak has many of the same charms as a good swordfish steak—it's moist, meaty (slightly mealy as well, without the negative that can convey), and satisfying, without however (to my taste) reaching the deepest level of sweetness and flavor of the "armed one"! But I don't think of them as "road-show" stand-ins, replacing the star when the show leaves Broadway; they fall somewhere between the delicacy of white meat and the richness of dark meat (but closer to dark), and they can be, in fact, even juicier than swordfish.

Most of the shark steaks we commonly see in the market are cut from mako and black-tip sharks, generally weighing in at about 125 pounds. But we know, from cable shows and movies like *Jaws*, that sharks can reach much heavier weights—up to 1,500 pounds, at which time the dinner spotlight turns on us! The steaks you buy can be entirely skinless or have a strip of thick black or gray inedible skin along one side. Either way, they're appealingly versatile and take well to sautéing, broiling, grilling, poaching, stir-frying, and frying. In England, they show up frequently as the fish in fish and chips! However, buy carefully when they're prewrapped in supermarket plastic "coffins"—they turn bad very quickly without exposure to air. Buy them only if they look white and fresh, and if their "sell-by" date gives one or two days grace. When you get them home, rinse the steaks in lightly salted water acidulated with lemon juice if there is a *mild* odor of ammonia. Take them right back to the store if the odor is strong.

Grilled Shark Steaks with
Cumin Vinaigrette

4 servings

PREP AND
COOKING
TIME
25–30
minutes

The smoky flavor from the grill enhances shark steaks—and that smokiness is mirrored by the ground cumin in the vinaigrette. With a little mustard and two kinds of vinegar, one for sharpness and one for earthiness, the whole dish plays between these points. I like to add some whole cuminseed for texture, and if they're lightly toasted, the flavor is magnified. The vinaigrette is also good with grouper and salmon fillets, swordfish steaks, and sea scallops

Optional: $^{1}/_{4}$ teaspoon whole cuminseed

1 teaspoon Dijon mustard, preferably French

1 teaspoon ground cumin

$^{1}/_{4}$ teaspoon dried oregano

$^{1}/_{8}$ teaspoon dried basil

2 teaspoons red wine vinegar

1 teaspoon balsamic vinegar

$^{1}/_{4}$ cup + 4 teaspoons olive oil

Salt and freshly ground black or white pepper to taste

Tabasco sauce to taste

Four 7-ounce shark steaks, each 1″ thick

Optional: 2–3 tablespoons diced ripe tomato

TO PREPARE: Start a hot fire in the grill (or preheat the oven broiler). Fifteen minutes before you're going to grill the steaks, put the grill grate 4″ or 5″ above the glowing coals if it isn't already there. (I also like to brush the top of the grate with vegetable oil just before grilling to help prevent sticking.)

If you're adding whole cuminseed, place them in a very small skillet over very low heat and toast them, shaking the skillet the entire time, until you smell the aroma of toasting cumin and you see the seeds *beginning* to color lightly, 1 to 2 minutes. Don't allow the seeds to get dark, or they'll taste bitter. Set them aside.

Place the Dijon mustard in a small mixing bowl (using the coiled snake towel trick if the bowl doesn't sit steady, see page 153) with the ground cumin, oregano, and basil. Whisk in the 2 vinegars until the mixture is smooth. Gradually whisk in the ¹/₄ cup of the olive oil to make a lightly thickened vinaigrette. Season the vinaigrette with salt, pepper, and Tabasco sauce to taste. Stir in the cooled cuminseed, if you're using them, and set the dressing aside. The vinaigrette can be made a week ahead, covered, and refrigerated. However, let it come to room temperature before using it. If it has separated, try whisking it vigorously while it's still cold or whirring it in a blender. Separated or not, it'll taste good.

Dry the steaks with paper towels, season them with salt and pepper, and rub them all over with the remaining 4 teaspoons of olive oil. Place them on the rack over the coals or on the broiler pan, and grill or broil them for 4 to 5 minutes on the first side, until they've browned. Turn them over and grill or broil the second side for 3 or 4 minutes more. Depending on the intensity of the coals, the steaks should be done at this point. To check, make a slit in the center of one—it should be white and opaque throughout.

TO SERVE: Place the shark steaks on warm dinner plates, spoon the cumin vinaigrette over them, and sprinkle each one with the diced tomato, if desired. Serve right away.

The best flavor you can get from a ground spice that was once whole, like cumin, fennel, cloves, and coriander, comes by grinding it yourself. This is, of course, why peppermills were invented. But here's how it works for lots of other spices. (If you're groaning over the thought of this, move on!)

You can grind many whole spices easily, and quickly, in a small electric coffee grinder. Grind what you need for the recipe—or a little extra—but don't defeat the purpose by grinding enough for a year, no matter how much fun you're having. Once you've done it, restrict your grinder to spices, unless you want to create a most extraordinary coffee!

Sautéed Shark with Fast Tomatoes, Garlic, and Hot Pepper Flakes

4 servings

PREP AND
COOKING
TIME
30 minutes

Something about tomato sauces always satisfies; they're so elemental, and they have the taste of the big three: tomatoes, olive oil, and garlic. What this is, is a really quick marinara with big, giving warmth. As soon as I see its beautiful red tomatoes, I know I'm about to eat something good for my mouth and good for my soul! Serve it with sautéed, grilled, or broiled shark steaks, with salmon or monkfish fillets, and swordfish or tuna steaks, or with shrimp, calamari, or lobster.

4 large garlic cloves, peeled
2 cups drained, canned whole plum tomatoes or crushed tomatoes
3 tablespoons olive oil
$^1/_2$ teaspoon crushed red pepper flakes, or to taste
Salt and freshly ground black or white pepper to taste
Four 7-ounce shark steaks, each about $^3/_4''$ thick
Flour for dredging

TO PREPARE: Preheat the oven to 400°.

Slice the garlic into long, very thin slices and then push the slices together in a mound and cut them into narrow slivers. If using whole plum tomatoes, slice them $^1/_4''$ thick or crush them in the palm of your hand over a bowl. Set both aside briefly.

Heat 2 tablespoons of the olive oil in a large skillet over high heat (so that the tomato juices will evaporate quickly), and when the oil is hot, add the tomatoes and garlic. (The tomatoes will spatter when you add them, so be careful.) Stir them into the oil, and cook them over high heat, stirring occasionally, for 3 to 5 minutes, or until the tomatoes have lost their excess liquid but are still very moist. (Some canned tomatoes are softer and wetter than others.) Stir in the red pepper flakes and cook for another minute or so, until the tomatoes are moist but not runny and the garlic is tender. Turn off the heat and season the sauce with salt and pepper. Set it aside while you prepare the steaks. The tomatoes can be refrigerated for up to a week.

Put the remaining tablespoon of olive oil into a skillet large enough to sauté the steaks comfortably in one layer, and set it over medium high heat. Season the steaks with salt and pepper, and dredge them lightly in flour, patting off any excess. When the oil is hot, slip the steaks into the skillet. Cook the steaks on the first side for 2 to 3 minutes, or until they're golden brown. Turn them over and place the skillet in the oven until the steaks are just cooked through, about 5 minutes. To check, place the end of a metal spatula or a paring knife in the thickest part of one steak and cut the flesh open slightly to see if the steak is white and opaque throughout. Gently reheat the tomatoes for the last minute the steaks are in the oven, or for a few minutes longer if the sauce has been refrigerated.

TO SERVE: Place the shark steaks on warm dinner plates. Coat the top of each with a thick layer of tomatoes, and serve right away.

It's a fact of life that sometimes the only "fresh" fish fillets we can buy come in prewrapped plastic supermarket packages. The packaging does allow you to see the top of the fillets (although I like to look at the back side too!) but it prevents you from touching and, to a large degree, smelling them. Bring the package to your nose anyway—if you can smell any odor through the plastic, it's not likely to be a good purchase. There is, or should be, a "sell-by" date stamped on the top of the package—look at it. I would be comfortable buying the fillets if the date showed at least one day's grace and the fillets looked freshly cut, not discolored. When you bring them home, unwrap them immediately to let them breathe again. Place them on a plate covered with clean plastic wrap, and refrigerate them until you're ready to cook. Home plastic wrap isn't going to create an oxygen-proof chamber.

Sautéed Shark with Red Peppers, Red Onions, and Orange

4 servings

PREP AND COOKING TIME 35–40 minutes

The combination of sweet red bell peppers, ground cumin, dry sherry, and freshly grated orange zest, all simmered together, makes an accompaniment for shark steaks that's lively and heartwarming! Salmon, trout, and delicate fillets like cod and snapper make good partners too.

3 tablespoons olive oil

2 cups thinly sliced red onions

3 cups sliced red bell peppers, about $^1/_3''$ wide × the length of the pepper

Salt and freshly ground black or white pepper to taste

Four 7-ounce shark steaks, each $^1/_2''$–$^3/_4''$ thick

Flour for dredging

2 teaspoons ground cumin

1 teaspoon grated orange zest (see page 133)

2 tablespoons dry sherry

TO PREPARE: Preheat the oven to 400°.

Place 2 tablespoons of the olive oil in a large skillet over medium heat. When the oil is hot, stir in the onions and peppers, season them with salt and pepper, and cook them, stirring occasionally, until they're a little brown and tender-crisp, about 8 minutes. While they cook, start the shark.

Put the remaining tablespoon of olive oil in a skillet large enough to hold the steaks comfortably in one layer, and set the pan over medium heat. Season the steaks on both sides with salt and pepper, and dip them into the flour, patting off any excess. Raise the heat to high, and brown the steaks on one side in the hot oil, about 3 minutes. Turn them over and place the skillet in the oven until they're just cooked through, 5 to 6 minutes. While the steaks cook, finish the pepper mixture.

When the onions are tender and the peppers still a little crisp, reduce the heat to low and stir in the cumin, orange zest, and sherry. Turn off the heat and adjust the seasoning, if necessary, with salt and pepper. Keep the vegetables warm while the shark finishes cooking.

When the steaks are done, they'll be white and opaque throughout. To check, insert the end of a metal spatula or the tip of a paring knife in the thickest part of one steak and gently push or cut the flesh open slightly.

Place the shark steaks on warm dinner plates with some of the red pepper mixture next to them, and serve right away.

I hate grating fruit rinds. But here's a way of doing it that makes it less aggravating:

Wrap a piece of plastic wrap over the perforations on the side of a box grater that you're going to use and grate as usual over the plastic. All the rind that normally ends up inside still does, but the rind on the outside—the maddening stuff that resides *between* the sharp perforations that you have to coax out with the tip of a knife—is now happily resting on the outside of the plastic wrap. Remove the plastic wrap, lay it out on the counter, and scrape the peel together with a rubber spatula. Voilà!

Stir-Fried Shark
with Sesame Noodles

4 servings

PREP AND
COOKING
TIME
40–45
minutes

Cut shark steaks into small pieces, marinate them briefly in soy sauce and Chinese five-spice powder, and then quickly stir-fry them in sesame oil with red bell peppers and scallions. Pour the hot stir-fry onto a bed of cool, earthy, buckwheat noodles that have been tossed in more sesame oil, sesame seeds, rice wine vinegar, and a few drops of hot pepper sesame oil. It makes a good light meal or unexpected and elegant first course for a party. You can substitute swordfish, tuna, mahimahi, or salmon fillets, or small shrimp or bay scallops, for the shark.

4 teaspoons sesame seeds

Salt to taste

One 8-ounce package Japanese buckwheat (soba) or other Oriental-style noodles (supermarket Oriental shelf)

4 teaspoons sesame oil

2 teaspoons brown rice vinegar or regular rice vinegar

1½ teaspoons hot pepper sesame oil or to taste, *or* other hot sauce to taste + 1½ teaspoons additional sesame oil

Three 8-ounce shark steaks, preferably mako

1 tablespoon soy sauce

¾ teaspoon Chinese five-spice powder (supermarket spice shelf, see page 135)

2 tablespoons vegetable oil

1 cup thinly sliced red bell pepper strips, about ⅛″ × 2″

¾ cup diagonally sliced scallions, white and green parts

TO PREPARE: Preheat the oven to 350° (or use a toaster oven).

Bring a large pot of water to a boil over high heat for the noodles. Place the sesame seeds in a small ovenproof pan and toast them in the oven for about 10 minutes, or until they're light gold. Set them aside.

Add a generous amount of salt to the water when it boils. Drop the noodles into the boiling water and cook them for 3 to 5 minutes, until al dente (or according to package directions—but check them sooner, sometimes the directions instruct you to cook them too long). Pour the noodles into a colander under cold running water to cool them down quickly. Drain them *very* well and place them in a large mixing bowl. Add 2 teaspoons of the sesame oil, the toasted sesame seeds, rice vinegar, and 1½ teaspoons (or more to taste) of hot pepper sesame oil (or 1½ teaspoons sesame oil plus hot sauce to taste), and salt, and toss it well. Put the noodles on a serving platter, loosely covered, and set them aside at room temperature (for up to 1 hour, or refrigerate them if the kitchen is very warm) while you prepare the stir-fry.

Trim the skin, any white membrane, and any dark fat from the steaks and discard it. Cut across the steaks the short way to make ½"-thick strips, and put them in a large mixing bowl. Sprinkle them with the remaining 2 teaspoons of sesame oil and gently toss them with a rubber spatula or chopsticks. Sprinkle them with the soy sauce followed by the five-spice powder. Gently toss them again and set them aside while you heat the oil in the wok. Place the wok or very large skillet over high heat with the vegetable oil. When the oil is beginning to smoke, slide in the shark strips and red bell peppers and stir-fry them for 2 to 4 minutes, or until the shark strips are *just* cooked. Turn off the heat and stir in the scallions.

TO SERVE: Spoon the shark stir-fry over the noodles and serve right away.

Chinese five-spice powder, also called five-fragrance spice powder (more poetic to my ear!), is a mixture of finely ground spices—sometimes more than five—that can differ depending on who's mixing them. Generally, though, the five biggies are star anise, cloves, fennel or aniseed, cinnamon, and Szechuan peppercorns. Ginger is also frequently included, as well as nutmeg. Unless the powder mixture is stale, it has a sweet and fragrant aroma and a lightly sweet, spicy-hot flavor. If you have trouble finding it, try mixing equal amounts of ground cinnamon, cloves, aniseed, and ginger, with half the amount of black pepper.

SWORDFISH

FLAVOR: Sweet, rich, and full but not strong

ORIGIN: Pacific and Atlantic oceans, Mediterranean Sea

GOOD SIGNS: Somewhat translucent, glistening flesh; white-ish beige to pearly pink, or even pale salmon in color; flesh dense and resilient with few, if any, obvious white circular membranes; looks and feels firm and full

BAD SIGNS: Dingy or discolored with flaccid muscle tone; pronounced white circular membranes throughout the flesh; mushy or soft, badly bruised sections; musty smelling, or any hint of ammonia

HEALTH TIPS: A raw 7-ounce serving of swordfish is approximately 240 calories with a moderate amount of omega-3 fatty acids and protein.

Think of swordfish this way: It's a very large fish weighing up to 1,000 pounds, whose body, looking something like a long bullet snuggly encased in thick black or battleship-gray skin, announces itself with its active sword. When *we* see it, however, it's another matter entirely!

At best, we see a thick cross-section of the fish with its central backbone. Or we see only a large, thick slice. Either way, this section gets cut into rough triangular- or rectangular-shape pieces called steaks. The best ones are cut from the middle of the fish—the center cut—and they're the prime, most tender cuts. Steaks cut close to the tail end have visible connective tissue—which look like white whorls circling through the flesh—and that makes them chewy.

Avoid steaks that are sitting directly on ice because the ice can "burn" the flesh and any melting ice can waterlog it. In fact, the best way to preserve and protect fish steaks and fillets is to hold them on trays *over* ice in a refrigerated case. Whole fish have skin and scales to protect their vulnerable flesh, so they can safely lie directly on the ice.

Freshly cut swordfish steaks naturally glisten—their shine is almost pearlescent. The flesh is resilient when pressed and feels firm and full. When they're old, they look like we all do when we're sick, with a gray, dingy pallor and a hangdog demeanor! Their flesh may be mushy—sometimes you can almost push your finger into it. If you see this, run the other way as fast as you can, or if you've gotten stuck with these steaks, run right back to the market and get your money back! Prewrapped supermarket swordfish steaks hold fairly well, but check the "sell-by" date closely.

The color of swordfish, whether pale beige or pinky salmon, doesn't indicate its freshness or quality. It does indicate what *it's* been dining on: Pink means you've brought home swordfish that preferred shrimp for supper!

You can happily sauté, stir-fry, grill, broil, bake, fry, and braise swordfish steaks. However, overcooking it changes its pleasing meaty texture into that of a mouthful of sand.

Grilled Swordfish Marinated in Lemon, Rosemary, and Fennel

4 servings

PREP AND
COOKING
TIME
20 minutes +
2 hours' to
2 days'
marinating
time

I started serving swordfish this way at my tiny Restaurant Leslie years ago, and never stopped. There's something so simple, and so right, about the combination. The steaks become quietly infused with lemon, rosemary, and fennel, particularly if they're marinated for 1 or 2 days. And they're equally good grilled in the summer, or broiled in the winter. Try the marinade with red snapper or bass fillets, tuna steaks, or shrimp, scallops, or pieces of lobster.

1 large garlic clove, unpeeled

Four 7-ounce swordfish steaks, each ³/₄″–1″ thick

2 tablespoons fresh squeezed lemon juice

1 tablespoon dry vermouth or white wine

3 tablespoons olive oil

¹/₂ teaspoon whole fennel seed

1 tablespoon roughly chopped fresh rosemary leaves, *or* 1 teaspoon dried

Salt and freshly ground black or white pepper to taste

TO PREPARE: Smash the garlic clove lightly with the side of a large knife, peel it, and rub the garlic all over the steaks. Place the steaks and the garlic clove in a shallow, nonaluminum pan and briefly set them aside.

Put the lemon juice and vermouth or white wine in a small mixing bowl and gradually whisk in the olive oil (use the coiled snake towel trick if the bowl doesn't sit steady, see page 153). Stir in the fennel and rosemary. Pour the marinade all over the steaks, turning them several times to coat them well. Cover the pan and refrigerate the steaks for up to 2 days, turning them once during this period. (If you're pressed for time, the steaks can marinate several hours only.)

Start a medium-hot fire in the grill (or preheat the oven broiler). Fifteen minutes before you're going to grill the steaks, put the grill grate 4″ or 5″ above the glowing coals if it isn't already there. (I also like to brush the top of the grate with vegetable oil before grilling to prevent sticking.)

When you're ready to cook the steaks, remove them from the marinade, reserve the marinade, and wipe most of the herbs and oil off the fish. (Removing the excess oil will prevent flare-ups on the grill but still leave the steaks oiled.) Season them with salt and pepper and place them on the grill (or on the broiler). Grill them, turning them once midway, for 5 to 7 minutes, or until they're just cooked through. (If broiling, do not turn them.) To check, make a small incision in the center of one steak to see if it's opaque all the way through, or use the wooden skewer trick (see page 53).

TO SERVE: Gently heat the reserved marinade in a small saucepan, season it with salt and pepper, and strain it. Place the swordfish steaks on warm dinner plates, drizzle them with a little marinade, and serve right away.

Do you want to impress yourself (and your family and friends!) with restaurant-style grill marks? You know, those lines that criss-cross the top of a fillet in a cool diamond sort of pattern. It's actually simple.

Begin by placing the fillet on the grill as you normally would. But halfway through its time on the first side, lift the fillet with your metal spatula, turn it about 45°, and place the fillet back down on the grill *at that angle on the same side*. Continue grilling it, like normal, until that side is done. Then turn the fillet over. What you should see are diamond markings covering the top of the fillet. Don't bother double-marking the second side in the same fashion (unless you want to practice)—this is all for show anyway!

Swordfish Sautéed with Onions and Tomatoes

4 servings

PREP AND COOKING TIME 35–40 minutes

*S*autéed onions are so sweet and giving, and like so many ordinary things we often don't pay much attention to, they're the best. Cook them with chopped tomatoes, oregano, and sage, and then make a small mountain of them on top of sautéed, grilled, or broiled swordfish steaks. These onions would also be good with tuna or shark steaks, or salmon, red snapper, sole, halibut, or grouper fillets.

2 tablespoons olive oil
1 tablespoon butter
4 cups thinly sliced onions (see page 141)
Salt and freshly ground black or white pepper to taste
$^3/_4$ teaspoon dried oregano
$^1/_2$ teaspoon dried sage leaves, crumbled
$^1/_2$ cup drained, seeded, chopped canned plum tomatoes, + 2 tablespoons juice from can
Four 7-ounce swordfish steaks, each $^3/_4''$–$1''$ thick
Flour for dredging

TO PREPARE: Preheat the oven to 350°.

In a large skillet, heat a tablespoon of the olive oil over high heat. Add the butter, and when it foams, stir in the onions. Lower the heat to medium and season the onions lightly with salt and pepper. Sauté the onions, stirring frequently, until they are nicely browned, 10 to 12 minutes, adjusting the heat if they brown too quickly. Stir in the oregano and sage during the last minute or so. (At this point, the onions can be covered and refrigerated for up to 4 days and finished with the tomatoes the day you're using them.) Stir in the tomatoes and their juice, and cook the mixture over low heat for another minute. Adjust the seasoning, if necessary, with salt and pepper and set the onions aside while you brown the steaks.*

*If you're serving the onions over grilled or broiled fillets, continue simmering them until they're tender and most of the liquid has evaporated. If a lot of liquid remains when the onions are ready, remove them with a slotted spoon and reduce the liquid over high heat to concentrate it, then stir the onions back in and adjust the seasoning if necessary.

Dry the steaks with paper towels. Place the remaining tablespoon of olive oil in an ovenproof skillet large enough to hold the steaks comfortably in one layer (or use 2 medium and divide the oil between them), and set it over medium heat. Meanwhile, season the steaks with salt and pepper and dredge them lightly in flour, patting off the excess. Turn the heat to high, and when the oil is almost smoking, brown the steaks on one side, 2 to 3 minutes. Turn them over and briefly brown the second side, 1 to 2 minutes. Turn off the heat and pour the onion mixture over and around the steaks. Place the skillet in the oven for 4 to 6 minutes, or until the steaks are just cooked through. To check, make a small slit in the center of one steak with a paring knife, or use the wooden skewer trick (see page 53). They should be opaque all the way through.

TO SERVE: Place the swordfish steaks on warm dinner plates. Mound the onions and tomatoes on top of them and let the onions cascade a little over the sides. Serve right away.

If you want to peel and slice an onion the way it's done in a professional kitchen, here's how:

Slice off about $\frac{1}{2}''$ at both ends of the onion. Make one cut through the skin and first layer of the onion, going from one flat end to the other. Slip your fingers inside the cut, grab the outer layer and attached skin, and peel it off—it'll come off in one circular shell-like piece. If you're planning on making a meat, poultry, or vegetable broth in the next 2 or 3 days, save these trimmings to use, otherwise discard them.

To slice the onion evenly, stand it on a flat end and cut it in half from top to bottom. Lay the halves on their newly cut flat side. With a sharp knife, slice the onion following the natural lines that you see on the top (round) side. The onion will fall into even, thin slices.

Baked Swordfish with Roasted Red Pepper and Mushroom Sauce

4 servings

PREP AND
COOKING
TIME
35–40
minutes + 25
minutes if
roasting your
own peppers

*S*tir together chopped roasted red peppers, mushrooms, garlic, red wine, and thyme, and pour the mixture over thick swordfish steaks that you've browned in olive oil. Bake it all in the oven, and when it's ready, the swordfish will be smothered in smoky-red, satiny peppers with sultry juices. The roasted pepper–mushroom mixture can be prepared in advance, which makes it good for a dinner party—but serve it to friends you know really enjoy food; don't waste it on annoying picky types! Substitute shark or tuna steaks, or salmon fillets. Or, make the sauce separately and serve it over grilled, sautéed, or broiled seafood.

2–3 large red bell peppers, *or* $^3/_4$ cup finely chopped, bottled roasted red peppers

$^1/_4$ pound fresh white mushrooms or exotic mushrooms (such as shiitakes or portobellos)

3 garlic cloves, finely chopped

1 tablespoon + 1 teaspoon chopped fresh (flat-leaf or curly) parsley

1$^1/_2$ teaspoons fresh thyme leaves, *or* $^1/_2$ teaspoon dried

2 tablespoons butter

Salt and freshly ground black or white pepper to taste

$^1/_4$ cup dry red wine

1 tablespoon olive oil

Four 7-ounce swordfish steaks, each $^3/_4''$–$1''$ thick

Flour for dredging

TO PREPARE: Preheat the broiler, putting the rack at the top rung and lightly oil a broiling pan. (Skip this step if using bottled roasted peppers.) Cut the peppers in half lengthwise and remove and discard the seeds and ribs. Place the pepper halves on the counter, cut side down. Flatten each half by pressing down with your palm. Place the peppers on the oiled broiling pan and broil them until the skins blister and blacken, 10 to 15 minutes. Transfer the peppers to a paper bag or a covered bowl to steam. While all that's happening, briefly rinse the mushrooms, dry them with paper towels, and chop them by hand or with a food processor to the size of small peas. You should have about $1^{1}/_{4}$ cups of chopped mushrooms.

Turn the oven down to 350°. When the peppers are cool enough to handle, peel away the blackened skin and discard it. (It helps to rinse your hands occasionally as you do this, but don't rinse the peppers because that will dilute their flavor.) Chop the peppers fine, by hand or in a food processor, to measure $^{3}/_{4}$ cup, and set them aside. Mix the chopped garlic, 1 tablespoon of the chopped parsley, and the thyme in a small bowl and set aside.

In a medium-size skillet set over high heat, melt the butter. When the butter foams, add the mushrooms and sauté them for 1 minute, stirring occasionally, or until their juices start to flow. (If you're using wild mushrooms with a low water content, sauté them over medium heat until they're tender.) Reduce the heat to low and stir in the garlic-herb mixture. Cook for 1 minute, stir in the chopped peppers, and cook for another minute to heat through. Season the mixture with salt and pepper. (At this point, you can cool, cover, and refrigerate the mixture for 2 to 3 days.*

Add the olive oil to an ovenproof skillet large enough to hold the steaks comfortably in one layer, and set it over medium heat. Season the steaks with salt and pepper, lightly dredge them in flour, and pat off the excess. Increase the heat to high, and when the oil is almost smoking, lightly brown the steaks on one side for 2 to 3 minutes, then turn them over and brown the other side for 1 to 2 minutes. Pour off any excess oil if necessary.

Pour pepper-mushroom mixture over and around the steaks and place the skillet in the oven, uncovered. Bake until the steaks are just cooked through, 5 to 8 minutes. To check, make a small slit in the thickest part of one steak to see of it's opaque all the way through or use the wooden skewer trick (see page 53).

Remove the steaks to a warm platter while you finish the sauce. Place the skillet over medium heat, adding any collected juices from the platter, and boil down the juices for 1 or 2 minutes to thicken them slightly—stirring frequently to keep the solids from sticking and burning. Adjust the seasoning with salt and pepper.

TO SERVE: Place the swordfish on warm dinner plates, smother them with the pepper-mushroom sauce, and sprinkle them with the remaining teaspoon of chopped parsley. Serve right away.

*Or, if you're using the sauce with broiled or grilled fish or seafood, add only 2 tablespoons of wine and simmer the mixture, stirring occasionally, until it's thick and rich, 5 to 8 minutes.) To use the sauce right away, add the wine, bring it to a quick boil, and set the mixture aside.

Swordfish Sautéed with Red Wine and Tomatoes

4 servings

PREP AND
COOKING
TIME
30–35
minutes

This is one of those "all-in-one-shot" kind of recipes—fish and sauce made together in the same pan. After you brown the swordfish steaks, add red wine with a little chopped tomato, and bake it all together. When the steaks are done, boil down the pan juices and stir in a little bit of cold butter. The result is an intense and delicious sauce. You can substitute salmon fillets and tuna or shark steaks.

$^1/_3$ cup seeded, chopped canned plum tomatoes

$^3/_4$ cup dry red wine

2 small bay leaves

1 tablespoon fresh squeezed lemon juice

1 large garlic clove, finely chopped

Four 7-ounce swordfish steaks, each $^3/_4''$–$1''$ thick

1 tablespoon olive oil

Salt and freshly ground black or white pepper to taste

Flour for dredging

$1^1/_2$ tablespoons butter

Optional: 4 fresh (flat-leaf or curly) parsley sprigs

TO PREPARE: Preheat the oven to 350°.

In a small bowl, mix the chopped tomatoes, red wine, bay leaves, lemon juice, and chopped garlic together and set it aside.

Dry the steaks with paper towels. Place the olive oil in an ovenproof skillet large enough to hold the steaks comfortably in one layer, and set it over medium heat. Season the steaks with salt and pepper, and lightly dredge them in flour, patting off the excess. Turn the heat to high, and when the oil is almost smoking, brown the steaks lightly on one side, 2 to 3 minutes. Turn them over and briefly brown the second side, 1 minute. Turn off the heat and pour the tomato-wine mixture over the steaks, bringing it to one fast boil (if it hasn't immediately done that from the retained heat of the skillet). Put the skillet in the oven, uncovered, and bake the steaks for 5 to 7 minutes, until they are just cooked through and opaque. To check, make a small slit in the center of one steak with a paring knife, or use the wooden skewer trick (see page 53).

Place the steaks on a platter, scraping any tomatoes on top of them back into the skillet, and keep them warm. Place the skillet over high heat, stirring occasionally, and boil down the pan juices—adding any collected juices from the platter—to about $1/3$ cup, 6 to 8 minutes. Turn the heat to low, discard the bay leaves, and stir in the butter until it's smoothly absorbed into the sauce. Adjust the seasoning with salt and pepper.

TO SERVE: Place the swordfish steaks on warm dinner plates, discarding any further collected juices, spoon the sauce over them, and garnish with a parsley sprig, if desired. Serve right away.

Grilled Swordfish with
Sun-Dried Tomato Puree

4 servings + 4 to keep

PREP AND
COOKING
TIME
30 minutes

This sun-dried tomato puree has deep, deep flavor with body to match. When I make it, I do a double batch, because it can be refrigerated for a month (it only needs to be refreshed with a squeeze of lemon juice). It's terrific tossed with shrimp, over tuna or shark steaks, mixed into pasta, and spooned onto chicken—all in all, a blessing to have on hand. In fact, I'll make the puree just so it's there—ready to go on nights when I'm ready to collapse! Broil, grill, or sauté the swordfish, the puree is happy any way!

1 cup sun-dried tomatoes packed in oil

1 1/2 teaspoons chopped garlic or roasted garlic (see Pantry, to Make)

1/4 cup packed, washed, and drained basil leaves

Up to 1/2 cup + 4 teaspoons olive oil

3 tablespoons fresh squeezed lemon juice

Pinch of crushed red pepper flakes

Salt and freshly ground black or white pepper to taste

Four 7-ounce swordfish steaks, each 3/4"–1" thick

Lemon wedges

TO PREPARE: Start a medium-hot fire in the grill (or preheat the oven broiler). Fifteen minutes before you're going to grill the steaks, put the grill grate 4" or 5" above the glowing coals if it isn't already there. (I also like to brush the top of the grate with vegetable oil just before grilling to help prevent sticking.)

Drain the sun-dried tomatoes, reserving 1/4 cup of the oil for the puree. (Add the rest back into the jar.) Cut them into rough pieces and place them in the food processor. Add the garlic, basil, and reserved tomato oil. Puree all the ingredients, scraping the bowl down once or twice and gradually adding up to 1/2 cup of the olive oil to make a thick but slightly liquid mixture.

Add the lemon juice and hot pepper flakes and season the puree highly with salt and pepper. Set aside half the mixture at room temperature for today and refrigerate the rest. (If the kitchen is very hot, refrigerate all of it and take out what you need an hour before serving it.)

Dry the steaks with paper towels, season them with salt and pepper, rub them

Maine Lobster with Avocado "Whipped Cream"

Seared Tuna with
Balsamic Vinegar,
Garlic, and Pine Nuts

Sautéed Trout with
Mustard-Curry
Vinaigrette

Broiled Sole with Red Onion-Herb Vinaigrette

Baked Swordfish with
Roasted Red Pepper and
Mushroom Sauce

Cod Baked with
Tomatoes and
Fresh Thyme

Grilled Salmon
with Basil
Vinaigrette

Poached
Salmon with
Purple
Cabbage,
Mushrooms,
and Scallions

Fried Calamari

Halibut Baked
with Rosemary
and Preserved
Lemon

Stir-Fried Shark with Sesame Noodles

Grilled Sea Scallops with Olives in Olive Oil

TROUT

FLAVOR:	Elusively sweet, mild, somewhat nutty
ORIGIN:	Farmed
GOOD SIGNS:	Translucent, glistening flesh, shiny bright skin; flesh firm and fine textured, pale beige-pink to orange in color; clean aroma
BAD SIGNS:	Dingy or discolored; flaccid muscle tone, separating flakes; mushy or soft; musty smelling
HEALTH TIPS:	A raw 7-ounce serving of trout is approximately 236 calories, with a moderate amount of omega-3 fatty acids and high protein content.

Unless you have an angler in the family, the trout you buy will most likely be a farmed rainbow trout bred for ideal serving size. The fillets cut from the fish will be 6 or 7 ounces in weight and, hopefully, completely boned. If not, the fillets will have a large number of tiny bones, called pinbones, running down half the length of each fillet. They're annoying in your mouth, but there's no reason for them to get that far—they're easy to pull out before cooking. See the directions on page 155.

Rainbow trout are delicate and mild, with a subtle nutty flavor. They're very versatile and take to almost any type of cooking—poaching, baking, sautéing, broiling, steaming, and grilling—and are delicious served chilled. I particularly like them grilled—the smoky crispness seems to heighten their juicy nuttiness. And they don't need fussy adornment; they have a gentle but rather noble character that stands on its own. Should you come across any trout relatives, snap them up: Arctic char, salmon trout, or sea-run forms known as sea trout or steelhead trout. Each is delicate, mildly sweet, and succulent in its own way. They lie at different points along a flavor-texture axis between trout and salmon, but are closer to trout in spirit and delicacy.

Trout "Poached" with Garlic and Fresh Herbs

4 servings

PREP AND
COOKING
TIME
30–35
minutes

*S*immer trout fillets in a little chicken or vegetable broth with lots of chopped garlic until they're just cooked through. The fillets add their delicate flavor to the broth, and when you swirl in some cold butter, fresh dill, parsley, and tarragon, they turn the broth into a lightly thickened sauce that is both gutsy from the garlic and spirited from the herbs. And, of course, you can add or subtract herbs to suit your taste. Substitute snapper, sole, halibut, bass, sea trout, or Arctic char fillets, or shrimp, lobster meat, or scallops.

Four 6–7-ounce trout fillets

Salt and freshly ground black or white pepper to taste

1 tablespoon butter

2–3 large garlic cloves, finely chopped

$^1/_4$ cup chicken or vegetable broth

1 tablespoon fresh squeezed lemon juice

$1^1/_2$ tablespoons *cold* butter, cut into small pieces

2 teaspoons chopped fresh dill, *or* $^3/_4$ teaspoon dried

1 tablespoon chopped fresh (flat-leaf or curly) parsley

$1^1/_2$ teaspoons coarsely chopped fresh tarragon, *or* $^1/_2$ teaspoon dried

TO PREPARE: Pull out any tiny pinbones from the fillets, if necessary (see page 155) and season them with salt and pepper.

In a skillet large enough to hold all the fillets in one layer (see Notes), melt the tablespoon of butter over low heat. Add the garlic and cook it, stirring, for 30 seconds to cook off its raw taste. Add the chicken or vegetable broth and the lemon juice. (If using dried herbs, add them now.) Place the fillets, skin side up, in the skillet—the liquid should come less than halfway up the fillets—and bring the liquid to a low simmer. Cover the skillet with a lid or foil and steam-poach the fillets over very low heat until they're just cooked through and opaque, 5 to 7 minutes. Lift the fillets out of the skillet with a metal spatula and put them on a platter. Keep the juices in the skillet over very low heat while you skin the fillets (see Notes).

Peel the skin off each fillet by picking up a corner of it from the wide end and pulling it down toward the tail. If the fillet is completely cooked, it will come off easily and smoothly. If it doesn't, slip the fillets back into the simmering liquid, skin side down, for 1 to 2 minutes more. Discard the skins. Measure the broth in the skillet along with any juices that have collected on the platter—you should have about $\frac{1}{4}$ cup. Pour the broth back into the skillet and place it over high heat, reducing it, if necessary, to about $\frac{1}{4}$ cup or adding a little extra chicken broth to make $\frac{1}{4}$ cup.

With the broth still boiling, scatter the pieces of cold butter over it and swirl the skillet by the handle. The broth will absorb the butter and thicken within a minute. As soon as the butter is almost completely absorbed into the broth, turn off the heat, but continue to swirl the skillet until the butter is completely absorbed. Stir in the fresh herbs, if using, and adjust the seasoning with salt and pepper.

TO SERVE: With a metal spatula, turn the trout fillets over onto warm dinner plates (the skinned side will now be on the bottom), and spoon the garlic-herb sauce over them. Serve right away.

NOTES: If you don't have a skillet large enough to hold all the fillets, bake them in a 375° oven instead of simmering them on the stovetop. Place the seasoned fillets, skin side up, in a shallow baking or roasting pan. Melt the butter in a medium skillet and cook the garlic as directed above. Add the broth, lemon juice, and dried herbs, if you're using them, to the skillet and bring the mixture to a simmer. (Reserve the skillet for finishing the sauce.) Pour the hot broth over the fillets, cover the pan, and bake them for 10 to 15 minutes, or until cooked through and opaque. (The cooking time will vary depending upon the thickness of the baking pan, see page 7.) Pour the cooking broth back into the reserved skillet and proceed as above.

The skin holds the delicate fillet together, so if you're nervous about moving the fillets without this insurance, don't peel off their skins.

If you're fortunate enough to have a market with a live trout tank (where they'll fillet the fish for you after they've been fished out of the tank), look for lively fish. They'll have the best texture and flavor once they've made it out of the skillet and onto your plate. And by all means, stay away from any sluggish-acting fish— they're sick and probably aren't long for this world.

Sautéed Trout with
Mustard-Curry Vinaigrette

4 servings

PREP AND
COOKING
TIME
25 minutes

*T*his mustard-curry vinaigrette had a previous life at the Inn at Pound Ridge when I was the chef there. I drizzled it over golden-brown roasted sea scallops sitting on Indian basmati rice flecked with finely chopped carrot. The dish became popular, which surprised me, because usually writing "curry" on an American menu is sure death to the dish! But, as a result of its popularity, I had to prepare it frequently during each night's dinner service. Plating it pleased me every time, its golden range of yellows and oranges never failing to warm my heart. (As if the heat of the kitchen weren't enough!) But here I've spooned the vinaigrette over lightly crisped, browned trout fillets. And the vinaigrette is just as good with salmon, bass, monkfish, and mahimahi fillets, or sea scallops or shrimp, all either sautéed or grilled.

> 5^1/$_2$ teaspoons + 4^1/$_2$ tablespoons olive oil
>
> 1^1/$_2$ teaspoons curry powder
>
> 1^1/$_2$ tablespoons Dijon mustard, preferably French
>
> 1^1/$_2$ tablespoons fresh squeezed lemon juice
>
> Salt and freshly ground black or white pepper to taste
>
> Four 6–7-ounce trout fillets
>
> Flour for dredging
>
> Optional: 2 teaspoons chopped fresh dill

TO PREPARE: Preheat the oven to 400°.

In a small skillet over low heat, stir 1^1/$_2$ teaspoons of the olive oil together with the curry powder for about 30 seconds, to cook off its raw taste. (Curry powder can burn, so watch it carefully.) Set the curry oil aside and make the vinaigrette base.

Put the Dijon mustard in a small mixing bowl, and whisk in the lemon juice (using the coiled snake towel trick if the bowl doesn't sit steady, see page 153). Gradually whisk in the 4^1/$_2$ tablespoons of olive oil to make a thick, creamy dressing. Whisk in the *cooled* curry oil and season the vinaigrette with salt and pepper. Set it aside or refrigerate it for up to 3 weeks, being sure to serve it at room temperature. (The vinaigrette may separate when it comes out of the refrigerator. If so, whisk it vigorously to recombine it, or whir it in a blender for a few seconds. Separated or not, it'll still be good.)

Pull out any tiny pinbones from the fillets, if necessary (see page 155), and season them with salt and pepper. Place 2 large skillets over medium heat, dividing the remaining 4 teaspoons of olive oil between them (or use 1 skillet at least 12″ in diameter). Lightly dredge the fillets in flour and pat off the excess. Turn the heat to high, and when the oil is very hot, brown the fillets, flesh side down, for 2 to 3 minutes. Turn the fillets over and immediately put the skillets in the oven for 3 to 5 minutes, or until the fillets are just cooked through and opaque. To check, gently separate part of the thick end of one fillet with a paring knife or the end of a metal spatula.

TO SERVE: Place the trout fillets, skin side down, on warm dinner plates and spoon some of the room temperature vinaigrette over them. Sprinkle each fillet with the chopped dill, if desired, and serve right away.

The coiled snake towel trick is a technique from the restaurant kitchen (although we never called it that—we just said "use a towel") that keeps a bowl steady while you whisk in ingredients. Heavy, flat-bottomed bowls generally don't need help, but when faced with a sliding, slippery critter, here's what you do:

Take a kitchen towel and make it completely damp. Hold opposite corners of the towel, one in each hand, and spin it, rotating your wrists toward your body so that the towel wraps around itself to form a snakelike shape. Then coil it on your counter into a ring that is slightly smaller than the base of your bowl, so the bowl will fit snugly. The dampness keeps it from sliding and the snugness cradles it in place. Whisk away!

Sautéed Trout Fillets with
Chili Rub, Lime and Avocado

4 servings

PREP AND
COOKING
TIME
20–25
minutes

The chili rub, a mixture of chili powder, ground cumin and coriander, with garlic powder, has a hot bite that starts working about a minute into eating the fillets. Slices of creamy, cool avocado and squeezes of lime give the fish another dimension. If you like it, make a quadruple batch of the rub and keep it on your spice shelf. You can also roast the fillets, lightly oiled and chili rubbed, in a very hot oven without searing them first. Substitute salmon, salmon trout, steelhead trout, Arctic char, sea trout, red snapper, catfish, or black bass fillets.

2 teaspoons chili powder

$^3/_4$ teaspoon ground cumin

$^1/_4$ teaspoon ground coriander

$^1/_8$ teaspoon garlic powder

Four 6–7-ounce trout fillets

Salt and freshly ground black or white pepper to taste

1 lime + additional lime wedges for garnish

1 ripe avocado, preferably Hass variety from California (the ones with pebbly skin)

2 tablespoons vegetable oil

Flour for dredging

TO PREPARE: Preheat the oven to 400°.

In a small bowl, mix the chili powder, cumin, coriander, and garlic together and set aside.

Pull out any tiny pinbones from the fillets, if necessary (see page 155). Season the fillets with salt and pepper and sprinkle the flesh side evenly with the chili mixture. Cut the lime in half, squeeze some of its juice (just enough to moisten) over the chili side of the fillets, and lightly rub it all in. Cutting lengthwise through the skin of the avocado, cut 12 long slices, removing one slice at a time. Peel each slice, and place it on a plate. Squeeze the rest of the lime juice over the avocado slices, season them with salt and pepper, and set them aside while you cook the fillets.

Place 1 very large (or use 2, with 1 tablespoon oil in each) ovenproof skillet over medium heat with 2 tablespoons of vegetable oil. Meanwhile, lightly dredge the fillets in flour, patting off any excess. Turn the heat to high, and when the oil is beginning to smoke, add the fillets, chili side down, and sauté them until they're a splotchy golden brown, about 3 minutes. Turn them over with a metal spatula, and put the skillet in the oven for about 5 minutes, or until the fillets are just cooked through and opaque. To check, gently separate part of the thick end of one fillet with a paring knife or end of a metal spatula.

TO SERVE: Place the trout fillets, chili-rubbed side up, on warm dinner plates, lay 3 slices of avocado diagonally over each, and garnish the plate with lime wedges. Serve right away.

Many times I've bought trout fillets, brought them home, and found that they still have their pinbones in them—those very fine bones that run along about half the length of the fillet and drive you mad when you get them in your mouth. To deal with these bones, buy a long-nosed pliers at the hardware store and do this:

Run your index finger down the fillet toward the tail to locate the bones, they'll be sticking out a little. Hold the pliers almost horizontal to the fish and grab as many of the bones as you can at a time and pull them out—they come out easily. Run your finger down the fillet to check for any bones you may have missed, and proceed with your recipe.

Trout Grilled with Walnut Oil

4 servings

PREP AND
COOKING
TIME
15 minutes +
optional
20–30
minutes'
marinating
time

*I*f you have sophisticated tastes that are extremely simple, and like the *au naturale* flavor of trout, try this. It's nothing more than a sprinkle of *herbes de Provence* over the fillets, and a gloss of walnut or hazelnut oil before you grill them. They're a pleasure to grill—they brown beautifully, and their skin and edges get deliciously crisp. For the best browning, I like to cook them three quarters of the way through on their flesh side first, then turn them over to crisp the skin and quickly cook them through. A final drizzle of nut oil and a squeeze of lemon when they're on the plate is all they need. Substitute salmon, snapper, or bass fillets, if you wish.

> Four 6–7-ounce trout fillets
> Salt and freshly ground black or white pepper to taste
> 1 teaspoon dried *herbes de Provence* or other dried herbs of your choice
> 2–3 tablespoons French walnut or hazelnut oil, + more for drizzling
> Lemon wedges

TO PREPARE: Start a hot fire in the grill (or preheat the oven broiler). Fifteen minutes before you're going to grill the fillets, put the grill grate 4″ to 5″ above the coals if it isn't already there. (I also like to brush the top of the grate with vegetable oil just before grilling to help prevent sticking.)

Pull any pinbones from the fillets, if necessary (see page 155). Season them on both sides with salt and pepper and sprinkle the *herbes de Provence* evenly over their flesh side. Drizzle them with enough nut oil to coat them all over, and gently rub it in. If time allows, let the fillets sit, covered, for 20 to 30 minutes, to let the herbs become more fragrant.

Place the fillets, skin side up, on the grill (or skin side *down* in the broiler) and cook them for about 4 minutes, until the flesh is nicely seared and brown. Turn the fillets over with a long metal spatula to support them, and grill (or broil) the skin side for 1 to 2 minutes, until brown and crisp. Depending on the intensity of the coals, the fillets should be done at this point. To check, slightly separate the flesh in the thickest part of one fillet with your metal spatula—it should be opaque throughout.

TO SERVE: Place the trout fillets, flesh side up, on warm dinner plates, drizzle with additional nut oil if you like, and serve with lemon wedges.

TUNA

description

om mild and subtle to beefy, depending on the type of tuna
lantic and Pacific oceans in both temperate and tropical wa-
s, and the Mediterranean Sea

anslucent, glistening flesh; flesh satiny smooth, fine, firm, and
ense, with color from light pink to deep maroon, depending on
the type of tuna; clean aroma

BAD SIGNS: Dingy or discolored; flaccid muscle tone, separating flakes;
mushy or soft; musty smelling

HEALTH TIPS: A raw 7-ounce serving of tuna has an approximate range of 216
calories for yellowfin to 344 calories for albacore. All tuna are very
high in protein but range from low to high in omega-3 fatty acids.

When I see stunningly fresh yellowfin tuna steaks, they look like deep, translucent garnet-colored pools, reflecting light like jewels—it's a thrill to see them. However, all types of tuna steak oxidize fairly quickly, losing their luster and becoming a dull brown. This oxidation doesn't necessarily mean they're no longer good, but it does mean they weren't cut that day, or perhaps even the day before. Use aroma and firmness as your next best sensory tools before you buy. One important warning: Tuna steaks that are prewrapped in supermarket plastic turn bad more quickly than those sitting over ice (on trays, we hope). If you have a choice, choose those that are still "breathing" and not in little plastic-wrapped coffins. However, if plastic-wrapped tuna is all you can get, look closely at the "sell-by" date and don't buy it if it doesn't have *at least* one more day to go.

The most commonly seen tuna steaks are cut from albacore, yellowfin, and bigeye tuna. The color of cut albacore is light pink to pale red with a mild flavor to match. Yellowfin tuna is the color of garnets, with a flavor that's rich, subtle, and delicate all at once. Bigeye tuna is heartier in all ways, from its beefy maroon color to its deeper, meatier flavor. It's a less subtle tuna than either the albacore or the yellowfin and excellent in its own way. Use them interchangeably and find the personality that suits you best! Tuna steaks are wonderful grilled, sautéed, baked, broiled, roasted, or stir-fried—it's best to keep them underdone to keep them moist.

Broiled Tuna with Caesar Vinaigrette

4 servings

PREP AND COOKING TIME
25 minutes

*T*his eggless vinaigrette is exactly what I would put on a Caesar salad. And it's just as good spooned over a piece of grilled, broiled, or sautéed tuna without the lettuce. But you could also cut the tuna into chunks (before or after cooking), toss it with some of the dressing, and then scatter it over a classic Caesar of romaine, croutons, and Parmesan cheese to make a perfect light summer supper. And fear not, you anchovy haters, the anchovy in the dressing only gives it richer flavor, not anchovy flavor! Consider keeping a jar of this vinaigrette in the refrigerator for salads or other cooked fillets—just be sure to let it come to room temperature before serving it. This dish works well with salmon fillets, and swordfish and shark steaks too.

Four 7-ounce tuna steaks, each 1/2"–3/4" thick

2 teaspoons + 6 tablespoons olive oil

Salt and freshly ground black or white pepper to taste

1 tablespoon Dijon mustard, preferably French

1 teaspoon Worcestershire sauce

1 teaspoon anchovy paste or finely chopped anchovy fillet

1 medium garlic clove, pureed (see page 59)

3 tablespoons fresh squeezed lemon juice

1/4 cup freshly grated Parmigiano-Reggiano cheese

4 halves sun-dried tomato, cut into thin slivers

TO PREPARE: Preheat the broiler with the rack at the top rung.

Rub the steaks with 2 teaspoons of the olive oil and season both sides with salt and pepper. Place them on a broiling pan and set them aside while you make the vinaigrette.

Put the mustard, Worcestershire, anchovy, and garlic in a small mixing bowl and whisk in the lemon juice. (Use the coiled snake towel trick if your bowl doesn't sit steady (see page 153). Gradually whisk in the remaining 6 tablespoons of olive oil to make a slightly thickened vinaigrette. (If you whisk slowly, and you're using good Dijon, the mustard will hold the oil in a light emulsion.) Season it well with salt and pepper and set it aside while you cook the steaks.

Broil the steaks for 2 to 3 minutes on the first side. Turn them over and broil the second side for 2 to 3 minutes more for medium-rare. For well done, cook each side for 1 or 2 minutes more. To check, make a small slit in the center of one steak to look for any redness.

TO SERVE: Place the tuna steaks on warm dinner plates. Sprinkle each one with the grated Parmigiano-Reggiano cheese, followed by a spoonful of vinaigrette. Garnish them with strips of sun-dried tomato, and serve right away.

Until the 1970s, tuna for most of us automatically meant canned, mixed with mayo and maybe a little celery and onion, and spread on slices of white or whole-wheat bread. Personally, I have no intention of abandoning those cans, particularly when the mix also has capers and a little lemon juice! However, fresh tuna finally won us over and became practically ubiquitous on up-scale and trendy menus. To add a little intellectual perspective, I'm glad to report that tuna has been appreciated for hundreds of years, poems have been written about it, and it's even been used medicinally. But the part I like best is knowing that the tail, which wasn't consumed for food by the ancient Greeks and Mediterranean people, "was nailed over doorways to ward off evil spirits." After about a week, I imagine it worked rather well for other unwanted visitors as well!

—National Fisheries Institute Information Series: *Blue Water Fishing: Tuna*

Seared Peppered Tuna with
Deviled Shallot Butter

4 servings

PREP AND
COOKING
TIME
30–35
minutes

*S*immer finely minced shallots in butter until they turn pale gold, turn off the heat, and stir in the "devil-producing" elements—dry mustard, Tabasco, and pepper flakes! The butter, hot but also naturally sweet from the browned shallots, is spooned over tuna steaks, which are lightly coated with coarsely ground black pepper and quickly seared in olive oil. You could also grill or broil the peppered steaks and top them with the butter. Substitute swordfish steaks, salmon, mahimahi, or grouper fillets, or soft-shell crabs without the pepper coating.

> 5 tablespoons butter
>
> Generous $^1/_3$ cup finely diced shallots or white onions (see page 161)
>
> 1 tablespoon fresh squeezed lemon juice
>
> 2 teaspoons English-style dry mustard
>
> 1 teaspoon Tabasco sauce
>
> $^1/_2$ teaspoon crushed red pepper flakes
>
> Salt to taste
>
> 1 tablespoon olive oil
>
> Four 7-ounce tuna steaks, each $^3/_4''$–$1''$ thick
>
> Generous $^1/_2$ teaspoon coarsely ground fresh black pepper, or more to taste

TO PREPARE: In a small skillet over medium heat, melt the butter and add the shallots. Reduce the heat to low and cook, stirring occasionally, until the shallots have turned pale gold, 6 to 10 minutes.

While the shallots are cooking, put the lemon juice in a small nonaluminum mixing bowl and stir in the dry mustard until it's smooth. Stir in the Tabasco and the red pepper flakes and set the mixture aside.

When the shallots are pale gold, turn off the heat, stir in the mustard mixture, and season it with salt. The mustard mixture won't blend in completely smoothly, that's okay. Set the devil butter aside while you sear (or grill or broil) the steaks. Or cover and refrigerate the butter for up to a week.

Place the olive oil in a large, preferably heavy, skillet over medium heat. While it heats, pat the steaks dry with paper towels and season them with salt. Sprinkle them on both sides with the pepper and gently press it in. Turn the heat to high, and when the oil starts to smoke, slip the steaks into the skillet. Sear the steaks until they are deep brown on the bottom, 3 to 4 minutes. Turn them over and sear them on the second side for about 3 minutes. The steaks will be medium to medium-rare at this point—a nice counterpoint to the hot shallot-y butter. If you'd like them well done, turn the heat to low and cook each side for 1 to 2 minutes more. To check, make a small slit in the center of one steak and look for any redness.

TO SERVE: Gently reheat the devil butter, if necessary, just to liquefy it. Place the tuna steaks on warm dinner plates and spoon the butter over them, making sure everyone gets a share of shallots. Serve right away.

I'm a fanatic about the way to cut shallots (and particular about dicing onions), just ask any long-suffering cook who's ever worked for me! I don't like what happens to shallots when they're chopped to death by knife or food processor (unless the knife or blade is very, very sharp). Both methods can bring out a gasolinelike potency (garlic is exempt from this problem, and is, in fact, handily chopped in a food processor). If you're a bug about Exxon in your food, here's how to chop, or ignore this and forget the subject ever came up!

Peel the shallot (or onion)—larger shallots are easier to deal with if you can get them—by slicing off both ends (but not entirely cutting off the root end because it holds them together) with a sharp paring knife (or a large knife for an onion). Then make a cut through the skin and the first layer, going from trimmed end to trimmed end, and slip off both. Save the trimmings for broth, or discard them. Cut the shallot (or onion) in half, from trimmed end to trimmed end, and lay one of the halves flat, parallel to you.

Secure the top of the shallot (or onion) with one hand while you prepare to cut it with the other, making sure the root end isn't facing the knife. Slice the shallot (or onion) into equal $^1/_8''$ to $^1/_4''$ (or larger) horizontal layers, going just to, but *not through* the root end. (I think it works best when you begin slicing from the bottom up.)

Then, with your knife at the top, slice down the shallot (or onion) vertically at $^1/_8''$ to $^1/_4''$ (or larger) intervals, once again *not cutting through the root end*. The shallot (or onion) is now completely scored except where it's held together by the root end.

Now, slice across the shallot (or onion) at $^1/_8''$ to $^1/_4''$ (or larger) intervals and watch it fall into $^1/_8''$ to $^1/_4''$ (or larger) dice. Chop or cut the root end into little pieces, save it for a soup or broth, or discard it. Repeat the process with the other half.

So, you can see that creating different sized dice—fine to small, medium, or large—is determined by how large the intervals are between cuts.

Once you get the hang of it, you'll see that doing this is a lot easier than reading about it!

Tuna Quickly Braised with Purple Cabbage

4 servings

PREP AND
COOKING
TIME
35–40
minutes

*S*auté purple cabbage with onions and tomatoes in a bit of delicious bacon or pancetta fat, or olive oil. (Pancetta is a rolled, spice-cured but not smoked, Italian bacon that looks like a fat white salami. It's sliced to order when you buy it.) When the vegetables are starting to become tender, sear the tuna steaks in the same skillet, surround them with the vegetables, and sprinkle everything with Marsala and a little red wine vinegar. Simmer it all together gently for 3 or 4 minutes—the steaks will emerge pink and tender. Serve them with the cabbage spooned on top, garnished with crisp bacon or pancetta bits. It's a wonderful fall or winter dish whose perfect accompaniment is the sound of ocean waves crashing in the background—I'm working on a recipe for that! You can substitute swordfish or shark steaks, or fillets of salmon or cod.

3 strips bacon, *or* two $1/8''$-thick slices Italian pancetta

$2^{1}/_{2}$ tablespoons olive oil

1 small head purple cabbage

1 small onion

Salt and freshly ground black or white pepper to taste

$3/_{4}$ cup drained, roughly chopped canned tomatoes

$1/_{4}$ teaspoon dried thyme

Four 7-ounce tuna steaks, each $1''$–$1^{1}/_{4}''$ thick

Flour for dredging

3 tablespoons dry Marsala

2 teaspoons red wine vinegar

TO PREPARE: Cut the bacon or pancetta into $1/_{2}''$ strips. In a skillet large enough to hold all the tuna steaks in one layer, cook the bacon or pancetta (using $1^{1}/_{2}$ tablespoons of the olive oil if using pancetta), over low heat, stirring frequently. While the bacon cooks, begin cutting the cabbage and onion. If you're not using bacon or pancetta, begin cutting the vegetables.

Cut the cabbage in half through its core. Cut out and discard the core from one of the halves. Slice enough cabbage into thin strips $1^{1}/_{2}''$ to $2''$ long to fill 2 cups, packed. *Thinly* slice enough onion (following the natural lines you see along its curved side—see page 141) into 1″-long by ¼″-wide pieces to fill ½ cup. Set both aside.

When the bacon is crisp or the pancetta pale gold, in about 10 minutes, remove it from the skillet with a slotted spoon, drain it on paper towels, and set it aside. There should be about 2 tablespoons of fat left in the skillet. If not, add enough olive oil to make up the difference.

Place the skillet over low to medium heat and stir in the cabbage and onion. Season them with salt and pepper, and cook them, stirring frequently, for 8 to 10 minutes, until they're starting to become tender and a little brown. Remove the vegetables to a bowl and stir in the tomatoes and thyme.

Pour the remaining tablespoon of olive oil into the same skillet set over high heat. Season the steaks with salt and pepper and lightly dredge on both sides in flour, patting off any excess. When the oil is hot, sear the steaks for 1 to 2 minutes, until they're light brown on one side. Turn them over, reduce the heat to low (the retained heat should lightly sear the second side without cooking the steaks too much) and return the vegetables to the skillet, coaxing them around and over the steaks. Sprinkle the Marsala and red wine vinegar over everything and cook the steaks, covered, over low heat for 3 to 4 minutes. (Be careful to watch the heat, the steaks will toughen if the contents boil.) The steaks will be medium to medium-rare at this point. If you prefer the steaks well done, continue cooking them for 3 or 4 minutes more.

Remove the steaks to a platter, but keep the vegetables in the skillet if there are any soupy juices. Place the skillet over medium heat and cook the juices down, stirring to prevent the vegetables from sticking, until they have become a little syrupy, about a minute or less. Turn off the heat and adjust the seasoning with salt and pepper.

TO SERVE: Place the tuna steaks on warm dinner plates, spoon the cabbage mixture on top, and sprinkle them with the crisp bacon or pancetta pieces. Serve right away.

Seared Tuna with Balsamic Vinegar, Garlic, and Pine Nuts

4 servings

PREP AND
COOKING
TIME
30–35
minutes

*T*his is one of my favorites. It's all pleasing tastes and textures: a little sweetness, a gentle vinegar bite, a little chewiness, a little nuttiness. The garlic slices taste almost candied after you cook them in olive oil and balsamic vinegar, and the toasted pine nuts add their elusively special flavor and soft crunch. Or you can prepare the dish with roasted garlic cloves and their roasting oil, which makes it mellower. If you grill the tuna steaks rather than sear them, let the garlic, olive oil, and vinegar mixture boil in its little skillet for less than half a minute, then add the pine nuts and pour the dressing over the steaks. This is so perfect with tuna I don't use it on anything else, but salmon, swordfish, or mahimahi fillets would be worth it, too.

> $^1/_4$ cup pine nuts
> 8 raw garlic cloves, peeled; *or* 3–4 tablespoons roasted garlic cloves with
> $^1/_4$ cup of their roasting oil (see Pantry, to Make)
> $^1/_4$ cup + 1 tablespoon olive oil
> $2^1/_2$ tablespoons balsamic vinegar
> Salt and freshly ground black or white pepper to taste
> Four 7-ounce tuna steaks, each $^3/_4''$–1$''$ thick
> Flour for dredging
> $^1/_4$ teaspoon dried oregano

TO PREPARE: Place a small skillet over low heat and add the pine nuts. Toast them, shaking or stirring frequently, for 3 to 5 minutes, or until they are *very lightly* browned. (They turn bitter if allowed to get too dark.) Set them aside in a little bowl and reserve the skillet.

The sauce with fresh garlic: Cut the garlic into very thin slices. In the reserved skillet over very low heat, heat the $^1/_4$ cup of olive oil with the garlic slices. Cook the garlic, stirring occasionally, for 5 to 6 minutes, or until it is *beginning* to become golden in color. Turn off the heat, add the vinegar, season the mixture well with salt and pepper, and set aside.

The sauce with roasted garlic: Stir the roasted garlic oil, the roasted garlic cloves, and the vinegar together in a small mixing bowl. Season the mixture well with salt and pepper, and set aside.

Dry the steaks with paper towels and season both sides with salt and pepper. Place a skillet, large enough to hold all the steaks comfortably in one layer (or use 2 medium skillets and divide the oil between them), over high heat and add the remaining tablespoon of olive oil. Dredge the steaks in flour and pat off the excess. When the oil is very hot and starting to smoke, sear the steaks on one side for 2 to 3 minutes. Turn them over and sear them for 2 to 4 minutes more. At this point, the steaks will be medium to medium-rare. If you prefer them better done, turn the heat to low and cook them for several minutes more on each side.

Turn off the heat and place the steaks on a platter. Pour either of the reserved oil mixtures and the pine nuts into the hot pan. Stand back a little—the oil will bubble up furiously. Stir the mixture and adjust the seasoning with salt and pepper. (The sauce will not blend—it will still look like oil and vinegar with pieces of garlic and nuts.)

TO SERVE: Place the tuna steaks on warm dinner plates and spoon the sauce over them, making sure each serving has its share of dark vinegar. Crumble the oregano between your fingers over the top of each steak, and serve right away.

Tuna Grilled with
Chinese Oyster-Ginger Sauce

4 servings

PREP TIME
25–30
minutes +
optional
30–60
minutes'
marinating
time

If you have time to marinate the tuna steaks in the sauce, all the better. But if not, the sauce is so flavorful from the Chinese oyster extracts, fresh ginger, and sesame oil, that you can just coat the steaks with it before grilling and spoon more on top when they're done. Substitute swordfish or shark steaks, or salmon, mahimahi, or bass fillets. Try it with grilled shrimp as an hors d'oeuvre, or drizzle it over soft-shell crabs as a first course.

2^1/$_2$ tablespoons bottled Chinese oyster sauce (supermarket Oriental shelf)
1^1/$_2$ tablespoons finely minced onion (see page 161)
2^1/$_2$ teaspoons chopped fresh ginger (see page 214)
2^1/$_2$ tablespoons rice wine vinegar
2^1/$_2$ tablespoons sesame oil
Four 7-ounce tuna steaks, each ^{3}/$_4$"–1" thick
Salt and freshly ground black or white pepper to taste

TO PREPARE: Start a medium-hot fire in the grill (see Note). Fifteen minutes before you're going to grill the tuna steaks, put the grill grate 4" or 5" above the glowing coals if it isn't already there. (I also like to brush the top of the grate with vegetable oil just before grilling to help prevent sticking.)

Place the oyster sauce in a small mixing bowl along with the minced onion and chopped ginger. Whisk in the rice wine vinegar, then gradually whisk in the sesame oil and set the sauce aside briefly, or cover and refrigerate it for up to 2 weeks.

Season the steaks with salt and pepper. Place them in a shallow dish and pour ^{1}/$_4$ cup of the oyster-ginger marinade over them. Coat them all over with the marinade, and, if you have time, let them marinate at room temperature for at least 30 minutes, covered with plastic wrap. (Refrigerate them if the kitchen is hot.) Otherwise, grill them right away.

Remove the steaks and reserve the remaining marinade. Place the steaks over the hot coals and grill the first side for 2 or 3 minutes, until browned. Turn the steaks and grill the other side for another 2 to 3 minutes. The steaks will be pink inside. Cook them for a few minutes longer on each side if you want them well done. To check, make a small slit with a paring knife in the middle of one steak to check for redness.

TO SERVE: Place the tuna steaks on warm dinner plates, spoon the rest of the oyster-ginger sauce over them, and serve right away.

NOTE: A large bed of extremely hot coals will crust the tuna if it's a thick steak. While the crust is delicious, the intense heat also dries out the first $1/2''$ of meat on both sides. So I sacrifice a little crust by grilling it over fewer coals to keep them moist. It's your choice.

Grilled Tuna with Tart-Sweet
Red Peppers and Mushrooms

4 servings

PREP AND
COOKING
TIME
40–45
minutes

Sauté sweet red bell peppers and sliced mushrooms in a generous amount of olive oil with splashes of red wine, balsamic vinegar, and lemon juice. The vinegars and lemon juice get sucked up by the peppers and mushrooms and make them tangy. Stir in some capers and spoon the vegetables, with their yummy olive oil, over grilled, seared, or broiled tuna steaks, and sprinkle them with lots of fresh basil. Substitute swordfish or shark steaks, grouper or salmon fillets, or veal, pork, or chicken!

$^{1}/_{4}$ cup + 1 tablespoon olive oil

2 cups red bell pepper strips, about $^{1}/_{4}'' \times 1^{1}/_{2}''$

$2^{1}/_{2}$ cups sliced mushrooms such as cremini, white, or Portobello

Salt and freshly ground black or white pepper to taste

4 teaspoons red wine vinegar

4 teaspoons balsamic vinegar

2 teaspoons fresh squeezed lemon juice

Four 7-ounce tuna steaks, each $^{3}/_{4}''$–$1''$ thick

1 tablespoon drained tiny capers (or large ones roughly chopped)

2 tablespoons chopped fresh basil

TO PREPARE: Start a medium-hot fire in the grill (see Note). Fifteen minutes before you're going to grill the tuna, put the grill grate 4″ to 5″ above the hot coals if it isn't already there. (I also like to brush the top of the grate with vegetable oil just before grilling to help prevent sticking.)

Heat $^{1}/_{4}$ cup of the olive oil in a large skillet over medium-high heat. Add the peppers and mushrooms and season them with salt and pepper. Sauté them, stirring occasionally, until they have browned a little and the peppers are still slightly crunchy, 6 to 7 minutes. (Creminis and Portobellos will brown faster because they have lower water content, so adjust the heat accordingly.) While the peppers and mushrooms are sautéing, mix both vinegars with the lemon juice in a small nonreactive bowl and set it aside.

When the peppers and mushrooms are done, raise the heat to high and add the vinegar mixture. Bring it all to one fast boil to amalgamate the flavors quickly, and turn off the heat. Adjust the seasoning with pepper—don't adjust the salt until after the capers are added. Set the vegetables aside while you grill the tuna steaks. Or make the vegetables 1 to 2 days ahead and refrigerate them, reheating them just before serving.

Rub both sides of the steaks with the remaining tablespoon of olive oil and season them with salt and pepper. Place them over the coals and grill the first side for 2 to 3 minutes, until lightly browned. Turn them over and grill the other side for another 2 to 3 minutes. The steaks will be pink inside. For well done, grill them for a few minutes longer on each side. To check, make a small slit with a paring knife in the middle of one steak to look for redness.

Reheat the peppers and mushrooms over low heat, stir in the capers, and adjust the salt if necessary.

TO SERVE: Place the tuna steaks on warm dinner plates, spoon the peppers and mushrooms over them, and sprinkle them with the basil. Serve right away.

NOTE: A large bed of extremely hot coals will crust the tuna if it's a thick steak. While the crust is delicious, the intense heat also dries out the first $1/2''$ of meat on both sides. So I sacrifice a little crust by grilling the tuna steaks over fewer coals to keep them moist. It's your choice.

Grilled Tuna with
Artichokes and Tomatoes

4 servings

PREP AND
COOKING
TIME
45–55
minutes for
fresh
artichokes,
25–30
minutes for
frozen

*A*rtichokes are one of the great—and strange—foods of life! Sliced artichoke bottoms—the meaty base without the fuzzy choke and leaves—sautéed in olive oil with garlic, tomatoes, and lemon are a wonderful and unexpected accompaniment for grilled (or broiled or sautéed) tuna steaks. When you're in a hurry, frozen artichoke hearts can do the job, if not quite as seductively. This vegetable combination also works well with swordfish or shark steaks, and salmon or pompano fillets.

1 large bay leaf (for fresh artichokes)

Salt and freshly ground black or white pepper to taste

3 medium or 2 large fresh globe artichokes, *or* 1 package frozen artichoke
   hearts or bottoms cooked according to package directions

2 large ripe tomatoes (see Notes), *or* 1 cup seeded, drained, chopped
   canned tomatoes

4 tablespoons olive oil

1 large garlic clove, finely chopped

2 teaspoons fresh squeezed lemon juice

Four 7-ounce tuna steaks, each 3/4"–1" thick

1 tablespoon coarsely chopped fresh (flat-leaf or curly) parsley

TO PREPARE: Start a medium-hot fire in the grill (see Notes). Fifteen minutes before you're going to grill the tuna steaks, put the grill grate 4" or 5" above the glowing coals if it isn't already there. (I also like to brush the top of the grate with vegetable oil just before grilling to help prevent sticking.)

With fresh artichokes and tomatoes: Put a large pot of water with the bay leaf over high heat, salt the water, and let it come to a boil while you trim the artichokes.

With a serrated, or other sharp knife, cut off and discard the entire top inch of the artichokes. With scissors, snip off the sharp pointed ends of the leaves, trim the stems by about 1/2", and set the artichokes aside while you prepare the tomatoes.*

*You can ignore these leaf-trimming directions if you choose—I've included them for safety's sake because those sharp points can be very nasty when you're handling them.

Cut out the core of the tomatoes and cut a shallow **X** through the skin on the other end. Drop the tomatoes into the pot of rapidly boiling water for *10 seconds,* or just long enough to peel the skin easily when lifting it from the **X**. Remove them with a slotted spoon or tongs and set aside briefly.

Drop the artichokes into the same pot of rapidly boiling water. Cover the pot, adjust the heat so the water boils at a medium pace, and cook them until a leaf can be pulled out with a little resistance, 18 to 25 minutes.

While the artichokes cook, peel the tomatoes, starting at the **X**. Cut the tomatoes in half, squeeze out the seeds, chop them somewhat coarsely, and set them aside. You should have 1 to 1¼ cups.

When the artichokes are done, immediately remove them from the pot and submerge them in a bowl of ice water to cool them quickly. When they're cool enough to handle, drain them and begin pulling off the leaves. (You can store the leaves in the refrigerator, in a plastic bag or covered dish, for up to 4 days and serve them cold with a vinaigrette as part of a midweek meal.) When you get to the point where there's a deep indentation around the lower part of the leaves (more than halfway through) and the leaves are beginning to look like an upside-down cone, pull out and discard that whole section—it should pull right out if the artichoke is cooked enough.

With a teaspoon, gently scrape out and discard the fuzzy fibers that cover the artichoke bottom. Slice off the stem flush with the underside and trim the stem by pulling off its outside fibers with a paring knife to reveal its lighter colored core. (The entire stem should be tender and edible, but sometimes they are slightly bitter—taste a piece before you go to the trouble of peeling them all.) Cut the peeled artichoke stem and the bottom into ⅓″-thick by ¾″-long slices—you should have about 1 cup. Set the artichoke pieces aside.

With frozen artichoke hearts or bottoms: Cut enough cooked artichoke hearts in quarters to measure 1 generous cup, reserving the rest for another use. Or cut cooked artichoke bottoms into ⅓″-thick by ¾″-long pieces.

For both fresh and frozen: Place 2 tablespoons of the olive oil in a medium-size skillet set over high heat, and when the oil is hot, add the artichokes. Cook them, stirring occasionally, until they begin to brown, 1 to 2 minutes. Turn the heat to low and add the garlic, stirring it for 10 seconds. Add the tomatoes and adjust the heat so the mixture simmers, stirring occasionally. In 3 to 5 minutes, the excess moisture should be evaporated and the tomatoes should have become a slightly chunky sauce that surrounds and coats the artichokes. (Be aware, *fresh* tomatoes can vary a lot in their water content.) Stir in the lemon juice and season the mixture with salt and pepper. Set it aside, or cool, cover, and refrigerate it for 3 or 4 days.

Season the steaks with salt and pepper and rub them all over with the remaining

2 tablespoons of olive oil. Place the steaks over the coals and grill the first side until brown, 2 to 3 minutes. Turn them over and grill the other side for 2 or 3 minutes more—they'll still be pink inside. Cook them for a few minutes longer on each side, on a cooler section of the grill, if you want them well done. To check, make a small slit with a paring knife in the middle of one steak.

Gently reheat the artichokes and tomatoes, adjust the seasoning, if necessary, with salt and pepper, and stir in the chopped parsley.

TO SERVE: Place the tuna steaks on warm dinner plates with a spoonful of artichokes and tomatoes on top, and serve right away.

NOTES: If you have *great* summer tomatoes, don't cook them at all. Rinse and dice them, skin, seeds, and all, and, right before serving (which should be at room temperature), season them with salt and pepper. Stir them into the sautéed artichokes, add the lemon juice, and pile the mixture on the tuna steaks.

A large bed of extremely hot coals will crust the tuna if it's a thick steak. While the crust is delicious, the intense heat also dries out the first $1/2''$ of meat on both sides. So I sacrifice a little crust by grilling the tuna over fewer coals (or at a lower temperature) to keep them moist. It's your choice.

3

Sea Animals

WITH SHELLS
AND ARMOR

CALAMARI OR SQUID

FLAVOR: Mild and sweet, not fishy, tender-chewy

ORIGIN: Atlantic and Pacific oceans

GOOD SIGNS: Flesh very firm; shiny, milky white bodies, deep maroon tentacles; clean smell

BAD SIGNS: Pink or yellowing bodies; any musty or apparent aroma

HEALTH TIPS: A raw 7-ounce serving is approximately 175 calories, low in fat and very high in protein.

First, let me make it clear that the calamari we're talking about have been purchased cleaned and ready to cook (or cleaned and frozen). Cleaning them is simple, but too time-consuming for the scope of this book. That said, calamari have much to recommend them: They're commonly available and inexpensive, they're an appealing change from the more familiar seafood main courses, and they take only seconds to cook. And, their serious name is "cephalopod," who could resist that word?

Before a calamari got to the state you see it now, it was a funny-looking critter of the sea. (Its flexible shell, called the "pen," resides *within,* just qualifying this little beast for this section.) From its elongated arrowhead-shape body a small globular head protrudes, waving its tentacles and arms like a hat. In cleaning, it loses its head, but keeps its hat! Both the sac (the body) and the tentacles are edible—the flavor of the tentacles seems sweeter and more concentrated, at least to me. And if you have a choice, choose calamari sacs that are under 4″ in length; they'll be more tender.

There's only one important piece of information you need to cook calamari right: Cook them quickly! Just as soon as they turn opaque, in about a minute, they're done. Almost as soon as you put calamari in the pan, you take them out—no day-dreaming allowed with these guys, or they'll be a dinner of rubber bands! However, if the worst happens, it can be remedied by continuing to cook them for another 20 minutes or so, until they become tender again. They're good deep-fried, sautéed, stir-fried, steamed, and braised.

"Curly" Grilled Calamari with Herbs and Greens

4 servings

PREP AND
COOKING
TIME
30–40
minutes

Lunch with your editor can produce many things, even a new recipe! Judy ordered a grilled calamari appetizer in a light vinaigrette with arugula, which was as simple, light, and tender as can be. Those calamari were much smaller than what we generally find in our markets, and they were grilled whole. Larger calamari—the bodies longer than 4″—are chewy grilled whole, because they have to be cooked too long for the heat to penetrate—a problem, unless you like to dine on hot, deflated beachballs. So, butterfly large calamari before grilling them (if you're lucky and find very small ones, grill them whole) and watch them curl after they're cooked. I get a kick out of seeing the silly squiggly pieces next to the greens in this dish! And, if you've got extra-virgin olive oil, use it in this recipe—it'll add pure intensity of flavor. Leftovers make a great chilled calamari salad (minus any soggy greens, that is). The vinaigrette and greens would also be good served with swordfish or tuna steaks, salmon fillets, sea scallops, shrimp, and delicate white fillets, too.

2 teaspoons fresh squeezed lemon juice

1 tablespoon red wine or other vinegar

8½ tablespoons olive oil, preferably fruity and full flavored

Salt and freshly ground black or white pepper to taste

2 pounds cleaned calamari, including some tentacles

3 tablespoons mixed, coarsely chopped fresh basil and parsley leaves

Optional: sprinkle of crushed pepper flakes

Optional: 1 teaspoon drained capers, preferably the tiny ones called nonpareils

6 cups lightly packed mixed greens (such as arugula, watercress, and frisée, or field salad or other nice lettuces), washed and dried

TO PREPARE: Start a hot fire in the grill. Fifteen minutes before you're going to grill the calamari, put the grill grate 4″ to 5″ above the glowing coals if it isn't already there. (I also like to brush the top of the grate with vegetable oil just before grilling to help prevent sticking.)

Put the lemon juice and vinegar in a small mixing bowl and gradually whisk in 6 tablespoons of the olive oil (using the coiled snake towel trick if your bowl doesn't sit steady, see page 153). The vinaigrette may thicken slightly as it's being made, but it will separate shortly thereafter—that won't affect the flavor. Season it with salt and pepper and set it aside. Or cover and refrigerate it for up to 1 week, being sure to serve the vinaigrette at room temperature.

If the calamari bodies are longer than 4″, butterfly them by slitting each one lengthwise *through one side only*. Leave smaller calamari, and any tentacles, whole. Rinse the calamari under cold running water and drain them on a double thickness of paper towels. Lay another double thickness of paper towels over them and pat them dry. Place all the pieces in a large mixing bowl, season them with salt and pepper, and toss them thoroughly with the remaining 2$\frac{1}{2}$ tablespoons of olive oil.

Doing 4 or 5 pieces at a time (or whatever is comfortable for you), place the calamari, with the *inside* of their butterflied bodies *down,* on the grill. Grill until the calamari turn milky white, 30 to 60 *seconds* depending on their thickness. With tongs, turn the pieces over and grill them on the other side until they turn milky white, 30 to 60 *seconds* depending on their thickness.* Continue grilling all the bodies in the same fashion, placing them in a large bowl as they're finished to keep warm—they'll do their curling trick in the bowl. Grill the tentacles until they're firm and white—if they're large, they'll take a few seconds longer than the bodies. Add them to the mixing bowl as they're grilled. (You can also do this in a ridged grill pan on top of the stove if you don't have access to an outdoor grill.)

Discard all the calamari juices that have accumulated in the bowl (there'll be a lot) by pouring the grilled calamari into a colander set in the sink or in a larger bowl. Briefly rewhisk the vinaigrette and, in a separate mixing bowl, toss 3 tablespoons of it with the drained calamari to coat all the pieces. Taste a piece, and adjust the seasoning with salt, pepper, and more vinegar or olive oil if it needs it. Add the fresh herbs and the hot pepper flakes and capers, if using them, and toss again.

TO SERVE: In a large salad bowl, toss the greens with the reserved vinaigrette and place them on 4 room-temperature dinner plates. Arrange the calamari curls and tentacles next to them and serve right away.

*If you grill the inside first, the calamari stay flat after you've turned them over. If you grill the outside first, you'll have to hold each piece down to keep it from curling on the grill once it's turned. And we don't want any curling going on until we say so!

Stir-Fried Calamari with Capers, Red Wine, and Basil

4 servings

PREP AND
COOKING
TIME
30 minutes

This isn't even remotely Chinese in flavor, but I use a wok to sauté the calamari because it provides lots of hot surface for contact. And that makes a difference, because calamari cook best two ways: very quickly, or very slowly. They stay tender if they're cooked only until turning white, almost a matter of seconds—or cooked a long time to break down their chewiness. Stir-fry the capers over high heat until they look like they're slightly "popped"—this mellows their flavor—then add the calamari and stir-fry them until they barely turn white, and remove them. Add the red wine, mixed with a little corn starch, to the wok and stir the calamari back in briefly. The calamari become coated, and purple-tinged, with the red wine sauce. Toss it all with a handful of chopped fresh, fragrant basil and parsley, and serve. You can also use scallops, shrimp, or pieces of lobster.

$1^3/_4$ pounds cleaned calamari, including some tentacles

1 tablespoon drained capers, preferably the tiny ones called nonpareil

$^2/_3$ cup dry red wine

2 teaspoons cornstarch

3 tablespoons olive oil

2 teaspoons fresh squeezed lemon juice

Salt and freshly ground black or white pepper to taste

3 tablespoons chopped fresh basil

1 tablespoon chopped fresh (flat-leaf or curly) parsley

TO PREPARE: Rinse the calamari and dry them well on paper towels. Cut the bodies into rings about $1/4''$ thick and cut the tentacles in half if they're small, or in quarters if they're large. Set the calamari aside.

Dry the capers on paper towels and set them aside. In a small bowl, combine the red wine and the cornstarch and set it aside.

Place a large wok over high heat and add the olive oil. When the oil is smoking, add the capers—stand back, they may spatter—and stir-fry them for 5 to 10 seconds, or until they look a little "popped." Immediately add the calamari, and stir-fry them, distributing them around the sides of the wok as well, so as much of them as possible contacts the hot surface. Stir-fry until they're almost white, 2 to 3 minutes. Take the wok off the heat, and remove the calamari with a slotted spoon to a colander set in a bowl large enough to contain them.

There will be a lot of calamari juices left in the wok. Place the wok back over high heat and boil down the juices, adding those that have collected in the bowl under the colander, until they've thickened slightly and are about $1/4$ cup in volume, 3 to 4 minutes. Stir the wine and cornstarch together to reamalgamate it, and add it to the juices in the wok. Stir it all together and let it come to a boil to cook the cornstarch. As soon as it has boiled, turn off the heat, stir in the calamari and lemon juice, and season it generously with salt and pepper. If the sauce seems thick, add a little more of the juices that have recollected in the bowl, otherwise discard them. Stir in the basil and parsley.

TO SERVE: Spoon the calamari onto warm dinner plates and serve right away.

Fried Calamari, Two Ways

*Y*ou may think frying calamari at home is too hard—it's such a restaurant dish—but actually, it's easy and delicious. Here are two recipes: one for a quick beer batter that makes the calamari pieces crisp and slightly puffy in a neat kind of way (the batter is just as good for other fried fillets and shellfish, too) and a simple variation where you merely flour the pieces. I would definitely serve one of these as an hors d'oeuvre at any easygoing dinner party, when I look forward to my guests making an occasional foray into the kitchen as I fry them. And here are three yummy ways of accompanying them:

1. Stir some chopped roasted garlic into mayonnaise along with lime juice and zest—it's nutty / garlicky and delicious.

2. Add some finely chopped Mexican chipotle chile to that same mixture and it's nutty / garlicky, hot, smoky, and even more delicious. (Chile chipotles are ripened, dried, and smoked jalapeños that are available in cans from specialty stores or by mail order.)

3. Forget the mayonnaise, dust the tops of the crisp calamari with chili powder, and serve them with lime wedges.

Or, how about forget the chili powder, and serve them with just lime wedges! Either of the sauces is also good with shrimp or scallops, and pompano or catfish fillets. And I don't want to tell you how good the chipotle mayo is with lobster! Think of serving shrimp—grilled, boiled, or fried—as an hors d'oeuvre and using the mayo as a dip.

Beer Batter Dipped

Vegetable oil for frying

1½ pounds cleaned calamari, including some tentacles

One 12-ounce can beer

1¼ cups all-purpose flour

1 teaspoon baking powder

¾ teaspoon salt

½ teaspoon paprika, preferably Hungarian sweet paprika

Freshly ground white or black pepper to taste

Optional: chili powder to taste

Optional: lime wedges

Optional: garlic-chipotle chile mayonnaise (recipe follows)

4 servings

PREP AND
COOKING
TIME
35 minutes

TO PREPARE: Pour the vegetable oil into a deep pot, filling it by no more than half but at least 3″ deep, and begin heating the oil over low heat. Or set your electric fryer to 400°. Preheat the oven to 500°. (No, that's not a mistake.)

Rinse and drain the calamari and lay them on sheets of paper towels, pressing and blotting them dry with another sheet laid on top. Cut the bodies into ½″ rings and cut the tentacles in half, or quarters if they're large. Set them aside or refrigerate them if the kitchen is hot.

Pour the beer into a large mixing bowl. Measure 1¼ cups flour by the "dip and sweep" method. (Dip a 1-cup nesting-type measuring cup into the flour to overflowing—don't jiggle or shake the cup after it's been filled or it will change the measurement—and sweep off the excess with a metal spatula or the blunt edge of a straight-sided knife, keeping one edge in contact with the measuring cup as you sweep across the top. Repeat this procedure with a ¼-cup measure.) Gradually whisk the measured flour, baking powder, salt, paprika, and a generous amount of pepper into the beer to make a smooth, somewhat thick, batter. Set the batter aside at room temperature until the oil is hot.

If using a conventional pot, turn the heat to medium-high until the oil reaches 400° on a frying thermometer or a pinch of flour makes sputtering noises and moves rapidly around the surface. (If the oil is too hot, it will begin tosmoke and the flour will brown too quickly. Turn down the heat and try the flour test again in a few minutes. If the flour just kind of lays there, the oil is too cool. Continue heating the oil for a few more minutes.) While the oil is heating, dry the calamari pieces again on paper towels. Line 1 or 2 large cookie sheets, or other ovenproof trays, with layers of paper towels and set them near the stove.

Stir the calamari pieces into the batter so that each piece is well coated. Lifting out a few pieces at a time, let the excess batter drip back into the bowl, and drop the pieces one by one into the hot oil. (The key is not to crowd the pieces and to keep the oil hot. If you fry too many at a time, the oil will cool down quickly and the batter will stay pale, soft, and soggy. It's better to take a couple of extra minutes to fry them carefully or you'll be disappointed with the result.) If the oil is hot enough, the pieces will pop up to the surface and begin to brown—if the oil is too hot, they'll brown too quickly. Raise or lower the temperature of the heat accordingly. Fry them for less than a minute, until they're light to medium golden, turning them over once. Remove them from the oil with a slotted metal spoon and drain them in a single layer on the prepared cookie sheet(s).

Remove and discard the cooked batter droplets from the oil between batches to keep them from burning and sticking to the freshly battered calamari. (I keep a separate plate covered with a paper towel next to the fryer for these cooked droplets; when I'm finished frying, I just dump the towel into the garbage.) Continue frying the rest of the calamari, being sure to allow the oil to come back up to the proper temperature between batches.

When all the calamari have been fried, place the cookie sheet(s) in the very hot oven for 2 to 3 minutes to reheat and recrisp the pieces. Remove the sheet(s) from the oven and sprinkle the calamari with the chili powder, if desired.

TO SERVE: Mound the calamari on warm dinner plates, garnish each plate with 1 or 2 lime wedges if you like, and serve right away, with the garlic-chipotle chile mayonnaise, if you're using it, on the side.

Simply Floured Variation

You'll need 2½ pounds of cleaned calamari for 4 people. Set yourself up as in the batter-dipped recipe: preheat the oven to 500°; rinse, cut, and dry the calamari pieces; heat the oil to 400°; and prepare 1 or 2 paper towel-lined cookie sheets. Place a generous amount of flour in a Ziploc-type plastic bag and season the flour generously with salt and pepper. Drop about a third of the calamari into the bag as loosely as possible. With the top of the bag tightly closed, shake it up and down, squeezing the sides to coat the pieces. After that, it's a good idea to put your hand *inside* the bag to give them a final toss and insure that they're well coated and not glopped together!

Lift all the pieces out of the flour, shaking them to remove excess flour, and place them in a colander set inside a larger bowl—it's easier to grab a few at a time this way. Pick up a small handful, shake them off again, and drop them into the hot oil, trying to let the pieces fall in as separately as possible. It's important not to crowd them in the oil so the temperature stays hot. The pieces will be very pale gold and just cooked in 30 to 60 seconds, drain them in a single layer on the prepared cookie sheet(s) and keep frying the remaining pieces in the same manner. When all the pieces have been fried, reheat them in the very hot oven for 2 to 4 minutes. Lightly sprinkle them with salt, and chili powder if you like, and serve them with the lime wedges and garlic-chipotle chile mayonnaise, if desired.

4 servings

Garlic-Chipotle Chile Mayonnaise

PREP TIME
12–15 minutes with fresh garlic or if roasted garlic is on hand

6 tablespoons storebought or homemade mayonnaise

4 teaspoons finely chopped roasted garlic (see Pantry, to Make); *or* 2 teaspoons finely chopped roasted garlic + 4 teaspoons oil from roasting; *or* 2 generous teaspoons very finely chopped fresh garlic

Grated zest of 1 lime (no bitter white pith, see page 133)

4 teaspoons fresh squeezed lime juice

Optional: 2 teaspoons finely chopped chipotle chile with a little sauce from the can (look for chile chipotles en adobo sauce)

Salt and freshly ground black or white pepper to taste

TO PREPARE: Place the mayonnaise in a small mixing bowl and stir in the roasted or fresh garlic, the roasted garlic olive oil, if you're using it, and the lime zest and juice. Stir in the chipotle chile, if you're using it. Season the mayo with salt and a generous amount of pepper. Set it aside while you fry the calamari, as in the preceding recipe, or cover and refrigerate it for up to 2 weeks.

CLANS

(Hard-shells: Littlenecks, Cherrystones, and Manila clams; Soft-shell Clams, also called Steamers)

FLAVOR: Briny and sweet, tender-chewy; Manilas and soft-shells more delicate

ORIGIN: All Atlantic Ocean except Manilas, which are from the Pacific

GOOD SIGNS: *Hard-shells:* thick, intact, tightly closed gray shell; *Manilas:* thinner, intact, tightly closed medium brown shell; *Soft-shells:* white, intact, partially open, brittle shell with taut protruding black neck; meat shimmering pink-ivory in color; practically clear juices; clean, gentle, briny aroma

BAD SIGNS: *Hard-shells:* open shells; *All:* broken or cracked shells; *Soft-shells:* limp black neck; *All:* dull or discolored meat, ripped or shredded; *Shucked meat:* lots of shattered shell, very cloudy juices; *All:* any strong aroma

HEALTH TIPS: A raw 7-ounce serving is approximately 120 calories, low in fat, low in omega-3 fatty acids, and high in protein. *Note:* Eating raw or partially cooked clams should be avoided by people who suffer from certain diseases such as chronic liver disease, cancer, or immunodeficiency disease, among others. Check with your doctor if you're unsure.

Clams are an excellent during-the-week-meal, whether in the shell or shucked, because they cook so fast and need so little to turn them into a mouth-watering, fun dinner.

In case you weren't sure, clams in the shell should be alive when you buy them *and* when you cook them. If you've chosen littlenecks, cherrystones (the same as littlenecks, only larger), or Manila clams in the shell, all they need is a scrub under cold running water. Soft-shells, however, need to be purged in a bowl of *salted* cold water ($^1/_3$ cup salt to 1 gallon water) for 30 minutes to disgorge their grit, then rinsed before proceeding with the recipe. (Incidentally, the black membrane covering the soft-shell's neck is peeled off and discarded as you're eating them.) Cherrystones and littlenecks benefit from this soaking too, but it's not essential. Then steam the clams with an interesting ingredient or two, *just until the shells open*—they'll toughen if they cook longer.

Shucked clams only need to be checked through for bits of shell before they're simmered very briefly and subsequently devoured!

Three crucial clam, oyster, and mussel points:

1. Be sure the shellfish you buy are from certified, unpolluted beds—ask your fish seller to show you the identifying tags if you have any doubts. All shellfish must be tagged, and the seller must keep these tags; it's the law.

2. If the shellfish have been bagged in plastic for the trip home, transfer them right away to an open paper or mesh bag, or to a bowl, covered with a damp towel, and put them in the refrigerator. Shellfish can't breathe in plastic, but properly stored, clams will be fine for 4 or 5 days, mussels 3 to 5, and oysters a week at least—if they were fresh when you bought them.

3. When you scrub clams, don't let them sit in the water (unless it's salted in the proportions given above), because plain water will do them in.

Pan-Roasted Clams Over
Olive Oil–Toasted Bread

4 servings

**PREP AND
COOKING
TIME
20 minutes**

ames Beard says pan-roasting clams in butter, mustard, and a little Worcestershire sauce is good. He's right. The clams remain tender and meaty when you cook them gently—not even simmering—for just a moment or two. (Pan "roasting" is something of a misnomer, since the point here is cooking over low heat, not the high temperature you associate with the word *roast.*) Spoon them, with their juices, over slices of chewy bread that you brushed with olive oil and toasted in a hot oven, and sprinkle them with lots of fresh chives and basil. It's just right for a light dinner or first course for a party.

8 slices country, Italian, French, or sourdough bread, each about 3″ × 4″

1 tablespoon olive oil

2 teaspoons Dijon mustard, preferably French

2 teaspoons fresh squeezed lemon juice

2 teaspoons Worcestershire sauce

4 dozen shucked littleneck clams (approximately 1$^2/_3$ cups drained—see Note)

3 tablespoons butter

Freshly ground black or white pepper to taste

3 tablespoons mixed, finely cut chives and chopped fresh basil or other fresh herbs

TO PREPARE: Preheat the oven to 425°.

While the oven is heating, brush both sides of the bread slices with olive oil and put them aside. Put the mustard in a small mixing bowl and stir in the lemon juice and Worcestershire sauce until the mixture is smooth. Set it aside.

Put the bread slices directly on the rack in the oven and bake them for 5 to 6 minutes without turning. When the edges become golden brown, and the bread is beginning to turn golden and dry, remove them and set them aside where they can stay a little warm. Turn off the oven.

Inspect the clams and juices for any broken bits of shell and discard them. In a large skillet, melt the butter over medium heat, add the drained clams, and stir them into the butter for about 30 seconds. Stir the Dijon mixture into the clams and continue stirring until their raw pink color turns gray, 1 to 2 minutes. Regulate the heat, if necessary, to be sure the liquid doesn't simmer—the gentle heat keeps the clams tender. Turn off the heat and grind in a generous amount of pepper.

TO SERVE: Slightly overlap 2 slices of toasted bread in each warm soup plate. Spoon the clams, and their cooking juices, over the spot where the 2 toasts meet (this gives you delicious soggy toast areas and crisper ones too—more fun to eat!) and sprinkle the fresh herbs over all. Serve right away.

NOTE: Refrigerate (or freeze) the drained clam juice for a soup or pasta, or add it to the seafood stew (on page 276) in place of some of the shrimp, lobster, or chicken broth.

Steamed Littleneck Clams with Olive Oil, Rosemary, and Sun-Dried Tomatoes

4 servings, or
6 with pasta

PREP AND
COOKING
TIME
40 minutes

*G*et out your cauldron! Steaming clams for 4 is really easy, but it helps to have a very large pot to do it in. However, if your *batterie de cuisine* doesn't include one, don't despair, because 2 good size pots with lids, or an oval covered roaster, will accomplish the same thing. So unless you want an excuse to buy new equipment, use what you have. The cooked juices in this preparation emphasize the clam's natural brininess, and they're great for sopping up with lots of crusty bread—but if that's too intense for you, pile the clams on top of pasta with some of their juices. With pasta, this is enough for 6 people, figuring on 8 clams per person. The recipe is also good with mussels.

4 dozen littleneck clams in the shell

Salt and freshly ground black or white pepper to taste

$^1/_2$ cup olive oil

8–10 large garlic cloves, chopped (approximately 3 tablespoons—see Note)

2 teaspoons finely chopped fresh rosemary leaves, *or* $^3/_4$ teaspoon dried, then roughly chopped

$^1/_2$ cup white wine or dry vermouth

$^1/_4$ cup drained, coarsely chopped sun-dried tomatoes

TO PREPARE: Scrub each clam with a stiff brush under cold running water and let them drain in a colander while you begin the recipe. (If there's time, cover them with cold water mixed with a small handful of salt—in the ratio of $^1/_3$ cup salt to 1 gallon water—and let them sit for up to 30 minutes to disgorge any sand. Rinse them and proceed with the recipe.)

Choose a very large (or use 2 medium) pot that will eventually hold all the clams without filling it more than halfway. Add the olive oil to the pot (or divide it between the 2 medium), and place it over medium-low heat, and stir in the garlic and rosemary. Cook, stirring occasionally, 3 to 4 minutes, or until the garlic is *just begin-*

ning to become light gold in color. (Be careful not to cook it any further or it will be bitter.) Add the white wine or vermouth and turn the heat to high. Add the clams to the pot, filling it by no more than halfway, cover the pot, and steam the clams just until they open, 6 to 10 minutes, removing them as they do. Stir them up from the bottom once or twice as they cook. When all the clams have opened, taste the juices and grind in fresh pepper—you won't need any salt. Discard any clams that haven't opened.

TO SERVE: Pile the clams into warm soup plates or big bowls, ladle the juices from the pot over them, leaving any sandy residue at the bottom, and scatter the sun-dried tomatoes over all. Serve right away.

NOTE: This amount of garlic is easily and quickly chopped in a food processor. Put all the cloves in at once and pulse them until they're finely chopped, less than a minute.

Steaming no more than 4 or 5 layers of clams or mussels in a pot gives you faster results and more even cooking. If you've got a pot that is wider than it is tall, but still deep, use it. The bivalves will cook at a more even rate, and you won't have to plunge your entire arm into the bowels of the pot to stir them—because, of course, they're going to open from the bottom first!

I have an ancient black iron pot with a lid, about 12″ in diameter and 5½″ deep, one of life's great stew and soup pots. I also use it for steaming clams and mussels. Look around your kitchen— you may have something you never thought of using.

Littleneck Clams Steamed in
Red Wine with Tomato

4 servings

PREP AND
COOKING
TIME
35–40
minutes

*S*auté fresh tomatoes and garlic in olive oil with some red wine before the clams go in the pot—the red wine blends with the clam juices, making them deep in color and rich in flavor. And I think the taste of the whole dish really "pops" when fresh thyme leaves are sprinkled over the clams just before you eat them! The fresh tomato skins remain crunchy in the broth, but you can substitute canned plum tomatoes if you'd rather. This would be good as a first course and with soft-shell clams or mussels, too.

> 4 dozen littleneck clams in the shell
> Salt and freshly ground black or white pepper to taste
> $^1/_4$ cup olive oil
> 4 medium garlic cloves, chopped
> 2 cups coarsely chopped fresh tomatoes (2–3 medium ones) or drained, canned plum tomatoes
> $1^1/_2$ tablespoons fresh thyme leaves
> $^1/_2$ cup dry red wine
> Optional: 1 tablespoon coarsely chopped fresh (flat-leaf or curly) parsley

TO PREPARE: Scrub each clam with a stiff brush under cold running water and let them drain in a colander while you begin the recipe. (If there's time, cover them with cold water mixed with a small handful of salt—in the ratio of $^1/_3$ cup salt to 1 gallon water—and let them sit for up to 30 minutes to disgorge any sand. Rinse them and proceed with the recipe.)

Choose a very large (or use 2 medium) pot that will eventually hold all the clams without filling it more than halfway (see page 189). Put the olive oil, garlic, tomatoes, and half of the thyme leaves in the pot over high heat (or divide these between the 2 medium), and cook, stirring occasionally, 2 to 3 minutes. Add the wine to heat through, 1 to 2 minutes. Add the drained clams, cover the pot, and cook them over high heat just until they open, removing them as they do, 6 to 10 minutes. Stir them up from the bottom once or twice as they cook. Discard any that haven't opened and grind a generous amount of fresh pepper into the juices.

TO SERVE: Place the clams in warm soup bowls, ladle the juices over the clams, leaving any sandy residue at the bottom, sprinkle them with the remaining thyme leaves and the parsley, if using. Serve right away.

CRAB MEAT AND SOFT-SHELL CRABS

(Including Blue, Maine, Stone, Snow, King, Dungeness, and Soft-shell Crabs)

FLAVOR: Mild, sweet, slightly nutty, delicate, and succulent

ORIGIN: Atlantic and Pacific oceans; soft-shell crabs are farmed

GOOD SIGNS: *Cooked, picked meat:* creamy white to pure white, has some red or brownish coloration depending on the type of crab; sweet, clean aroma, smelling a little of the sea; *Soft-shells:* alive and moving their legs when picked up; very soft top shell

BAD SIGNS: *Cooked, picked meat:* darkening, discolored meat; evidence of much broken shell or cartilage; any hint of ammonia or off-smell; *Soft-shells:* limp or hanging legs when picked up; any off-smell or suggestion of ammonia

HEALTH TIPS: A raw 7-ounce serving (not including shells) is approximately 180 calories with a medium amount of omega-3 fatty acids, and high protein content.

Picked, Cooked Crab Meat

"Rave on" as Buddy Holly sings, about crab meat, irresistible in all its varieties and forms! From Atlantic crab meat of the hard-shell blue crab—which in late spring and summer becomes the completely edible soft-shell crab—to the sweet and nutty Jonah crab meat of Maine, to the rich, firm stone crab claws of Florida,* to the mild and sweet long-limbed beauties (Yes, beauty *is* in the eye of the beholder!) who inhabit the Pacific: snow and king, and to the West Coast Dungeness, whose distinctive flavor some feel is the best of all.

Picked, cooked crab meat—and you can buy it fresh, pasteurized and canned, or

---

*Recipes for stone crab claws don't appear in the book, but don't let that stop you, serve them with the ginger-cilantro sauce for shrimp on page 254, the avocado "whipped cream" for lobster on page 217, the mustard-scallion mayo for soft-shell crabs on page 205, the melted butter with ginger and herbs for lobster tails on page 213, or any number of other possibilities you find in the "Do-All" category on page 296.

frozen—is very perishable stuff. And very expensive. Freshly picked meat is packed in containers with an easily opened lid—try asking the fish seller to open the container so you can see and smell it. You may not get your request, but you'll have made your point, and yourself, visible, in case you discover a problem when you get it home! (If I have an ongoing relationship with a fish market, I trust them, although now they open the container for me without my asking!) If it's fresh, it smells sweetly of the ocean. If there's a suggestion of mustiness, or heaven forbid, ammonia, pass the meat up. Ideally, buy it the day you plan on using it. Pasteurized crab meat, which comes in closed refrigerated cans, holds well for several months (check the "sell-by" date stamped on the can and keep it refrigerated—don't freeze it), but use it within a day or two once you've opened it. It can be good, but it has a more pronounced cooked flavor and has lost some of its delicacy.

When choosing frozen crab meat, inspect it as you would any other frozen seafood (see the guidelines on page 266) and plan on defrosting it slowly, in the refrigerator, to preserve its juices, and hence its texture and flavor. Frozen crab meat is frequently watery, but you can remedy that by squeezing out the defrosted meat, a handful at a time, before using it. And taste a piece, particularly king and snow, to check for saltiness; the processors can get carried away with their brine! A salty batch can be briefly soaked in milk to remove the excess salt before you squeeze it out, and save the crab-infused milk to make a sauce or to enrich a seafood stew. (See the recipe headnote for King Crab with Fine Spaghetti on page 194 for these instructions.)

Maine Jonah crab meat comes fresh or frozen in small, firm lengths of claw meat and tender pieces from the body. Snow crab is a mass of delicate long fibers with occasional pieces of claw meat. King is another story: long, chewy-meaty chunks of firm, sweet meat. It's always packed frozen, whether as picked meat or in its own natural packaging as bright red, two-foot-long, stiff, bumpy legs! Dungeness, which can be bought live on the West Coast from December into April and on the East Coast as well during July and August, is available as fresh-picked or frozen meat the rest of the time, or in whole cooked form. Its character is sort of a felicitous blend of all the best crab meat attributes: sweet and nutty with a flavor that's rich yet delicate, and a texture that's tender and succulent, yet slightly firm at the same time!

Soft-Shell Crabs

Soft-shell crabs, as I've mentioned, are the molted form of the Atlantic blue crab. Bought alive (they're also available frozen), they're cleaned either by the fish seller or by you (see page 206), and the sooner you cook them after cleaning the better, because their bodies deflate, their juices going down the tubes, as they sit. To cook them, rapidly sauté or deep-fry them until they're crisp, then eat the entire body, legs and all. The largest ones in our markets are "jumbos," about 5 inches across. Some people prefer the smaller, more delicate ones, and more of them! It's your choice—and the fishmarket's. Remember two things: 1) The shells should be soft when pressed; and 2) Don't buy precleaned crabs; have them cleaned when you buy them (or do it yourself).

Picked, cooked Atlantic blue crab meat is graded by size: "Jumbo lump" has the largest, most succulent pieces, and is, of course, the most expensive. "Lump," followed by "flake" and "claw," are the next levels down, and obviously, cost proportionately less. When cleaning any of this crab meat, look particularly closely through the smaller sizes for bits of shell and cartilage, it often has more. And always keep it *very* cold until you use it.

King Crab with Fine Spaghetti, Garlic, and Olive Oil

4 servings

PREP AND
COOKING
TIME
30 minutes

It's hard to imagine anything more satisfying than hunks of slightly briny, chewy king crab meat cooked in lots of garlic and olive oil, and tossed with pasta and a little chopped fresh tomato. (I also add some butter to the olive oil because it enhances the natural sweetness of both the crab meat and the garlic.) On the plate, the pasta looks demure—with pretty pink-red chunks of crab meat and bits of tomato. But don't let its looks fool you, it's right up there with energetic flavor! Taste the crab meat before you use it; it can be excessively salty. If so, cover it with cold milk for 10 minutes—the milk will remove the salt and become infused with the flavor of the crab meat itself. Save the milk to make a soup, as an enrichment for seafood stew, or as the base for a crab sauce for another dish.* Substitute fresh or canned lump blue crab meat, Maine, Dungeness, or snow crab meat, surimi, scallops, shrimp, or small cubes of swordfish or salmon fillets, too. And serve this as a first course at a party, providing your guests agree about garlic!

1 pound king crab leg meat, defrosted in the refrigerator overnight; *or* other crab meat

Optional: Approximately 1 cup cold milk (see headnote)

4–6 large garlic cloves (6 if you love garlic)

2 medium ripe tomatoes, *or* 1 cup drained, chopped canned plum tomatoes

Salt and freshly ground black or white pepper to taste

9 tablespoons olive oil

2 tablespoons butter, preferably sweet butter

1 pound dried spaghettini *or* other dried pasta, such as linguine fini, penne, or shells

3 tablespoons chopped fresh (flat-leaf or curly) parsley

TO PREPARE: Bring a very large pot of water to a boil over high heat for the pasta.

*To make the white crab-meat sauce, use half the amount of butter, flour, and milk in Surimi Seafood Baked with Red and Green Peppers (page 250), substituting the crab-meat soaking milk for the regular milk.

Pick through the crab meat for pieces of cartilage (see page 197; king crab meat has long, thin pieces with sharp ends running down the length of each leg and some small pieces may still be in the meat—pull them out). If you're using king crab meat, taste a piece to see if it's very salty. If it is, place it in a shallow pan, cover the crab meat with about a cup of milk, and let it sit for 10 minutes while proceeding with the recipe.

Chop the garlic in the bowl of a food processor (or by hand) until it's finely chopped, scrape it out with a rubber spatula, and set it aside. (You'll have $1^1/_2$ to 2 tablespoons.) If using fresh tomatoes, cut out and discard the cores and make a shallow X through the skin on the opposite end. When the water for the pasta has boiled, drop the tomatoes into the boiling water for *10 seconds* to loosen the skins. Immediately remove the tomatoes and let them sit briefly until they're cool enough to handle. As soon as the tomatoes are out, salt the water to taste, cover the pot, and let the water come back to a boil.

If you've soaked the crab meat, drain it in a colander set over a bowl (if you're saving the milk) and squeeze small amounts of it out with your hand. Cut the crab meat, if necessary, into $^1/_2''$ pieces, and set them aside.

Place 6 tablespoons of the olive oil and all the butter in a large skillet set over low heat. When the butter has melted, add the garlic and cook it, stirring frequently, about 1 minute. Add the crab meat, season it generously with pepper (and salt if necessary), and heat it over low to medium heat, stirring occasionally, 3 to 5 minutes, or until it's heated through. Remove the skillet from the heat.

Add the pasta to the boiling water and cook it al dente (firm) according to the package directions. Meanwhile, peel the tomatoes by lifting the skin starting from the X cut. Cut each tomato in half, squeeze out and discard the seeds, and cut the flesh into small dice. You should have about 1 cup of diced tomatoes. Set it aside while the pasta cooks.

A minute before the pasta is done, place the crab meat mixture back over low heat to warm through, stirring occasionally.

When the pasta is done, drain it well and pour it back into its cooking pot over very low heat. Stir in the remaining 3 tablespoons of olive oil and season the pasta to taste with salt and pepper. At this point, stir the tomatoes and parsley into the warm crab meat and immediately pour the mixture over the pasta, scraping it out with a rubber spatula. With tongs or another appropriate implement, lift and stir the crab meat into the pasta as best as possible—it won't mix in very well (unless you're using a short pasta like penne or shells), but don't worry, it flavors it all nicely. Continue lifting and stirring until everything is hot and fragrant, about 1 minute.

TO SERVE: Divide the pasta onto warm dinner plates, top with spoonfuls of crab meat (most of the meat will probably be in the corners of the pot), and serve right away.

Crab-Meat Hash with Corn and Cheddar Cheese

4 servings

PREP AND
COOKING
TIME
35–40
minutes

I love crab meat in all forms, but it is quite a luxury. So, when you have it, really have it! Sauté lots of jumbo lump crab meat with shallots, red bell peppers, and corn. (Definitely make this in late summer, at least once, when incomparable local corn is around.) Moisten the mixture with a little bit of cream or chicken broth, add some freshly grated Parmigiano-Reggiano, and stir in small cubes of Cheddar cheese just to *begin* to melt. Take a bite—the crab meat's succulence hits you first, then milky little corn kernels pop in your mouth, and when you come upon the Cheddar, it's a good, sharp little surprise. I like to bring the crab meat to the table in its cooking pan, so, if you have a pan you love, use it. Try this with chunks of king crab, pieces of Maine or Dungeness crab, or snow crab. For an economy version, use surimi. It also makes a luscious first course for a party.

1 pound fresh or canned jumbo lump crab meat or frozen and defrosted king or snow crab meat (see Note), or surimi

2 tablespoons butter

$^1/_2$ cup thinly sliced shallots, about 1″ long; *or* white onions

$^3/_4$ cup red bell pepper strips, about $1^1/_2″ \times ^1/_4″$

$^1/_4$ teaspoon dry mustard

$^1/_4$ cup heavy cream or chicken broth

$^1/_8$ teaspoon cayenne, or to taste

1 generous cup fresh corn kernels (about 4 ears); *or* canned, drained; *or* frozen and defrosted (see page 198)

$^1/_4$ cup thinly sliced scallions, both white and green parts

3 tablespoons freshly grated Parmigiano-Reggiano cheese

Salt and freshly ground black or white pepper to taste

$^1/_3$ cup medium-sharp Cheddar cheese cubes (about $^1/_2″$)

TO PREPARE: If you're using fresh lump crab meat, it needs to be picked through for pieces of cartilage and shell. (See page 197, for cleaning instructions.) Often there isn't much, but it is annoying getting any in your mouth, so it's worth the bother. (King and snow crab have long, thin pieces of cartilage with sharp ends running the length of each leg, and some small pieces may still be in the meat—pull them out. Taste a piece of the meat if you're using king crab, because it can be very salty. If so, place the meat in a shallow pan, cover it with milk, and let it sit for 10 minutes while starting the vegetables. Whether you've soaked the crab or not, frozen crab meat needs to be squeezed dry in your hands before proceeding.)

Here's how to clean fresh picked or pasteurized crab meat: Dump the container of crab meat into a medium bowl and have another medium bowl right next to it. (If it's very hot in the kitchen, I suggest setting each of the bowls in another, larger bowl of ice—fresh crab meat is very perishable. I empty the uncleaned crab meat into a bowl because it's easier to grab, and you break it up less while cleaning it.)

Pick up a small handful of uncleaned meat. With the fingers of your other hand, lightly feel around all the pieces as best you can without shredding the meat any further. When you come across cartilage or shell, it will feel sharp and pointed. In fact, you'll feel the pieces before you actually see them. As you do this you're getting an "overview" of each handful, not actually feeling every tiny piece—you're relying on the feel of your fingers at least as much as your eyesight. Pick out the cartilage/shell and discard it. Then put the cleaned handful in the second bowl. Continue picking through the remaining crab meat. It sounds laborious, but it goes quickly once you've felt your first cartilage and know what you're "looking" for! When the crab meat is all cleaned, refrigerate it if you aren't using it immediately.

In a large skillet, melt the butter over medium heat and add the shallots and red peppers. Sauté them, stirring occasionally, until the shallots are wilted and the peppers are slightly crisp, 3 to 5 minutes. While the veggies cook, put the dry mustard in a little mixing bowl and stir in $1/2$ teaspoon of the cream or broth until the mixture is smooth. Stir in the remaining cream or broth and the cayenne, and set the mixture aside. Gently stir the corn and crab meat into the veggies, and heat them through, stirring frequently, 3 to 5 minutes. When the crab meat is hot, stir in the cream or broth mixture to heat through. When the entire mixture is hot, stir in the scallions and Parmigiano-Reggiano cheese. Turn the heat to low, season the mixture with salt and pepper, and stir in the Cheddar. Heat the mixture less than a minute, just long enough for the cheese to begin to soften.

TO SERVE: Bring the skillet to the table, if you like, and serve right away, on warm dinner plates.

NOTE: The crab meat comes already cooked when you buy it, what you're doing is merely heating it through with other good things.

Beware of prehusked corn! Yes, you can see what the corn actually looks like, but who knows how long it's been husked! Precious moisture (and therefore flavor) has probably long since gone. Fresh husks feel almost waxy when you run your hand along them—they're a fresh green, and the silk that protrudes from the top should actually be silky and moist with a light, fragrant aroma. Look at the end where the corn was severed from the stalk—it should look freshly cut, not shriveled or discolored. You can tell a lot about its age and storage treatment from that cut.

To cut kernels off the cob, first remove the husks and silk—if the corn is really, really fresh, first smell its milky sweetness and stroke the silkiness of the silk, and be sure to swoon over its elemental beauty! Of course, none of the oohing and aahing applies if the corn is old and dry.

Once that moment of pleasure is over, snap off the stalk and stand the corn on its wide end. If it doesn't stand flat, trim it with a knife so it stands more steadily. Cut down along the cob, starting close to the top, just slightly away from where the kernels and cob meet. Better to leave a little corn on the cob than to take any cob with you as you cut. (You can always scrape the cob after you've removed the kernels to release the last of its precious fluids!) Then cut down the cob in long vertical sections, all the way around, to release the kernels.

Shredded Crab Tacos

*T*his is a version of a soft taco that's traditionally served as an appetizer in Mexico. But for me, having a few big bites wouldn't be enough. "They go down so easily," my husband says—maybe too easily—so we made it an official meal. You can also use surimi, small shrimp, or pieces of lobster (cooked or raw), or big flakes of cooked fillets.

4 servings

PREP AND
COOKING
TIME
35–40
minutes

2 medium ripe tomatoes

1 large garlic clove

1 small onion

4 pickled serrano or jalapeño chile peppers, or to taste (in cans or jars on supermarket Mexican shelf)

$^1/_4$ cup vegetable oil

1 pound fresh or canned lump crab meat or frozen and defrosted king or snow crab meat

1 tablespoon fresh squeezed lime juice

Salt and freshly ground black or white pepper to taste

Corn or flour tortillas, steamed (supermarket refrigerated section or specialty store)

Shredded mild Cheddar, Colby, or Monterey Jack cheese

Sour cream

Sliced ripe avocado

Thin tomato wedges

Lots of fresh cilantro leaves

TO PREPARE: Preheat the oven to 450°.

Rinse and dry the tomatoes and cut out the core. Slice the tomatoes in half and place them, cut side down, on a baking pan. Roast the tomatoes until they are soft throughout and the skin is blistered, or even a little blackened, about 15 minutes. While the tomatoes are roasting, start the vegetables.

Finely chop the garlic clove and set it aside. Finely chop the onion and set it aside. Finely chop the chiles and set them aside. When the tomatoes are roasted, let them cool enough to handle and chop them into medium pieces. You should have $^1/_2$ to $^3/_4$ of a cup. Discard any liquid left in the roasting pan.

Place the vegetable oil in a large skillet set over medium heat and add the chopped garlic and onion. Cook them without browning, stirring occasionally, until they're tender, 8 to 10 minutes. While the onion is cooking, clean the crab meat (see page 197). If you're using king or snow crab meat, check for thin sections of cartilage within the pieces, and pull them out. Taste a piece of the meat. If it's very salty, place the meat in a shallow pan, cover it with milk, and let it sit for 10 minutes. Drain and squeeze the meat dry in your hands before proceeding with the recipe. If you like, the soaking milk can be saved and used for a sauce or stew. (See the headnote page 194). Chop the meat into small pieces if necessary.

When the onion is tender, stir in the chopped tomato and the chiles, and cook them together for 1 minute. Stir in the crab meat to heat through, 2 to 3 minutes, and stir in the lime juice. Season the crab mixture generously with salt, pepper, and more chopped chiles, if you wish. The mixture can be made a day ahead and refrigerated. (Reheat it in a large skillet over low to medium heat, stirring frequently, for about 10 minutes, or until hot. Or, place it in a shallow, covered, ovenproof casserole in the preheated oven for about 20 minutes, or until hot.)

TO SERVE: Serve the crab meat right away on a warm platter with a basket of tortillas that have been wrapped in aluminum foil and heated in a preheated 400° oven until steaming. Serve bowls of grated cheese, sour cream, sliced avocado, tomato wedges, and fresh cilantro leaves to stuff into the tacos.

Crab Cakes with Tomatoes, Olives, and Preserved Lemon

*T*hese crab cakes are served with a Moroccan-inspired sauce that gets its texture and character from chopped fresh tomato, ripe Mediterranean olives, and preserved lemon, with a teaspoon of *harissa,* the Moroccan hot red pepper sauce, stirred in at the end. (Harissa comes prepared, often from France, in a tube, and lasts in the refrigerator for at least a year! It's available in specialty stores or by mail order.) You might want to serve these cakes with other sauces—or just wedges of lemon or lime—and the sauce is good with fillets such as sole, bass, snapper, monkfish, grouper, swordfish, tuna, shark, or catfish, or with sea animals like lobster, fried calamari, or shrimp.

4 servings

PREP AND
COOKING
TIME
40–45
minutes

1 pound fresh jumbo lump crab meat or king, snow, Dungeness, or other frozen crab meat (about 2¹/₂ cups), defrosted overnight in the refrigerator, *or* surimi seafood

1 large egg

1 tablespoon Dijon mustard, preferably French

2 tablespoons storebought or homemade mayonnaise

2 tablespoons + approximately ¹/₂ cup dry bread crumbs

Optional: 2 tablespoons roughly chopped fresh (flat-leaf or curly) parsley, *or* other fresh herb

Salt and freshly ground black or white pepper to taste

¹/₄ cup + 3 tablespoons olive oil

1 teaspoon harissa; *or* 1 teaspoon fresh or jarred roasted red peppers, pureed with hot pepper sauce to taste; *or* hot pepper sauce to taste

¹/₂ cup ripe tomato, cut into ¹/₄″ dice

1 tablespoon coarsely chopped ripe Mediterranean olives (such as kalamata, Gaeta, or other Greek-style)

4 teaspoons chopped preserved lemon (see Pantry, to Make), *or* 1 teaspoon grated lemon zest (see page 133)

TO PREPARE: Preheat the oven to 375°.

If you're using fresh lump crab meat, it needs to be picked through for pieces of cartilage and shell. Often there isn't much, but it is annoying getting any in your mouth, so it's worth the bother. (See page 197 for cleaning instructions.)

If you're using king or snow crab meat, they have long, thin pieces of cartilage running the length of each leg, and some small pieces may still be in the meat— you can feel their sharp ends—pull them out. Taste a piece of the meat if you're using king crab, because it can be very salty. If it is, place the meat in a shallow pan, cover it with milk, and let it sit for 10 minutes. Whether soaked or not, frozen crab meat needs to be squeezed dry in your hands before proceeding. Otherwise, cut the king crab meat, if necessary, into $1/2$" pieces, chopping a quarter of it somewhat finer to help bind the cakes, and set it aside in a large mixing bowl.

Lightly beat the egg in a small bowl and stir in the mustard and mayonnaise until they're fairly well combined—don't worry about small lumps. Pour this mixture over the prepared crab meat and fold it together until it's well combined, being careful to break up the pieces as little as possible. Sprinkle 2 tablespoons of the bread crumbs and the parsley or other herb, if using, over the top of the crab meat, seasoning it with salt and pepper. (Be cautious with salt if you're using frozen crab meat.) Fold the ingredients together well. The mixture should just hold together when squeezed in the palm of your hand. If it's dry, add a little more mayonnaise, or if it's wet, add a little more bread crumbs. Check the seasoning by sautéing a teaspoon of the mixture— formed into a patty—in a small skillet over medium heat with a little vegetable oil. Adjust the seasoning with more salt and pepper if necessary.

Place the remaining $1/2$ cup of bread crumbs on a large plate or platter. Form eight 2" cakes and press them into the crumbs, lightly coating them top and bottom. Refrigerate them, uncovered, in a single layer, while you prepare the sauce, or at least 10 minutes, to firm them up. They can also be refrigerated overnight. (And, if you prefer, they can be sautéed, after forming and chilling, without being dipped in crumbs.)

Place $1/4$ cup of the olive oil in a medium mixing bowl, stir in the harissa until well combined, and stir in the diced tomatoes, olives, and preserved lemon. Season the sauce with salt and pepper and set it aside, or refrigerate it for up to 3 days, being sure to let it come to room temperature before serving.

Place a large ovenproof skillet (or use 2 medium) over medium heat with the remaining 3 tablespoons of olive oil (or divide the oil between the 2). When the oil is hot, add the cakes. Brown the first side, adjusting the heat as necessary, until they're a lovely *light* golden brown, 2 to 3 minutes. Turn the cakes over with a metal spatula and place the skillet in the oven. Cook the cakes until they're hot throughout and golden on the bottom, 6 to 8 minutes.

TO SERVE: Place the cakes on warm dinner plates, top them with a spoonful of tomato-olive-lemon sauce, and serve right away, with more sauce on the side.

Soft-Shell Crabs with Tomatoes and Basil

4 servings

PREP AND
COOKING
TIME
30 minutes

*D*iced red-ripe summer tomatoes, dripping with their own juices, mixed with minced shallot, fresh basil and cilantro, lemon juice, and a tiny spoonful of balsamic vinegar create a room temperature "sauce" for the crabs—all the dressing-up they could ever need. And if you like hot and spicy, turn this into a salsa by adding Tabasco or chopped hot chiles. I've deep-fried the crabs in this recipe and they come out light and crisp, practically greaseless, much less so, in fact, than when pan-fried. I fry them in a heavy, old pot which works as well—even if it's not as foolproof—as an electric fryer. The sauce is also good with salmon, snapper, sole, or bass fillets, with tuna or swordfish steaks, with scallops, or just about anything!

Vegetable oil for frying
1$^1/_2$–2 cups milk
Salt and freshly ground black or white pepper to taste
8 jumbo soft-shell crabs (or more small ones), cleaned in the fish store or alive
$^3/_4$ cup ripe tomatoes, cut into small dice (see page 204)
1 tablespoon finely minced shallot or white onion or white of scallion
1 teaspoon balsamic vinegar
1$^1/_2$ teaspoons fresh squeezed lemon juice
1 tablespoon chopped fresh basil
2 teaspoons chopped fresh cilantro (or all basil)
Flour for dredging

TO PREPARE: Pour the vegetable oil into a heavy, deep pot, filling it by no more than half, but at least 3″ deep, and begin heating the oil over low to medium heat. Or set your electric fryer to 375°. Preheat the oven as low as possible.

Pour the milk into a pan or container big enough to hold all the soft-shell crabs, and salt it moderately. Place the cleaned crabs in the milk, turning them over several times, to soak while you prepare the tomatoes. If the crabs are still alive, see page 000 for cleaning instructions.

Place the diced tomatoes in a small mixing bowl and stir in the shallot, vinegar, lemon juice, basil, and cilantro. Season the mixture well with salt, a generous amount of pepper, and a few more drops of balsamic vinegar, if you wish. Set it aside while you fry the crabs.

If you're using a conventional pot filled with oil, turn the heat to medium-high until it reaches 375° on a frying thermometer, or drop a pinch of flour into the oil. If the flour makes sputtering noises it's ready. (If the oil is too hot, it will begin to smoke and the flour will brown too quickly; turn down the heat and try the flour test again in a few minutes. If the flour doesn't sputter, the oil is too cool. Continue heating the oil a few more minutes.)

Line a cookie sheet, or other ovenproof tray, with 2 layers of paper towels and set it near the stove. Place the flour in a large brown paper bag, on a plate, or in another shallow container. Drop 1 or 2 of the crabs in the flour (only flour as many as will fit in the fryer at one time with lots of room), roll the top of the paper bag to seal it, and shake the bag up and down a few times to coat the crab thoroughly (or dip the crab into the flour to coat well on both sides). Immediately, and carefully, lower the crab into the hot oil—holding the crab with a metal tongs or your hand. The oil will bubble furiously as the crab begins to cook and its juices flow into the oil—place a wire basket on top of the crab to submerge it while it's frying, or hold it down with metal tongs or a metal kitchen spoon. However, remember that the metal implement you use to keep the crab in the oil is going to get very hot. The crab is cooked through when the bubbles subside, in 3 to 4 minutes.

The crab will be a very light gold when it's done. The color isn't much to write home about, but the crisp lightness is. Remove the crab to the towel-lined tray and put it in the oven while you finish frying the remaining crabs. When the oil is cool, if it looks salvageable, strain it and refrigerate it for another use, or if it's become very dark, discard it.

TO SERVE: Place the crabs on warm dinner plates, top them with a large spoonful of the tomatoes and basil, and serve right away.

To cut a tomato into small dice, skin and all, first rinse and dry it with paper towels. Remove and discard the core and place the tomato, core side down, on a cutting board. Using either a very sharp conventional knife or a good serrated one, cut the tomato into $1/4''$ slices and stack about half of them on top of one another. Cut through the stacked slices into $1/4''$-wide strips, keeping them in their original formation. Turn the stack so the strips are horizontal to you. Cut across the strips at $1/4''$ intervals and the tomatoes will fall into even dice. Do the same thing with the other half of the tomato.

Soft-Shell Crabs with Mustard-Scallion Sauce

4 servings

PREP AND
COOKING
TIME
25–30
minutes

Sometimes nothing's better than a lightly creamy, slightly piquant, mayonnaise for crispy soft-shells. And you can throw it together in a couple of minutes. The sauce, a thinned mayo, doubles as a dip for vegetable crudité and, in greater volume, it's a base for homemade potato salad—my daughter Rachel's favorite. It's also good with catfish and perch fillets, fish and chips, and chilled shrimp or crab meat.

1$^1/_2$–2 cups milk, or more if needed

Salt and freshly ground black or white pepper to taste

8 jumbo soft-shell crabs, cleaned in the fish store or alive

$^1/_4$ cup homemade or storebought mayonnaise

2 generous tablespoons Dijon mustard, preferably French

4 teaspoons fresh squeezed lemon juice

1$^1/_2$ tablespoons very thinly sliced scallion, white and green parts

$^1/_2$ cup vegetable oil + more if necessary

Flour for dredging

TO PREPARE: Pour the milk into a pan or container large enough to hold all of the crabs, and salt it lightly. Place the cleaned crabs in the milk, turning them over several times, to soak while you prepare the mayo. If the crabs are still alive, see page 206 for cleaning instructions.

Place the mayonnaise in a small bowl and stir in the mustard to make a smooth mixture. Stir in the lemon juice and scallion. (Adding the scallion at this point lets its flavor permeate the sauce. If you prefer, you can sprinkle the scallion over the cooked crabs as a garnish.) Season the sauce with salt and pepper and set it aside, or refrigerate it for up to 2 weeks. (I like the flavor as it develops over time—it becomes richly scallion flavored, which is what happens to a potato salad if you use this as a base.)

Put a very large skillet (or 2 smaller ones) over low heat and add the vegetable oil (or divide it between the pans). While the oil is heating, place the flour in a brown paper bag or on a plate. Remove the crabs from the milk (you can drain them all in a colander) and discard the milk. Drop 3 or 4 of the crabs at a time into the paper bag and roll the top to seal it. Gently shake the bag up and down a few times to coat the crabs thoroughly (or flour them on the plate).

Turn the heat under the skillet to high, and as soon as the oil is very hot, place the crabs, belly side down (that's the white side), in the hot oil. Continue flouring and cooking the remaining crabs in the same fashion. Cook the crabs on their belly side until golden brown, 3 to 4 minutes. Turn them over and cook the second side for another 3 to 4 minutes. Add more vegetable oil any time the pan seems dry. Season the crabs with salt and pepper. As the crabs are cooked, drain them briefly on a paper towel-lined cookie sheet or tray.

TO SERVE: Place the crabs on warm dinner plates, spoon some of the mustard-scallion sauce over them, and serve right away.

If you can deal with cleaning your own soft-shell crabs, do it. It's not technically difficult, but it can be emotionally rough because they're alive when you clean them. I know—I feel like running away screaming as I'm writing this. But the closer to their cooking time the crabs are cleaned the better—they're composed of a lot of water and much of it gets lost in cleaning. Stay with me if you want, or you can be excused to enter a state of instant, and effective, denial!

Pick up one crab and turn it over so its pale underside faces up. You see a section called, for fairly obvious reasons, the "apron"—it's flush with the underside but is clearly defined. Slip your fingers under the "apron" at its long point in the middle of the underside, it'll pull up easily. Pull the point toward you, pulling out the entire "apron" as you do so. When you reach the end of the body, twist it a little and rip it off the body. Discard it. Incidentally, males have a narrower, pointier apron than females. It makes sense, doesn't it?

Turn the crab over, top side up, and lift up one of the pointy wing-like sides—there's one on each side. Under these sides are filament-shaped spongy lungs. Pull them out and discard them.

Now, here's another option. Many people cut across the front of the face (see the eye stalks?) with a scissors. That part really bothers me and I only do it if the crabs have gone beyond their very soft stage and are a little hard, their facial protuberances being quite sharp then. It's up to you. No, they don't make any discernible noise during all of this trauma, but if you're an empathetic being, it can't help but touch you.

So there you have it, they're clean and ready to cook.

Pan-fried Soft-Shell Crabs with Chinese Black Bean–Garlic Ginger Vinaigrette

4 servings

PREP AND COOKING TIME 20–25 minutes

Chinese black beans are small soy beans—fermented, intense, and quite salty. When you buy them loose, you need to rinse or soak them before you can cook with them. But you can also buy a prepared black bean–garlic paste that's a good starting point for quick sauces to suit lots of fillets and shellfish. For these soft-shell crabs, I've added chopped ginger, rice wine vinegar, and vegetable oil to make a vinaigrette. By adding these elements, I've both sharpened and softened the sauce at the same time, and "raised its pitch," so that it relates better to the crabs. You'll see what I mean when you compare the bottled preparation with your finished vinaigrette. Substitute lobster, or sea scallops, swordfish steaks, or fillets like bass, catfish, and monkfish. Or mix a little of the vinaigrette into chilled crab meat for a salad, or to serve on toast as an hors d'oeuvre. Use it as a dip for grilled shrimp, or as a flavoring base for a seafood stir-fry.

1$^1/_2$–2 cups milk, or more if needed

Salt and freshly ground black or white pepper to taste

8 jumbo soft-shell crabs (or more small ones), cleaned in the fish store or alive

2 tablespoons prepared black bean–garlic sauce (supermarket Oriental shelf)

2$^1/_2$ teaspoons chopped fresh ginger (see page 214)

2 tablespoons rice wine vinegar

9 tablespoons vegetable oil + more if necessary

Optional: 2 tablespoons sesame oil

Flour for dredging

TO PREPARE: Pour the milk into a pan or container large enough to hold all the soft-shell crabs, and salt it lightly. Place the cleaned crabs in the milk, turning them over several times, to soak while you prepare the vinaigrette. If the crabs are still alive, see page 000 for cleaning instructions.

Put the prepared black bean–garlic sauce in a small mixing bowl and stir in the ginger and rice wine vinegar. (Use the coiled snake towel trick if your bowl doesn't sit steady. See page 153.) Gradually whisk in 3 tablespoons of the vegetable oil and season the vinaigrette with pepper. Set it aside while you cook the crabs, or cover and refrigerate it for up to 1 month.

Put 2 large skillets over low heat and add 3 tablespoons of vegetable oil and 1 tablespoon of sesame oil (or 4 tablespoons vegetable oil) to each. While the oil is heating, place the flour in a brown paper bag, on a plate, or in another shallow container. Remove the crabs from the milk (you can drain them all in a colander) and discard the milk. Drop 2 or 3 of the crabs into the paper bag and roll the top to seal it. Gently shake the bag up and down a few times to coat the crabs thoroughly (or flour them on the plate).

Turn the heat under the skillets to high, and as soon as the oil is very hot, place the crabs, belly side down (that's the white side), in the hot oil. Flour the remaining crabs and place them in the hot oil in the same fashion. Cook the crabs on their belly side until golden brown, 3 to 4 minutes. Turn them over and cook the second side for another 3 to 4 minutes, adding more vegetable oil any time the pan seems a little dry. Season the crabs with salt and pepper. When the crabs are cooked, drain them briefly on a cookie sheet or a tray lined with paper towels.

TO SERVE: Place the crabs on warm dinner plates with their bellies facing up (that's the traditional way, at least at the Waldorf-Astoria!), spoon the black bean vinaigrette over them, and serve away.

Soft-Shell Crabs with Lemon-Dill Mashed Potatoes

4 servings

PREP AND
COOKING
TIME
35–40
minutes

I think "yum" says it all! You can make the mashed potatoes, which are full of fresh lemon flavor, up to an hour ahead, by keeping them warm in a very low oven or over a water bath. I pour a little more hot milk over them while they're sitting, and when I'm ready to serve them, I stir it in with the fresh dill. Try the potatoes with salmon fillets, or swordfish or tuna steaks also.

Salt and freshly ground black and white pepper to taste
1 pound boiling potatoes
$^1/_3$ cup + 3 tablespoons milk for potatoes, + $1^1/_2$–2 cups milk for crabs + more if necessary
Grated zest of 3 lemons (about $1^1/_2$ teaspoons—see page 133)
2 tablespoons butter
$1^1/_2$ tablespoons chopped fresh dill, *or* 1 generous teaspoon dried dill
8 jumbo soft-shell crabs (or more small ones), cleaned in fish store or alive
$^1/_2$ cup vegetable oil + more if necessary
Flour for dredging

TO PREPARE: Put a large pot of salted water over high heat to cook the potatoes. Meanwhile, peel them, cut them into 1″ chunks, and keep them in a bowl covered with cold water. When the water is boiling, drain the potatoes and add them to the pot. Cook them at a low boil (so they don't break up), uncovered, until they're very tender, about 10 minutes. While they're cooking, gently heat $^1/_3$ cup + 3 tablespoons of milk with the grated lemon zest and butter. Season the milk with salt and white pepper and set it aside.

Pour the milk for the crabs into a pan or container large enough to hold all of them, and salt it lightly. Place the cleaned crabs in the milk, turning them over several times, to soak while you mash the potatoes. If the crabs are still alive, see page 206 for cleaning instructions.

When the potatoes are tender, drain them very well and put them back in their cooking pot. Keeping the pot over very low heat, mash the potatoes (or put them through a ricer) while gradually adding all the warm milk but *reserving 3 table-spoons*. Season the potatoes with salt and white pepper (stir in the *dried* dill now but not the fresh, if you're using it) and transfer them to a small pot or bowl to keep warm. Pour the reserved milk over their surface but don't stir it in. Cover the potatoes and keep them in a very low oven or over simmering water while you cook the crabs.

Put 2 large skillets over low heat and add $\frac{1}{4}$ cup of vegetable oil to each. While the oil is heating, place the flour in a brown paper bag, on a plate, or in another shallow container. Remove the crabs from the milk (you can drain them all in a colander) and discard the milk. Drop 2 or 3 of the crabs into the paper bag and roll the top to seal it. Gently shake the bag up and down a few times to coat the crabs thoroughly (or flour them on the plate).

Turn the heat under the skillets to high, and as soon as the oil is very hot, place the crabs, belly side down (that's the white side), in the hot oil. Flour the remaining crabs and place them in the hot oil in the same fashion. Cook the crabs on their belly side until golden brown, 3 to 4 minutes. Turn them over and cook the second side for another 3 to 4 minutes. Add more vegetable oil any time the pan seems dry. Season the crabs with salt and black pepper. When the crabs are cooked, drain them briefly on a paper towel-lined cookie sheet or tray.

Uncover the mashed potatoes and stir in the layer of milk and the fresh dill. Adjust the seasoning, if necessary, with salt and white pepper.

TO SERVE: Make a small hill of mashed potatoes on warm dinner plates. Lean the crabs against the potatoes with their browned bellies facing up, and serve right away.

LOBSTER

(Including the American "Maine," Spiny Lobster Tails, and Slipper Lobster Tails)

FLAVOR: Mild, sweet, firm, and succulent

ORIGIN: *American "Maine":* the Northern Atlantic from Canada to North Carolina; *Spiny:* Florida and the Bahamas through the Carribean; South African and Australian lobster tails are called "rock" lobster tails; *Slipper:* China, Thailand, and Australia

GOOD SIGNS: *American "Maine":* lively flapping tail when picked up; *Spiny:* a frozen product, see guidelines, page 266; *Slipper:* a frozen product, see guidelines, page 266

BAD SIGNS: *American "Maine":* listless or utterly lifeless when picked up; *Spiny:* a frozen product, see guidelines, page 266; *Slipper:* a frozen product, see guidelines, page 266

HEALTH TIPS: A raw 7-ounce serving (not including shells) is approximately 200 calories, with a low level of omega-3 fatty acids and high protein content.

American "Maine" Lobster

Let's get it straight right now: American "Maine" live lobsters are ruthless, thoughtless creatures who think nothing of eating their own, young or old, when placed in too tight quarters in tanks. Fortunately, we don't have to watch that spectacle, because the bands or pegs on their claws keep these shocking instincts from prevailing. It must be nature's way of telling them their population needs to be thinned—nature is not known for its gentility!

Whole American lobsters need to be very lively before they're cooked; pick one up by its midsection and watch it angrily flap its tail and threaten you with its (pegged) claws. Those are the ones you want. Dead and dying lobsters make terrible, mushy eating.

The best lobsters I've ever had are those known as "soft-shells" (generally available from July to October). But it's a comparative soft-shell—unlike a soft-shell crab which you can, and do, eat shell and all. Soft-shell lobsters have a more malleable, but still inedible shell. The meat is tender and very sweet, but it doesn't fill out its shell (particularly the claws) as much as it does when in its hard-shell phase (lobsters molt often), but I think the trade-off is worth it. Cook live lobsters boiled, grilled, or broiled. The meat, apart from its shell, can be sautéed, stir-fried, steamed, and fried.

Spiny and slipper lobster tails are found in the frozen food section of the market, or better yet, on a beach in the Carribean or Australia, being grilled, just pulled from the water, over a driftwood fire! Spiny tails, or "rock" lobster as they're often called commercially, have a somewhat large, robust tail that's mild and sweet, but somewhat less briny-succulent and lush than its American counterpart. Defrosted overnight in the refrigerator, they're a quick meal grilled, steamed, boiled, or broiled.

Eating a slipper lobster tail can be likened to meeting a well-bred "lady," if you don't mind the clichés attributed to that sort of femininity: high refinement, gentle tenderness, and delicate breeding! Actually, I don't know a thing about their breeding, but when they're on the plate, they're extraordinarily delicate and fine, quite different from "rock" and "Maine." It's simple to remove them from their shells and slip off their "slipper" skins for sautéing, poaching, or broiling or grilling over a low fire.

To boil live lobsters properly, plunge them into boiling water head first. Let the water come back to a low boil and time them at 5 minutes for their first pound and 3 more for each additional pound. Remove them to a platter and continue cooking any that didn't fit into the pot in the first round.

It's common wisdom live lobsters are best boiled in sea water, no doubt true, but I don't keep much of that around. Perhaps you do. Nor do I add any salt to their cooking water to compensate. You can.

Grilled Lobster Tails with Ginger-Herb Butter

4 servings

PREP AND
COOKING
TIME
40 minutes

*S*outh African lobster tails can be as good as they are easy. Defrost them overnight in the refrigerator—one tail is the right amount for a smallish serving, but you'll want another if you're a lobster fiend—then butterfly and grill them. (You can butterfly the tails and make the basic ginger butter the day before.) Melt the butter with finely grated ginger—which thickens the butter and gives it zing—and, right before serving, stir in a mixture of fresh chives, thyme, tarragon, and basil. Serve them by themselves for yourselves, or for a special summer party—perhaps as part of an assortment of grilled seafood that could also include sea scallops, shrimp, oysters in the shell, and small fillets of your favorite fish. You can also spoon the butter over Maine lobster, slipper lobster tails, sea scallops, salmon, tuna, swordfish, snapper, bass, or sole fillets, and just about anything else with or without fins!

> 5 tablespoons butter
>
> 1¹/₂–2 teaspoons peeled and finely grated fresh ginger (see page 214)
>
> Salt and freshly ground black or white pepper to taste
>
> Four 6- or 7-ounce frozen rock lobster tails in the shell, defrosted in the
>   refrigerator overnight
>
> 2 teaspoons vegetable oil
>
> 1 tablespoon snipped fresh chives, *or* 1¹/₂ tablespoons thinly sliced scallion,
>   green part only
>
> 1¹/₂ teaspoons fresh thyme leaves, lightly chopped
>
> ¹/₂ teaspoon coarsely chopped fresh tarragon
>
> 1¹/₂ tablespoons chopped fresh basil

TO PREPARE: Start a medium-hot fire in the grill (or preheat the oven broiler). Fifteen minutes before you're going to grill the lobster tails, put the grill grate 4″ or 5″ above the glowing coals if it isn't already there. (I also like to brush the top of the grate with vegetable oil just before grilling to help prevent sticking.)

Place the butter and grated ginger in a small skillet over very low heat. Stir the butter several times while it's melting, and season it with salt and pepper. Set the butter aside to allow the ginger flavor to permeate, while you prepare the lobster tails. Or cover and refrigerate the ginger butter for up to 1 week, or freeze it for up to a month.

Slide the lower blade of a pair of poultry shears or large scissors between the flesh of the tail and the top shell of the lobster tail. Keeping the shears in the middle of the shell, cut lengthwise down the entire shell leaving about ¹⁄₂″ of the flipper *uncut*. As you cut, you'll be slicing into about ¹⁄₂″ of the flesh as well.

Holding each side of the tail with the flesh side facing you, gently, but surely, snap the sides away from you to butterfly it. (You may need to cut the flesh a little more to butterfly it without tearing, but don't cut all the way through.) The small, uncut flipper section should stay together, making the butterflied tail look like a beautifully marked wigwam! And you've created one flat side that's perfect for grilling. (If you cut too far, don't worry, it'll still grill fine.) Repeat this process with the other tails. Rub the exposed flesh of the tails with vegetable oil and season them with salt and pepper.

Place the tails over the glowing coals, flesh side down (or in the broiler, flesh side up)—they should lie perfectly flat. Grill them until the flesh is golden, 6 to 7 minutes. Turn the tails over and grill them on the second side, until the flesh is completely opaque, another 2 to 3 minutes. To check, make a small slit with a paring knife in the flesh of the thickest part of one tail. Place the tails, flesh side up, on a warm platter while you finish the ginger-herb butter.

Reheat the butter over low heat to warm it, and adjust the seasoning with salt and pepper. Turn off the heat and stir in the fresh herbs.

TO SERVE: Place the lobster tails on warm dinner plates, spoon some of the ginger-herb butter over the meat of each tail, and serve right away. (Or pull the meat out of the shells before buttering them, if you prefer—it comes right out.)

Fresh ginger (it's commonly referred to as a root, but it's really a rhizome—like the bearded iris in the garden) is very firm, with knobs and bumps, and it has smooth, slightly shiny, light brown skin when it's fresh. When it's old, it becomes wrinkled, somewhat soft, and shrunken.

Peel the ginger with a small paring knife to reveal its moist, aromatic interior. Using the medium side of a box grater, rub the ginger up and down against the sharp perforations. The pulp *inside* the grater will be finely grated, soft and juicy. The pulp on the *outside* of the grater is fibrous—most of the long fibers get stuck there. Use only the ginger *inside* the grater for this butter and save the fibrous stuff for another use or discard it. (Simmer it in chicken broth, strain it, and save the broth for a stew or soup. Or heat the ginger fibers in sesame oil and save the strained oil for a stir-fry.) You'll find that you'll need considerably more ginger to start with when you're grating instead of chopping it. So, why should I do this, you may ask? Because much more of the ginger juice is released in grating, and that means tons of flavor!

GREAT FISH, QUICK

Slipper Lobster Tails with Lemon, Pine Nuts, and Dill

Slipper lobster tails are very small, about 2″ long, and they come frozen in their shells from Taiwan. They're amazingly tender, succulent, and mild in flavor. But they can't handle assertive companions—they're too delicate for wild dolling up! A little bit of white wine, lemon juice, fresh dill, and toasted pine nuts enhances without overwhelming them. They are expensive, but they do make a great family treat, or a party appetizer or main dish. You can, of course, substitute other lobster, or shrimp, in this dish—but I think the voluptuous texture of scallops would work better.

1¹⁄₂ pounds slipper lobster tails in their shells (12 to 14 pieces), defrosted overnight in the refrigerator

2¹⁄₂ tablespoons pine nuts

1 tablespoon butter

Salt and freshly ground black or white pepper to taste

6 tablespoons white wine or dry vermouth

3 tablespoons fresh squeezed lemon juice

2 tablespoons *cold* butter

2¹⁄₂ tablespoons chopped fresh dill

TO PREPARE: Holding the tail belly up, slide the lower blade of a pair of poultry shears, or kitchen scissors, between the flesh of the lobster tail and the under side of its shell. Cut down the entire length of the shell. With your hands, snap back the sides of the shell to expose the flesh and pull out the entire tail—it'll come right out. The dark intestine also comes out as you remove the meat, conveniently staying attached to the shell; discard it all together. Sometimes the tail meat is enclosed in a membrane that covers it like a slipper (hence, the name, I gather!), and sometimes the membrane remains stuck inside the shell, and sometimes it isn't there at all! If the tail comes out covered with this membrane, slip it off and discard it. (There seem to be a number of reasons for this lobster to be called "slipper"!) Pat the tails dry with paper towels and set them aside, or refrigerate them if you aren't cooking them right away.

Place the pine nuts in a large skillet over low heat. Shake the pan frequently until the nuts have golden spots on them, 3 to 5 minutes, watching them closely because they scorch easily. Remove them from the skillet and set them aside.

Add 1 tablespoon of butter to the same skillet, set it over low heat, and add the slipper tails. Season them with salt and pepper, and cook them for about 30 seconds on each side to firm them slightly. Add the white wine and lemon juice, and bring the liquid to a simmer. Cover the skillet and gently simmer the tails for 4 to 5 minutes, turning them once midway, until they're just cooked through. To check, make a cut in the thickest part of one to see if it's opaque throughout. If necessary, cover and cook them another minute or so. When the tails are done, remove them to a platter and keep them warm.

Place the skillet over high heat to concentrate the juices rapidly (you'll have $^1/_3$ to $^1/_2$ cup), adding any collected juices from the platter. Boil them down to about $^1/_4$ cup, and add the 2 tablespoons of cold butter, swirling the pan by the handle, or stirring the butter into the juices as they boil. The juices will absorb the butter in about a minute and become a light, creamy sauce. When the sauce has thickened, turn the heat to low and stir in the reserved pine nuts, the slipper tails, and dill to warm very briefly.

TO SERVE: Place the slipper lobster tails on warm dinner plates with a little sauce and a share of pine nuts. Serve right away.

Maine Lobster with Avocado "Whipped Cream"

4 servings

PREP AND COOKING TIME 25–30 minutes + optional 30 minutes to anesthetize the lobsters in ice (see page 218)

*T*here is no cream of any sort in this dish! When you puree avocado with onion, garlic, lime juice, ground cumin, and oil, its innate luxuriousness is heightened and it becomes a softly whipped, gently mounded "cream." Behind its luminous, pale green "face," there's surprisingly assertive flavor, which holds its own with the lobster. Try it as a dip, or with other seafood such as "rock" (spiny) or slipper lobster tails, shrimp, scallops, or sole, bass, snapper, salmon, or pompano fillets. And a big dollop would be perfect on top of a chilled crab meat or lobster cocktail.

> $^1/_2$ ripe avocado (about $^2/_3$ cup when diced or sliced)
>
> 3 tablespoons fresh squeezed lime juice
>
> 2 tablespoons very thinly sliced onion
>
> 1 small-to-medium garlic clove, very thinly sliced
>
> $^3/_4$ teaspoon ground cumin
>
> 2 tablespoons olive oil mixed with 1 tablespoon vegetable oil or all vegetable oil
>
> Salt and freshly ground black or white pepper to taste
>
> Four $1^1/_2$-pound Maine lobsters, tails vigorously flapping when purchased

TO PREPARE: Bring 1 or 2 very large pots of water to a boil over high heat.

Place the avocado, lime juice, onion, garlic, cumin, and oil in a blender jar. Puree the ingredients until the avocado is velvety smooth, scraping the jar down several times during the process, 2 to 3 minutes. Season the puree with salt and pepper, cover it, and set it aside while you cook the lobsters. Or, cover and refrigerate it for up to 1 day—it will still be a pretty pastel green tomorrow, but I can't promise anything after that! Be sure to remove it from the refrigerator an hour before serving to take the chill off.

When the water is boiling furiously, pick up each lobster by holding it firmly around the middle of its back. Don't be afraid, their claws are kept closed by a thick rubber band or with short wooden wedge-shape pegs—they can only make you nervous. Plunge each lobster, head down, into the boiling water. Cover the pot, let the water reach the boil again, and cook the lobsters at a low boil for about 8 minutes. The lobsters will be bright red and their tails tightly curled. (If the tails are flaccid, it means the lobsters were dead when they were cooked, and the meat will be stringy and spongy.)

TO SERVE: Spoon the avocado "whipped cream" into individual bowls. Place the lobsters on warm dinner plates and serve right away. Supply crackers for the shells, a big bowl for the empty ones (see Note), and individual damp towels for sticky hands (or at least lots of napkins).

NOTE: If you like, break up some of the leftover cooked shells into smaller pieces, first by hand, then by chopping them with a large knife or cleaver, smashing them with a mallet, or pulsing them in a food processor. Then freeze them. Sections of shell, such as the claws, that are very hard, are best not chopped in the processor—for the machine's sake. Use the lobster shells in place of raw shrimp shells to make a lobster broth or oil (see Pantry, to Make), for a soup, or for the seafood stew on page 276.

Numbing a whole live lobster by surrounding it in ice for 30 minutes before cooking is said to make it more tender. I tried it several times, feeding it to friends and comparing it to a cooked, un-iced lobster, and I wish I could say we found a clear difference. But only once did we find the iced lobster more buttery and succulent. I'm not sure it's worth the trouble, but you might try it for yourself. It does seem more humane, although the official word from the Maine Lobster Promotion Council is that ". . . the nervous system of a lobster is very primitive, and contains far fewer nerve cells than our nervous systems. It is unlikely that the nervous system is sophisticated enough to sense pain as we know it."

Grilled Maine Lobster with Olive Oil, Tarragon, and Pernod

This is an unusual, and delicious, dipping option for grilled, broiled, or boiled lobster. The anise flavor from the tarragon and Pernod, the French apéritif, really complements this succulent beast, particularly when it arrives slightly charred from the grill! However, when you taste the mixture alone, you'll probably be underwhelmed—it needs its clawed partner to show how good it is. And when the Pernod–olive oil sits for a few minutes, it looks like a translucent, pale green pool with deep green flecks. You can also use this dip with shrimp and scallops or spoon it over broiled, poached, or grilled fillets of any kind.

4 servings

PREP AND COOKING TIME

30 minutes + optional 30 minutes to anesthetize the lobsters in ice (see page 218)

6 tablespoons + 2 teaspoons olive oil, preferably full flavored and fruity

3½ tablespoons Pernod, *or* 3 tablespoons Ricard (another French anise-flavored apéritif)

1 tablespoon coarsely chopped fresh tarragon, *or* 1 teaspoon dried

Salt and freshly ground black or white pepper to taste

Four 1½-pound Maine lobsters, tails vigorously flapping when purchased

TO PREPARE: Start a medium-hot fire in the grill (or preheat the oven broiler). Fifteen minutes before you're going to grill the lobsters, put the grill grate 5″ or 6″ above the coals if it isn't already there. (I also like to brush the top of the grate with vegetable oil just before grilling to help prevent sticking.)

Pour the 6 tablespoons of olive oil into a small mixing bowl and stir in the Pernod or Ricard, and the tarragon. Season the mixture with salt and pepper and set it aside at room temperature, or cover and refrigerate it for up to 2 months (!), making sure to bring it to room temperature before serving.

Remove a lobster from the ice, if using (see page 218), and lay it on its back. Insert the point of a large, sharp knife into the center of the upper part of the abdomen where the top legs meet, and cut through the head first (which will kill the lobster instantly), then through the tail, splitting it in half lengthwise. Repeat the process with the other lobsters. (If this utterly freaks you out, plunge the lobsters into boiling water just long enough for them to stop moving and begin to turn red, 2 to 3 minutes. Then split them.) Pull out the small, gravelly-looking section that's directly behind the head and discard it (that's called the sand sac). Pull out the dark green tomalley (the liver) and the roe, if any, if the lobster is female (the roe runs from beneath the sand sac into the tail). Put the tomalley and roe in a small skillet, season with salt and pepper, and stir in 2 teaspoons of the olive oil. Set the skillet aside. Remove the rubber bands or wooden pegs from the claws and crack them lightly on both sides so the heat will penetrate. Twist the arms, claws attached, to separate them from the bodies. Grilling them separately makes them easier to handle, and lets you cook them longer, if necessary, without overcooking the tails.

Season the cut sides of the lobsters lightly with salt and pepper, brush each half with about $^{1}/_{2}$ teaspoon of the Pernod–olive oil, and drizzle a little into the cracked claws. Place the split lobsters, flesh side down, on the grill (or in the broiler, flesh side up) with the arms/claws, and cook them for about 5 minutes. Turn the pieces over and continue grilling (or broiling) them for about 3 minutes more, or until the flesh is just firm and completely opaque. If the claws are particularly large, they may take another minute or two. Place the skillet with the tomalley/roe on the grill or on a burner over medium heat. Cook it, stirring occasionally, for 1 to 2 minutes. The tomalley will be khaki green and the roe will be bright orange-red.

TO SERVE: Divide the remaining Pernod–olive oil into individual bowls and place the lobsters, garnished with the tomalley and roe, on warm dinner plates. Supply crackers for the shells, a big bowl for the empty ones (see Note), and damp towels for sticky hands (or at least lots of napkins). Serve the lobsters right away.

NOTE: Use the lobster shells to make a broth for a soup, or for the lobster oil (see Pantry, to Make), or for the seafood stew on page 276.

To broil a whole live lobster, place the already split, prepped lobster, flesh side up, on a broiling pan with its arms and claws next to it. Place the pan 3″ or 4″ away from the *preheated* broiling element, and cook the lobster for about 5 minutes. Turn over and continue broiling the lobster for an additional 3 minutes. Remove from the broiler, but if the arms/claws are large, continue cooking them for about 2 minutes more.

MUSSELS

(Including Blue Mussels and Green-Lip Mussels)

FLAVOR: Sweet, slightly smoky, rich, and tender

ORIGIN: Atlantic and Pacific oceans, wild and cultivated

GOOD SIGNS: Deep blue-black (in Green-lip, brown to green) tightly closed shells that don't slide across one another; feel full but light in your hand; sweet, clean aroma; *Cooked meat:* full, plump, and juicy; color ranges from creamy beige to orange in color

BAD SIGNS: Partially open shells that don't close when tapped or pressed; feels heavy in your hand—probably full of mud; any musty or off-smell; *Cooked meat:* appears flattened, stringy, or dry looking

HEALTH TIPS: A raw 7-ounce serving (not including shells) is approximately 170 calories, high in omega-3 fatty acids, protein, and iron.

Mussels are alive when you buy them and should be alive when you cook them, unless you've bought partially cooked, and frozen, New Zealand green-lip mussels. And mussels, like clams and oysters, need to come from certified, unpolluted waters. If you have any doubts, ask your fish seller to show you their certification tag. When you bring live mussels home, make sure you store them in the refrigerator in an open paper or mesh bag, or in an open bowl covered with a damp towel, so they can breathe. They'll stay alive for 3 to 5 days if they were fresh when you bought them.

Depending on their source, mussels may need a preliminary scrubbing, as the shells may be encrusted with dried sea grass and mud. Some cultivated mussels, however, are quite clean and need only a good rinse or light scrub and debearding. An example of these is Prince Edward Island mussels, which are excellent and have small and tender meat. I've never had a problem with grit and only rarely do they have a beard, that annoying little tuft of fibers that sticks out of the shell from one side. (Sure, sure, I know the mussel needs that beard to attach itself to its "home.") For years I gave up eating mussels, because no matter how I cleaned them, I would still be ambushed by foreign matter when I was chewing. The loud crunch of a tiny pebble put me into mini-shock! When I learned about Prince Edward Island mussels, I was happy.

The debate rages on whether or not to purge mussels by soaking them overnight in water mixed with a little salt and a small handful of flour or cornmeal! Some people contend it dilutes their flavor. And there may be some truth to that, but it also encourages the mussel to take in the food and expel the grit, and in doing so, plumps them a bit. However, if I've got a clean, farmed product, I don't usually bother. But if I've been spectacularly organized and bought the mussels the day before I plan on cooking them, I'll go ahead and soak them anyway—I figure I can't lose. Either way, it's important to snip off with scissors the little inedible extrusion of fibers, called the "beard," from the edge of the shell.

If you have the time, and want to be fastidious about purging mussels of sand or grit, make a paste of 1 or 2 tablespoons of cornmeal or flour and a little cold water. Dilute the paste with enough cold water to cover the mussels and soak them overnight in the refrigerator. The mussels will chow down on the grain, become plumper, and expel most, if not all, of their grit. Before you use them the next day, give them a good rinse in cold water (sometimes they need a little scrubbing with a brush; it'll be obvious if they do) and clip off the beards with small scissors. I'm impatient and often try to rip the beards out—most books recommend it—but I usually find it more frustrating than productive.

Mussels cook very quickly, in a matter of a few minutes, and they have so much flavor they don't need much else; but that said, it's fun to play around with what to add. Whatever you do, don't keep cooking them after their shells are well opened (green-lip mussels need only to open about $^1/_4$ inch to be done) or they'll become hard and mealy. And discard those that haven't opened, they were probably dead when they went into the pot.

Don't discard the shells after you've eaten the meat without looking at them: Their inner walls shimmer and resonate in silvers and blues (or luminescent green), like thinly rolled out pearls reclining perfectly within stretched and shallow cups— and when you run your finger over the surface, it's like satin and stainless steel. Years ago, at Restaurant Leslie, my lilliputian store-front, hole-in-the-wall bistro, I used to slice jewel-like, stunning, raw tuna and halibut for sashimi, top it with a dab of black caviar, and serve it in the scrubbed silver-blue shells. Wondrous nature within wondrous nature!

Mussels Steamed in White Wine with Butter, Curry, and Fresh Herbs

I've taken James Beard's basic steamed mussels à la marinière—white wine, onions, butter, and herbs—and added curry power and additional fresh herbs to make the juices even more fragrant and aromatic. Try it also with soft-shell clams ("steamers") or littleneck clams, for a main course or as an appetizer.

4 servings

PREP AND COOKING TIME 25–30 minutes

3¹/₂ pounds cultivated mussels

3 tablespoons butter

¹/₄ cup thinly sliced shallots or white onion

1 bay leaf

1¹/₂ teaspoons curry powder

¹/₄ teaspoon dried thyme

¹/₄ cup white wine or dry vermouth

Salt and freshly ground black or white pepper to taste

2 tablespoons mixed chopped fresh basil and parsley

TO PREPARE: Rinse the mussels well (scrub them if they look muddy), clip off any beards with small scissors, and let the mussels drain in a colander in the sink. (Or soak them in a diluted paste of cornmeal or flour in the refrigerator overnight (see page 222).

Place 1 tablespoon of the butter in a pot twice the size of the volume of the mussels (or use 2 pots and divide the butter between them) over medium heat. Add the shallots or white onion and the bay leaf and cook them, stirring occasionally, until the vegetables begin to wilt, 2 to 3 minutes. Stir in the curry powder and thyme and cook, stirring constantly, for 30 seconds. Add the white wine and pour the drained mussels into the pot, filling it by no more than half. Raise the heat to high, add the remaining 2 tablespoons of butter, and cover the pot. Steam the mussels until they just open, 3 to 6 minutes, stirring once or twice from the bottom, and removing them to a bowl as they open. Discard any mussels that haven't opened and season the juices with salt and pepper.

TO SERVE: Pile the mussels into warm soup plates or big bowls, ladle the juices over them, and sprinkle them with the mixed herbs. Serve right away.

Steamed Mussels with
Cumin and Preserved Lemon

4 servings

PREP AND
COOKING
TIME
35–45
minutes

These mussels take on a Moroccan spin with cumin, tomato, and preserved lemon all mixed in with their juices. If you can find Prince Edward Island mussels from Canada, grab them. They're generally beard free and very clean—all they need is a good rinse and they're ready to cook. Ask the fish man where the mussels come from—all shellfish is required by law to be tagged with its place of origin, and the store has to keep these tags.

3^1/$_2$ pounds cultivated mussels

2 tablespoons olive oil

^{3}/$_4$ cup finely chopped onion

3 garlic cloves, finely chopped

1^1/$_2$ tablespoons ground cumin

^{1}/$_2$ cup well-drained, chopped canned plum tomatoes

3 tablespoons drained and finely chopped preserved lemon (see Pantry, to Make), *or* 1–2 tablespoons fresh squeezed lemon juice

^{1}/$_3$ cup white wine or dry vermouth

Salt and freshly ground black or white pepper to taste

Optional: 1^1/$_2$ teaspoons chopped fresh mint

TO PREPARE: Rinse the mussels well (scrub them if they look muddy), clip off any beards with small scissors, and let the mussels drain in a colander in the sink. Or soak them in a diluted paste of cornmeal or flour in the refrigerator overnight (see page 000).

Heat the olive oil in a pot twice the size of the volume of mussels (or use 2 pots and divide the oil between them) over medium heat. When the oil is hot, turn the heat to low and add the onion and garlic. Cook, stirring occasionally, until the onion is almost tender, about 5 minutes. Stir in the cumin and cook for a few seconds more. Add the tomatoes, preserved lemon or 1 tablespoon of lemon juice, and the white wine.

Pour in the drained mussels and cover the pot tightly. Steam the mussels over high heat until they've all just opened, 3 to 6 minutes, discarding any that haven't opened. Taste the juices and adjust their seasoning with salt and pepper. The preserved lemon should come through as a mild and mellow undertone. (If you used lemon juice, add the other tablespoon of fresh juice if you'd like a sharper edge.)

TO SERVE: Pile the mussels into warm soup plates or deep soup bowls, ladle the juices over them, and sprinkle them with mint if you like. Serve right away.

"The blue-black bivalves are bound to their beds with silken anchor threads. These byssus threads are secreted by the mussel and are composed of a protein which hardens upon contact with seawater. In ancient Greece the threads of the mussels were collected and woven into byssus gloves for the hands of fishermen. These gloves had to be kept wet or they would lose their durability. They were stored in buckets of seawater, and lasted so long they were handed down from generation to generation."

—from the beautifully written and entertainingly scholarly book *The Encyclopedia of Fish Cookery,* by A. J. McClane.

Mussels Roasted with
Olive Oil, Garlic, and Shallots

4 servings

PREP AND
COOKING
TIME
35–45
minutes

The Joy of Cooking has a recipe for baked mussels on the half-shell served with garlic butter. It sounded appealing, so here's my take on that story: Toss the mussels with a generous amount of olive oil, chopped garlic, and sliced shallots (briefly sautéed first), put them in a large roasting pan, and roast in a 500° oven. As soon as they open, stir in a nugget of butter to sweeten the juices further, and some bread crumbs to thicken them slightly. With the oven temperature so high, this method obviously makes a good fall or winter dish—as it certainly helps the central heating! But you can prepare them in the summer in the traditional way—in a big covered pot on top of the stove or on the grill.

> 4 pounds cultivated mussels
> 1 tablespoon + ¹/₄ cup olive oil
> ¹/₃ cup peeled, very thinly sliced shallots
> 1 tablespoon finely chopped garlic
> Salt and freshly ground black or white pepper to taste
> Optional: 1 tablespoon butter, cut into small pieces
> Optional: 2–3 tablespoons dry bread crumbs
> 2 tablespoons coarsely chopped fresh (flat-leaf or curly) parsley

TO PREPARE: Preheat the oven to 500°.

Rinse the mussels well (scrub them if they look muddy), clip off any beards with small scissors, and let them drain in a colander in the sink. Or soak them in a diluted paste of cornmeal or flour in the refrigerator overnight (see page 222).

In a small skillet, heat 1 tablespoon of the olive oil over low to medium heat and cook the shallots, without browning, until they're translucent and tender, about 5 minutes. Reduce the heat to low, add the garlic, and cook it, stirring, for 1 minute. Turn off the heat, lightly season the mixture with salt and pepper, stir in the remaining ¹/₄ cup of olive oil, and set it aside.

Pour the mussels into a colander, shaking it to drain off any excess water. Pour the mussels into a large roasting pan, preferably no more than 1 or 2 layers in depth (if they're deeper, they'll take longer and will need to be stirred occasionally, letting heat escape, but it won't affect the flavor), and toss them with the garlic–olive oil mixture. Roast them just until they open, about 15 minutes, discarding any mussels that haven't opened. Turn off the oven.

Pile the mussels into warm soup plates or deep soup bowls and keep them warm in the turned-off oven with the door ajar while you finish the pan juices, if you are. Add the butter to the juices in the roasting pan to melt, and stir in 2 tablespoons of bread crumbs, if desired. In a moment, the crumbs will soften and very lightly thicken the juices. If you'd like them thicker, stir in up to 1 more tablespoon of crumbs. Either way, season them with salt and pepper. If they've cooled during this time, put the roasting pan over low to medium heat to warm them again briefly— but don't let them boil.

TO SERVE: Pour the juices over the mussels in the bowls, sprinkle them with chopped parsley, and serve right away.

Steamed Mussels
with Mustards

4 main course
or 8 to 10
appetizer
servings

PREP AND
COOKING
TIME
25–30
minutes

ake a vinaigrette with 3 different mustards—whole-grain, Dijon, and English-style dry. Then simply steam the mussels in the water that clings to their shells after they've been rinsed. Pile them into bowls with some of their natural juices, and drizzle them with the vinaigrette—the sweet, unadorned mussel flavor predominates, highlighted by mini-mustard bursts in your mouth. You can serve the mussels as a first course, or serve the vinaigrette with almost any fillet or shellfish you can think of.

4 pounds cultivated mussels

$1^{1}/_{2}$ teaspoons + $^{1}/_{4}$ cup olive oil

$^{1}/_{3}$ cup mixed green and red bell peppers, cut into $^{1}/_{4}''$–$^{1}/_{3}''$ dice (see page 271)

Salt and freshly ground black or white pepper to taste

Generous $^{1}/_{4}$ teaspoon dry mustard

$1^{1}/_{2}$ tablespoons fresh squeezed lemon juice

1 tablespoon Dijon mustard, preferably French (see Note)

$1^{1}/_{2}$ teaspoons whole-grain mustard, preferably Pommery from France; *or* $4^{1}/_{2}$ teaspoons Dijon only

TO PREPARE: Rinse the mussels well (scrub them if they look muddy), clip off any beards with small scissors, and soak the mussels in a bowl of cold water to cover while you prepare the vinaigrette. Or soak them in a diluted paste of cornmeal or flour in the refrigerator overnight (see page 222).

In a small skillet, heat $1^{1}/_{2}$ teaspoons of the olive oil over low to medium heat and add the diced peppers. Sauté them, stirring occasionally, until they're crisp-tender, 3 to 4 minutes. Season them with salt and pepper and set them aside on a small plate to cool.

Place the dry mustard in a small bowl and stir in about $^{1}/_{2}$ teaspoon of the lemon juice to make a smooth mixture. (Use the coiled snake towel trick, see page 153, if your bowl doesn't sit flat.) Stir in the remaining lemon juice and the Dijon and Pommery mustards.

In a slow stream, gradually whisk the $^{1}/_{4}$ cup of olive oil into the mustards—the dressing will emulsify and thicken lightly. Stir in the cooled peppers, season well with salt and pepper, and set the dressing aside while you steam the mussels. Or make and refrigerate the dressing up to a week ahead—it will probably separate, so stir or vigorously shake it together right before serving. Be sure to serve it at room temperature.

Pour the mussels into a colander, shaking it to drain any excess water. Pour them into a large pot (or 2 medium)—filling it by no more than half—and cover the pot tightly. Steam the mussels over high heat until they've all *just* opened, 3 to 6 minutes, stirring them up from the bottom of the pot once or twice during cooking. Discard any mussels that haven't opened, taste the juices, and adjust the seasoning with salt and pepper.

TO SERVE: Pile the mussels into warm soup plates or deep soup bowls, adding ¹/₄ cup of broth to each bowl. (You'll have broth left—cool and refrigerate or freeze it for Seafood Stew, page 276, save it for another use, or eat more of it!) Drizzle 2 tablespoons of mustard vinaigrette over each portion, and serve right away.

NOTE: You may wonder why I keep suggesting *French* Dijon. There are two reasons: First, it's the real thing—Dijon mustard originated in France—Dijon, France, of all places! And its flavor is what Dijon mustard should be. And second, it has wonderful thickening ability, holding oil in emulsion better than American mustard marketed with a "Dijon" label.

OYSTERS

FLAVOR: From mild to strong, slightly to very briny, tender, plump meat

ORIGIN: American Continent: Atlantic ocean inlets and bays from Canada to the Gulf of Mexico and Pacific ocean inlets and bays from Washington State to California; France, England, Japan, Chile, and Australia

GOOD SIGNS: *In Shell:* tightly closed intact shell, or closes when tapped; *Shucked Meat:* plump, firm, intact, and juicy; meat is creamy beige in color, juices are slightly cloudy; clean, briny fragrance

BAD SIGNS: *In Shell:* broken shell, or doesn't close when tapped; *Shucked Meat:* mangled or ripped, soft or "milky" looking; dry or shriveled looking; discolored or blotchy; many pieces of broken or shattered shell; any ammonia odor

HEALTH TIPS: A raw 7-ounce serving of shucked meat is approximately 160 calories and high in omega-3 fatty acids. (Atlantic oysters are marginally lower in calories and protein than Pacific oysters, but higher in iron.) *Note:* Eating raw or partially cooked oysters should be avoided by people who suffer from certain diseases such as chronic liver disease, cancer, or immunodeficiency disease, among others. Check with your doctor if you're unsure.

Think of serving oysters as dinner for a change. When you buy them shucked, it takes only minutes to prepare a good, hot supper. Look for plump ones, large or small, and stir-fry, pan-fry, deep-fry, simmer, or add them to seafood stews, casseroles, and chowders. When you buy them shucked, fresh or frozen, they're likely to be either a Pacific or Atlantic oyster, wild or farmed, and fine for any recipe.

While there are three basic types of oysters, Atlantic, Pacific, and European, oysters are, at heart, a local kind of thing. Habitat determines their taste and texture, and a particular type grown in one locale, say around Cape Cod, will be very different from a family member, like the Apalachicola, that spent its formative years off the Florida Panhandle. If you're in the market for oysters to grill (see Grilled Oysters on the Half-Shell with Horseradish Butter, page 234) or to serve on the half-shell, there are fascinating varieties about which to inquire. And if you're in or near an oyster-growing area, choose those first—they're likely to be the freshest and to reflect the distinctive character of the area's bays and inlets.

From the North and East come the Long Island Blue Point, the Cape Cod Cotuit, the Wellfleet, the Chincoteague, the Malpeque, and the powerfully flavored Belon. The South gives us the Apalachicola and the New Orleans. West Coast oyster lovers count the tiny, prized Washington State Olympia a delicacy—although it's not often available far from its home ground, while British Columbia gives us the Golden Mantle, and California the Kumamoto. If you're extremely lucky, maybe you have a fish market that prides itself on the variety of oysters it sells, and you can buy a sampling. Try tasting any of these on the half-shell or just off the grill and slightly smoky, to see what you think. Or visit your local high-quality restaurant raw bar to check some out.

Like fresh clams and mussels, oysters in the shell should be removed from any plastic wrapping as soon as you get them home. Store them in the refrigerator in a bowl, covered with a damp towel, or in an open paper or mesh bag, so they can breathe. And never let them sit in water.

We've all heard that eating oysters in the months that don't have an "r" isn't healthy for us. Well, that's not it. Northern hemisphere oysters are spawning then and their bodies have gone to wrack and ruin with the effort. They've become "milky," soft, and well, boring. We're just giving them a chance to return to their plump, succulent selves before pouncing on them again.

Classic Oyster Stew

4 servings

PREP AND
COOKING
TIME
15–20
minutes

*B*efore I ever found out what it was, I pictured oyster stew as a . . . stew! You know, filled with oysters and chunks of vegetables like potatoes and carrots and who knew what else, all mixed in a white gravy. But it's not like that. Basically, it's the simplest, most comforting, oyster soup you could have. To make it—and it's real quick—gently cook shucked oysters, with their liquor, in half and half until their fine little edges start to curl. Add a dash of paprika and a pinch of cayenne plus a good sprinkle of fresh thyme, snipped chives, and a little pat of butter and you're in business. The oysters are so tender and they flavor the liquid so fully—what a delicious thing it is! You can substitute bay or sliced sea scallops or shrimp if you want, but they won't infuse the half and half with as much flavor.

2 cups half and half or milk or light cream
$1/4$ teaspoon paprika, preferably sweet Hungarian
$1/8$ teaspoon cayenne, or to taste
2 teaspoons fresh thyme leaves
3 cups shucked oysters with their liquor (about 4 dozen large)
Salt and freshly ground black or white pepper to taste
4 teaspoons butter
2 tablespoons snipped fresh chives

TO PREPARE: Heat the half and half with the paprika, cayenne, and thyme. Add the oysters and their liquor, and cook them over low to medium heat, stirring frequently, *just* until their bodies have contracted somewhat and their edges have curled slightly, 3 to 5 minutes. Turn off the heat and season the stew with salt and pepper.

TO SERVE: Pour the stew into warm soup bowls, making sure everyone gets an equal share of oysters. Top each portion with a pat of butter and sprinkle each with the chives. Serve right away.

Stir-Fried Oysters with Scallions and Bacon

This is all about oysters—the dish is packed with them in an unexpected, kind of Chinese way. Briefly toss the shucked oysters in a very hot wok with bacon fat, chopped ginger, lengths of white and green scallion, and a little soy sauce. Then sprinkle them with the bits of crunchy, chewy bacon that gave us its fat in the first place! The oysters are like tender little cushions, and it all tastes smoky and good. Or try it with scallops or shrimp.

4 servings

PREP AND COOKING TIME 20–30 minutes

2¼ cups well-drained, shucked oysters (approximately 4 dozen large)
¾ teaspoon cornstarch
2 tablespoons soy sauce
3 strips smoked bacon, *or* 3 tablespoons vegetable oil
2 tablespoons finely chopped fresh ginger (see page 214)
1¼ cups scallions, both white and green parts, cut into 1″ lengths
Optional: cooked rice or Oriental-style noodles, *or* lightly steamed spinach leaves

TO PREPARE: Feel around the oysters with your fingers for any small pieces of shell and discard them. In a small mixing bowl, combine the cornstarch with the soy sauce and set it aside.

Cut the bacon strips into ½″ pieces and cook them in a wok, or a very large skillet, over medium-high heat. Stir-fry them until they're brown and crisp, and place them on paper towels to drain. If you're not using bacon, go to the next step.

Measure the fat left in the wok and add vegetable oil, if necessary, to bring it to 3 tablespoons. Or place 3 tablespoons of vegetable oil in the wok if you're not using bacon.

Place the wok over high heat, and when it begins to smoke, add the ginger and stir-fry it for about 10 seconds. Add the oysters and scallions and stir-fry them until the edges of the oysters have started to curl, about 1 minute. Quickly stir the soy sauce mixture to amalgamate it and pour it over the oysters. Let the liquid come to a quick boil, stir-frying, and turn off the heat.

TO SERVE: On warm dinner plates, spoon the stir-fried oysters over the rice, noodles, or lightly steamed spinach, if using, and serve right away.

Grilled Oysters on the Half-Shell
with Horseradish Butter

4 servings

PREP AND
COOKING
TIME
20–30
minutes

*J*ust scrub and place the oysters—still in their shells—directly on the grill for a couple of minutes, until they pop open. Pull off the top shell and spoon melted horseradish butter over their plump little bodies! I wish I could say that grilling oysters for 4 people isn't a bit of a pain in the neck—after all, it is a lot of oysters, but it's also fast and easy. And if you love oysters, it's worth it. Or, grill enough for just 2 of you. They also make an ideal hors d'oeuvre or first course for a dinner party.

36–40 large oysters in their shells
$^1/_2$ cup butter, slightly softened
Scant 3 tablespoons, slightly drained, grated prepared horseradish, or to taste
Salt and freshly ground black or white pepper to taste
Optional: coarse or rock salt (see Notes)

TO PREPARE: Start a hot fire in the grill, and preheat the oven to 250°. Fifteen minutes before you're going to grill the oysters, put the grill grate 5″ to 6″ above the glowing coals if it isn't already there. Scrub each oyster with a stiff brush under cold running water and let them drain in a colander while you prepare the horseradish butter. Or scrub the oysters the day before you're going to use them and keep them in the refrigerator, covered with a damp cloth.

Place the butter in a medium-size bowl and stir in the horseradish until it's well combined. Season the mixture with salt and a generous amount of pepper, and set it aside. Or refrigerate it for up to 2 weeks, or freeze it for up to 2 months.

Place the oysters, *round shell down,* over the coals (see Notes). In 2 to 4 minutes the shells will pop open slightly. At this point, the oysters are still quite raw—remove them from the grill if that's how you like them. Or, leave them on the grill for 2 to 3 minutes more—until their bodies have contracted somewhat and their edges are slightly curled. Remove the top shell from one to check its doneness. Continue grilling the oysters until they're all done, and place them, round side down, in the oven with the door ajar, on ovenproof platters that have been covered with a $^1/_2$″ layer of coarse or rock salt, if using.

Place the horseradish butter in a small saucepan over very low heat. While the butter is melting, remove, and discard the top shell—the flat one—of each oyster, taking one platter out of the oven at a time. (Find a helper if you can!) As soon as the butter is melted, turn off the heat and keep it warm in the oven while you finish removing the top shells from the oysters.

TO SERVE: Spoon some horseradish butter over each oyster, bring the platters of oysters to the table, and serve right away. (Or serve the oysters on warm dinner plates.)

NOTES: The coarse salt keeps the shells from rolling and holds the heat efficiently.

Grilling the oysters with their round shell down keeps all the juices inside the natural "bowl" of the shell to mix deliciously with the butter when the oysters are served.

If you don't have access to a grill, you can put the oysters on baking pans in single layers and set them in a preheated 500° oven until their shells open, then proceed with the recipe as written.

SCALLOPS

(Including Sea, Bay, and Calico)

FLAVOR:	Nutty rich, sweet to remarkably sweet, firm and succulent
ORIGIN:	*Sea:* the northern Eastern seaboard; *Bay:* predominantly Long Island to Cape Cod; *Calico:* Atlantic and Gulf coasts of Florida
GOOD SIGNS:	*Sea:* $3/4''$ to $1^1/4''$, moist, cylindrical-shape meat; translucent creamy ivory to beigy-pink in color; tiny rectangular side muscle firmly attached to main body; sweet, briny aroma of the seashore, but may exhibit an aroma of musk, which is okay; *Bay and Calico:* $1/2''$ to $3/4''$, firm, smooth, somewhat plug-shape meat; translucent creamy white to light pink; sweet, slightly briny aroma; *All:* firm, intact, moist, well-shaped meat
BAD SIGNS:	*Sea:* flabby tone with loose, or nonexistent tiny rectangular side muscle; opaque and dull-looking or slippery in feel; *Bay and Calico:* apparent shell debris; *All:* darkly discolored or mangled meat; aroma of iodine or sourness
HEALTH TIPS:	A raw 7-ounce serving has a calorie range of approximately 160 for bay and calico scallops to approximately 180 for sea scallops. Sea scallops are also slightly higher in protein than the other two.

Scallops are the castanets of the sea! Imagine them clacking their shells together as they glide through the water—or has Disney already commandeered the image of them clattering away in animated conversation with one another? Although serving scallops in their shells with their roe has become an elegant and spectacular restaurant offering, we, unfortunately, don't generally get scallops that way.

The three common, and super-popular, American scallops are the sea, bay, and calico. The sea scallop is the largest, with its main muscle, the part we eat, sometimes reaching up to 2 inches—though I've never seen it that big. The way to buy them is fresh and "natural." Natural, in this context, has a very specific meaning: It means the meat isn't treated with chemicals, or "washed" as it's sometimes known in the trade. There's a world of difference in quality between the two. Natural sea scallops are translucent, moist, and firm, with a satisfying toothsomeness that washed ones never have. The flavor of natural scallops is rich and deep, with a musky sweetness only tasted in the real thing; washed ones taste like scallops mixed with chemicals. And the way they look is a turn-off too: slippery-shiny, flabby, and without substance.

Sea scallops, the great ones and the less great, are ideal for pan-frying, broiling, and grilling. And we must listen when the brilliant Madeleine Kamman tells us, ". . . scallops should not be steamed, because they develop that tiny little film of overcooked fibers on their outside, which contrasts unpleasantly with their tender inside." But prepared any other way, cook them ever-so-slightly-underdone; they'll be like satin on your tongue.

Bay scallop meats are different from calico scallop meats though they look quite similar at first glance. They're both very small, about half an inch in size, although bay scallops are stubbier in shape and much sweeter in taste than calicos. And truth be known, calicos are frequently pawned off as the classier, more profoundly sea-flavored bays. Calicos, unfortunately, are also commonly washed (treated with tripolyphosphates) and packed off to us, the unsuspecting public. They're a good small scallop, but without big flavor resonance. Bays and calicos are best rapidly sautéed, stir-fried, or marinated raw for seviche-type dishes. Careful, though, depending on the size, since bays and calicos cook in practically seconds. Overcooked, they're like dry wads of bubble gum.

It's interesting to note that, unlike their colleague the mussel who spends his life stuck on something, scallops are free spirits, being able to propel themselves through the water by clicking their shells together. This enables them to swim away from any pollution.

Broiled Sea Scallops with a Sauce of Roasted Tomatoes and Garlic

4 servings

PREP AND COOKING TIME
30 minutes

I love this sauce with sea scallops, whether they're broiled, grilled, roasted, fried, or sautéed. And I love it just as much with fried calamari, Maine lobster, salmon fillets, and swordfish steaks! Not stopping there, it's also good with halibut, monkfish, and grouper fillets, tuna and shark steaks, as a pasta sauce in its own right, or on a vegetable frittata. This sauce is one of the reasons to keep roasted garlic around at all times!2 large very ripe tomatoes

1³/₄ pounds sea scallops, ³/₄″–1″ in height

3 tablespoons roasted garlic olive oil from roasting garlic, at room temperature

2 generous teaspoons coarsely chopped, roasted garlic cloves (see Pantry, to Make)

2–3 teaspoons fresh squeezed lemon juice

Salt and freshly ground black or white pepper to taste

2 generous tablespoons olive oil

4–5 teaspoons dry bread crumbs

TO PREPARE: Preheat the oven to 450°.

Rinse and dry the tomatoes and cut out the cores. Slice the tomatoes in half and place them, cut side down, on a baking pan. Roast the tomatoes until they're soft throughout and the skin is blistered, or even a little blackened, about 15 minutes. While the tomatoes are roasting, clean the scallops.

Clean the scallops by peeling off and discarding the little strip of muscle that is attached to one side. (If your scallops are somewhat old, the muscle strip may not be there.) Place the scallops in a colander and wash them well under cold running water—keep an eye open for specks of dark sand. Drain the scallops well and roll them in paper towels to dry them thoroughly. Set them aside while you prepare the sauce, or refrigerate them if the kitchen is very hot.

When the tomatoes are done, remove them from the oven, turn the oven to "broil," and place the rack near the top. Let the tomatoes cool long enough to handle, and chop them fine, skin and all, discarding any liquid in the baking pan. You should have about 1 cup of chopped tomatoes. Put them in a small mixing bowl and slowly add the roasted garlic olive oil, stirring constantly until it's absorbed. (Use the coiled snake towel trick if the bowl doesn't sit steady, see page 153.) Stir in the chopped, roasted garlic and lemon juice to taste. Season the mixture with salt and a generous amount of pepper and set it aside. Or cover and refrigerate it for up to a week, being sure to let it come to room temperature before serving.

Place the scallops in a large mixing bowl, drizzle them with the olive oil, and season them with salt and pepper. Toss them gently but thoroughly with your hands or a rubber spatula.

Place them in one layer on a broiling pan and sprinkle their tops with bread crumbs. (Or place the crumbs on a plate, *lightly* dip one end of each scallop into the crumbs, and place them, crumb side up, on the pan.) Broil them without turning until their sides feel springy-firm when you gently squeeze one, and the crumbs have browned, 4 to 6 minutes. To check, cut a scallop in half—it will be slightly translucent if it's medium. For well done, broil a minute or two longer.

TO SERVE: Spoon the roasted tomato-garlic sauce on warm dinner plates and place the scallops on top. Serve right away.

Stir-Fried Scallops with
Snow Peas and Mushrooms

4 servings

PREP AND
COOKING
TIME
30–35
minutes

*T*he elements speak for themselves—they're succulent, rich, crunchy, and chewy. The sauce, just enough to coat everything, is mellow and brings out the natural flavor of the scallops. Try it with pieces of lobster, king crab, shrimp, or surimi.

1¹/₄ pounds bay scallops (or sea scallops cut into ¹/₂″ pieces)
¹/₄ pound shiitake mushrooms
6 ounces snow peas (about 1¹/₂ cups—see page 241)
2 tablespoons soy sauce
1 tablespoon dry sherry
1 teaspoon cornstarch
¹/₄ cup vegetable oil
1 cup thinly sliced white mushrooms (about 4 large)
2 teaspoons finely chopped fresh ginger (see page 214)
¹/₃ cup drained, sliced water chestnuts (supermarket Oriental shelf)
Optional: hot chili oil, hot pepper sesame oil, or plain sesame oil, to taste
Salt to taste

TO PREPARE: Rinse the scallops under cold water and drain them well. Dry them on paper towels and set them aside while you begin the other preparations, or refrigerate them if you're not using them immediately.

With a paring knife, trim the shiitake stems flush with the underside of the cap. Save the stems to flavor a broth (they're too tough to eat) or discard them. Cut the caps into ¹/₂″-thick slices—you should have about 2 cups—and set them aside.

Rinse the snow peas in cold water and dry them on paper towels. Remove their string by pinching a tiny piece of the pointed end, snapping it back, and pulling it down the edge—the string will come with it. (It'll come down the edge that looks like a seam if you look at it closely.) Do it again from the other end and pull the string *up* along that same edge. Cut them in half on the diagonal and set them aside.

In a small mixing bowl, stir the soy sauce, sherry, and cornstarch together and set aside.

Put a large wok over high heat and add the vegetable oil. When the oil is almost smoking, add both kinds of mushrooms and the ginger. Stir-fry them for about 1 minute and add the scallops, snow peas, and water chestnuts. Stir-fry everything for 2 to 4 minutes, or until the peas are bright green and the scallops half-cooked. Stir the reserved soy sauce mixture to reamalgamate it, and pour it into the wok. Bring the liquid to a boil, stir-frying, and turn off the heat. Stir in the hot chili, or other oil, and salt to taste.

TO SERVE: Transfer the scallops and vegetables to a warm platter or dinner plates and serve right away.

The highest-quality soy sauce is a liquid made from soybeans, wheat, salt, and water (and often a preservative). The sauce is the end result of a complex brewing process that involves months, or even years, of aging in stainless-steel vats. Lower quality soy sauces, on the other hand, are produced quickly—in a matter of days—with corn syrup and caramel coloring added in the processing. You can easily tell one from the other—the ingredients are clearly listed on the label.

Good, fresh snow peas are a deep, bright green. They're resilient when you bend them; they're not yellow, wrinkled, or flabby. The best ones are young, $1^1/_2''$ to $2''$ long, and feel firm and smooth to the touch. If the pods feel thick between your fingers, and you can feel well-developed peas inside, they're going to be tough. Pass.

Roasted Sea Scallops with Provençal Herbs and Lemon Peel

4 servings

PREP AND
COOKING
TIME
30 minutes +
10 minutes
for
marinating

*T*oss big, luscious sea scallops with fruity olive oil, dried lemon peel, and *herbes de Provence*—the dried mixture of French herbs that always includes thyme and rosemary but will also have some, or all, of these: basil, tarragon, marjoram, fennel seed, and my favorite, lavender. Roast the scallops in an intensely hot oven—just until they've browned a little on the outside but are still tender and sensuous on the inside—and serve them drizzled with a little of their concentrated juices. They stand alone, like small seas of aromatic simplicity. Or rub the herbs, lemon peel, and olive oil over red snapper, sea bass, halibut, or sole fillets and roast or bake them.

> 2 pounds sea scallops, at least $^3/_4''$ to 1" in height
> $1^1/_2$ tablespoons olive oil
> 1 tablespoon dry sherry
> $1^1/_4$ teaspoons dried *herbes de Provence* or a mixture of dried thyme, rosemary, basil, marjoram, fennel seed, tarragon, and lavender to your taste
> Generous $^1/_4$ teaspoon dried lemon peel (supermarket herb and spice shelf)
> Salt and freshly ground black or white pepper to taste
> 3 tablespoons white wine or dry vermouth

TO PREPARE: Preheat the oven to 550° with the rack at the top. At the same time, place a large cookie sheet with sides as far back on the rack as it will go, with the long side facing out.*

Clean the scallops by peeling off and discarding the little strip of muscle that is

*If you prefer, the scallops can be browned first in an ovenproof, nonstick skillet. Finish them by popping the skillet into a preheated 425° oven until they're cooked medium (3 to 5 minutes, depending on their size), or to your taste. After removing the cooked scallops, add the white wine to the skillet and concentrate the juices over a burner as described in the recipe.

attached to one side. (If your scallops are somewhat old, the muscle strip may not be there.) Place the scallops in a colander and wash them well under cold running water—keep an eye open for specks of dark sand. Drain the scallops well and roll them in paper towels to dry them thoroughly.

Place the scallops in a large mixing bowl and drizzle the olive oil over them. Toss them gently but thoroughly with a rubber spatula. Sprinkle them with the sherry, herbs, and lemon peel. Toss them again gently but thoroughly, and let them sit for 10 minutes for the peel to soften and begin to release its flavor, and the herbs to "bloom." Or marinate the scallops the day before, covered and refrigerated, to allow the flavors to penetrate even further. If you're roasting them today, season them with salt and pepper.

Before you begin to roast the scallops, keep in mind that the goal is to try to pour them out of the bowl *over* the surface of the hot cookie sheet, in one layer, without letting too much of the oven heat escape.

Pick up the bowl of scallops, open the oven door, pull the cookie sheet to the front of the rack. Moving the bowl above and along the sheet, let the scallops fall onto it. (The scallops won't all fall into the desired position, of course. But don't try to move them—unless they've all ended up in a pile—because it's more important that the oven stay hot.) Push the cookie sheet to the back of the oven and immediately close the door.

Roast the scallops for 6 to 10 minutes, without turning them and without opening the oven door, until they're lightly browned on the bottom and springy-firm when gently squeezed on their sides, or slightly translucent in the center when cut with a knife. They'll be medium at this point. For well done, cook for another minute or two. If the bottoms of the scallops aren't golden brown by the time they're cooked to your taste, don't worry, they'll still taste delicious.

Remove the scallops, brown side up, to a platter, and keep them warm while you scrape up any brown bits stuck to the bottom of the cookie sheet. Pour the white wine onto the cookie sheet and place it directly over low to medium heat, scraping up the bits with a metal spatula. Push the liquid into a corner of the cookie sheet with your spatula, keeping only that corner over the heat so you can control it and keep the sheet from burning. Let the liquid boil down for about 1 minute, to thicken it slightly and concentrate its flavor. You won't end up with more than a few drops for each scallop, but those few drops definitely heighten their flavor.

TO SERVE: Place the scallops on warm dinner plates, drizzle them with the wine juices, and serve right away.

Grilled Sea Scallops with
Olives in Olive Oil

4 servings

PREP AND
COOKING
TIME
25–30
minutes

If you're an olive freak as I am, this will be right up your alley. Rich, deeply sweet—almost musky—sea scallops grill beautifully when they're big, big, big. They get golden and smoky, and are right at home luxuriating in fruity olive oil with chopped green and purple/black Mediterranean olives, coarse black pepper, ground coriander, and herbs. Thread the scallops through their sides with wooden skewers so they'll lie flat on the grill, and then you can do a lot easily. Toss any leftovers with the olives in oil and have them cold. Try the recipe with lobster tails, shrimp, stir-fried calamari, salmon fillets, or with swordfish, tuna, or shark steaks.

6 tablespoons full-flavored, fruity olive oil

3 tablespoons mixed black and green chopped, pitted olives (such as purple/black kalamata, Gaeta, or niçoise, and green Amfissa, Atalanti, or Sicilian)

$^1/_8$ teaspoon somewhat coarsely ground fresh black pepper, + more to taste

Salt to taste

1 teaspoon fresh thyme leaves, very lightly chopped

$^1/_8$ teaspoon very finely chopped fresh rosemary leaves

1 teaspoon chopped fresh sage leaves

1 teaspoon coarsely chopped fresh (flat-leaf or curly) parsley

$^1/_2$ teaspoon ground coriander

Pinch of crushed red pepper flakes

$1^1/_2$ pounds sea scallops, at least 1″ in height

Wooden skewers, soaked in water for at least 30 minutes before using

TO PREPARE: Start a medium-hot fire in the grill (or preheat the oven broiler). Fifteen minutes before you're going to grill the sea scallops, put the grill grate 5″ to 6″ above the glowing coals if it isn't already there. (I also like to brush the top of the grate with vegetable oil just before grilling to help prevent sticking.)

Place 4 tablespoons of the olive oil in a small mixing bowl and stir in the chopped olives, $1/8$ teaspoon of the pepper, and all the seasonings. Set it aside while you prepare the scallops. The olives in olive oil can be made up to 2 weeks ahead, adding the parsley at the last minute to preserve its color, and refrigerated. Just be sure to let the mixture come to room temperature before serving it.

Clean the scallops by peeling off and discarding the little strip of muscle that is attached to one side. (If your scallops are somewhat old, the muscle strip may not be there.) Place the scallops in a colander and wash them well under cold running water—keep an eye open for specks of dark sand. Drain the scallops and roll them in paper towels to dry them thoroughly.

Place the scallops in a large mixing bowl, drizzle them with the remaining 2 tablespoons of olive oil, and season them with salt and pepper. Toss them gently but thoroughly with a rubber spatula.

Remove the wooden skewers from the water and thread the scallops onto the skewers through their sides. (If you push the skewer through their ends, there's a good chance they'll split, plus they won't lie flat on the grill.) Leave about $1/4''$ space between scallops (so they cook all around) and at least $1/2''$ at each end so you can handle the skewers.

Place the skewers over the coals (or in the broiler) and grill the first side golden brown, 4 to 5 minutes. Turn the skewers over and grill (or broil) the scallops for 1 to 2 minutes more, or until they're springy-firm when gently squeezed on their sides, or slightly translucent in the center when cut with a knife. They'll be medium at this point. For well done, cook for another minute or two.

TO SERVE: Push the scallops off the skewers onto warm dinner plates and spoon the olives in olive oil over them. Serve right away.

Grilled Scallops in Portobellos with Parsley and Feta Cheese

4 servings

PREP AND
COOKING
TIME
40–45
minutes

Grill sea scallops and really big Portobello mushroom caps until they're tender and faintly charred. Then mound the scallops inside the caps and drizzle them with bright green parsley vinaigrette and crumbled feta cheese. For a party—and this dish is festive—you can pull it all together in 10 to 15 minutes if you make the vinaigrette ahead and have the skewers and caps ready to grill. Or try this dish with the basil vinaigrette on page 116. Or substitute shrimp, medallions of lobster tail, small grilled salmon fillets or tuna, or swordfish steaks.

1 1/2 pounds large sea scallops, at least 1″ in height

4 very large Portobello mushrooms (see Note)

1/2 cup packed, fresh (flat-leaf or curly) parsley leaves, washed and drained well

1 tablespoon thinly sliced shallot

1/2 small garlic clove, thinly sliced

1 1/2 tablespoons cider or white wine vinegar

1 tablespoon water

6 tablespoons + 2 teaspoons olive oil

Salt and freshly ground black or white pepper to taste

Six to eight 8″ wooden skewers, soaked in water for at least 30 minutes before using

3 tablespoons crumbled feta cheese

TO PREPARE: Start a medium-hot fire in the grill. Fifteen minutes before you're going to grill the scallops and Portobellos, put the grill grate 4″ to 5″ above the glowing coals if it isn't already there. (I also like to brush the top of the grate with vegetable oil just before grilling to help prevent sticking.)

Snap the stems off the Portobellos and save them for another use. Briefly rinse the top of the caps, or wipe them off with a dampened paper towel, and set them aside while you make the vinaigrette.

Put the parsley, shallot, garlic, vinegar, water and 4 tablespoons of the olive oil in a blender jar or food processor and puree them 2 to 3 minutes, scraping the jar or bowl down once or twice, until you have a thick, creamy liquid. (The food processor makes a rougher, less homogenized vinaigrette than the blender. It's good either way; the smoothness can be to your taste.) Season the vinaigrette highly with salt and pepper and set it aside. Or you can refrigerate it for 2 to 3 days. (The color will be a beautiful bright green the first day, but then it will begin to turn slightly khaki. The flavor, however, will still be good.) Be sure to take it out an hour before you serve it.

Clean the scallops by peeling off and discarding the little strip of muscle that is attached to one side. (If your scallops are somewhat old, the muscle strip may not be there.) Place the scallops in a colander and wash them well under cold running water, keeping an eye open for specks of dark sand. Drain the scallops and roll them in paper towels to dry them thoroughly.

Place the scallops in a mixing bowl, drizzle them with the 2 teaspoons of olive oil, and season them with salt and pepper. Toss them gently but thoroughly with a rubber spatula.

Remove the wooden skewers from the water and thread the scallops onto the skewers through their sides. (If you push the skewer through their ends, there's a good chance they'll split, plus they won't lie flat on the grill.) Leave about $1/4''$ space between scallops (so they cook all around) and at least $1/2''$ at each end so you can handle the skewers. Rub the *tops* of the Portobello caps with the remaining 2 table-spoons of olive oil and season them generously, inside and out, with salt and pepper.

Place the Portobellos, gills up, along the edges of the grill where the heat isn't so intense. Grill them for 3 to 4 minutes, then place the scallop skewers on the hot part of the grill. Grill the scallops and Portobellos for 3 to 4 minutes more (turning the mushrooms over as they brown), or until the scallops are golden brown on the first side.

Turn the skewers and Portobellos over. Grill the scallops for another minute, or until they're springy-firm when gently squeezed on their sides, and slightly translu-cent in the center when one is cut with a knife. They'll be medium at this point. For well done, cook them for another 1 or 2 minutes.

The Portobellos should be cooked through by this time as well. Check by push-ing a wooden skewer all the way through a cap to feel for tenderness—if it seems hard, grill them for another minute or two. Take the mushrooms off the grill and place them, gill side down, on a platter to drain excess liquid while you get ready to assemble the dish.

TO SERVE: Place the Portobellos on warm dinner plates with the gills facing up now. Remove the scallops from the skewers and mound them in the upturned caps. Spoon the parsley vinaigrette over them, top with the feta cheese, and serve right away.

NOTE: To get the Portobellos ready ahead of time, snap off their stems and briefly rinse or wipe them clean. Wait until you're almost ready to grill before you oil and season them—salting them ahead of time will draw out their juices.

SEA LEGS

(Surimi Seafood)

FLAVOR: Mild and lightly sweet, tender

ORIGIN: Made from fillets of Alaskan pollock and/or whiting

GOOD SIGNS: Snowy white, slightly firm flesh; high-quality product lists "pol-lock" as the first ingredient; clean, fresh, slightly sweet aroma

BAD SIGNS: Lower-quality product has black flecks of skin; lower-quality product lists "whitefish" as an ingredient at the middle to the bottom of the list; mushy or extremely firm texture; any sugges-tion of sour aroma

HEALTH TIPS: A 7-ounce serving is approximately 180 calories, with very good protein content and low fat.

Sea legs are effortless to use—they're precooked and cut into pieces—and inexpensive for a large family. If you like their sweet blandness and their crab meat-like texture, (and I do), they can be a boon for making a quick meal after an exhausting day.

The highest-quality surimi (which means "minced fish" in Japanese) is made from Alaskan pollock, a little shellfish meat, and starches. There isn't much else to know in order to buy it carefully, except, of course, to check its "sell-by" date. It's usable both cold and hot: as the ever-present seafood-type salad in salad bars; mixed with vegetables, grains, or beans, cold or hot; in a stir-fry; as the main ingredient in a casserole; in crab-type cakes; mixed with pasta; or tossed into stews and soups.

Stir-Fried Surimi Seafood ("Sea Legs") with Broccoli

*M*ild, soft "sea legs" mix well with lots of fresh crunchy broccoli, ginger, and scallions. And while it probably looks like a lot of liquid going in to make the sauce, most of it gets guzzled up by the broccoli and the legs, and little ends up as sauce on your plate. Crab meat, of course, or scallops, shrimp, or pieces of lobster would be an appropriate substitute.

4 servings

PREP AND
COOKING
TIME
30 minutes

1/4 cup soy sauce

2 tablespoons white wine or dry vermouth

3/4 cup chicken broth, room temperature or cold

Optional: 3/4 teaspoon (or to taste) prepared Chinese black bean-garlic
   sauce, *or* 1/2 teaspoon (or to taste) prepared Chinese chili-garlic sauce
   (supermarket Oriental shelf)

1 tablespoon cornstarch

1/4 cup vegetable oil

5 cups lightly packed 1″ broccoli florets (including some peeled, sliced
   stems, if you want)

4 1/2 teaspoons finely chopped fresh ginger (see page 214)

1/3 cup scallions, white and green parts, cut into 1/4″ lengths

1 1/4 pounds surimi seafood, at room temperature

TO PREPARE: In a small bowl, stir together the soy sauce, white wine, chicken broth, and garlic sauce, if using. Stir in the cornstarch until smooth.

Place the vegetable oil in a wok over high heat, and when the oil is beginning to smoke, add the broccoli. Stir-fry it for about 2 minutes, or until it has turned bright green (it may brown a little—that's fine) but is still *very* crisp, and stir in the ginger and scallions.

Stir the soy sauce mixture very briefly to reamalgamate the cornstarch and pour it into the wok, stirring as you pour. The liquid will come to a boil almost immediately but will still look mostly cloudy. Turn the heat to low right away and simmer the mixture, stirring frequently, until the liquid has become shiny and clear, less than a minute. (When the liquid has turned clear, it means the cornstarch is cooked and won't taste grainy.) Add the sea legs and combine all the ingredients well. Cook the mixture just long enough to heat the sea legs, 1 to 2 minutes.

TO SERVE: Spoon the stir-fry onto warm dinner plates and serve right away.

Surimi Seafood ("Sea Legs") Baked with Red and Green Peppers

4 servings

PREP AND
COOKING
TIME
40 minutes

*B*aking "sea legs" in an old-fashioned white sauce brings out their inherent tenderness, and adding bell peppers and mustard gives them needed flavor. Having somewhat disparaged these poor faux-legs, I must now tell you that I think this dish is really good! Of course, you can substitute crab meat of any sort, shrimp or lobster, or big flakes of cooked white fish fillets. And this is a good time to use some of your "I'm-so-clever" frozen shellfish broth (see Pantry, to Make).

2 cups milk, *or* 1 cup milk and 1 cup shellfish broth (see Pantry, to Make)
3 tablespoons butter
2 tablespoons flour
$^{1}/_{2}$ large red bell pepper
$^{1}/_{4}$ large green bell pepper
Salt and freshly ground white pepper to taste
1 pound surimi seafood
2 tablespoons Dijon mustard, preferably French
2 tablespoons dry bread crumbs
1 tablespoon freshly grated Parmigiano-Reggiano cheese

TO PREPARE: Preheat the oven to 450° with the rack at the top.

Heat the milk or milk and broth in a small saucepan while cooking the butter-flour thickener for the white sauce.★

In a medium saucepan over low heat, melt 2 tablespoons of the butter and stir in the flour with a whisk or wooden spoon until the mixture is smooth. Cook the roux over low heat, stirring frequently, for about 2 minutes.

Add about a third of the hot liquid to the roux while stirring it with a whisk. Continue whisking in the remaining liquid in a steady stream. (The sauce thickens very quickly at first, and then thins out as you add the rest of the liquid.) Simmer

★When you cook butter, or other fat, together with flour you create a thickening agent (that doesn't taste of raw flour) called *roux* (roo) in French cooking terminology. The amount of butter and flour you use per cup of liquid (whether it be milk, meat, poultry, or fish broth) determines how thick the sauce will be.

the sauce over low heat for 10 to 12 minutes, stirring occasionally, making sure to get into the corners of the saucepan. While the sauce simmers, cut enough of the red and green pepper into $1^1/_2'' \times ^1/_2''$ strips to measure $1^1/_2$ cups total.

In a large skillet, melt the remaining tablespoon of butter over medium heat. Add the peppers, season them with salt and white pepper, and sauté them for 5 to 6 minutes, until they're still somewhat crisp. Stir in the sea legs and heat them through, about 2 minutes. Stir the mustard into the simmering white sauce, season it with salt and white pepper, and stir the sauce into the peppers and sea legs, combining them well.

In a small bowl, stir the bread crumbs and grated cheese together. Pour the sea legs and vegetables into a shallow 9" baking dish, and sprinkle the top with the bread crumb–cheese mixture. Put the baking dish onto the top rack of the oven, and bake until the topping is golden brown and the sauce bubbly, about 20 minutes.

TO SERVE: Bring the baking dish to the table and serve right away.

SHRIMP

(Including White Shrimp, Gulf Shrimp, and Tiger Shrimp)

FLAVOR: Mild and sweet, firm to crisp

ORIGIN: *White:* Eastern seaboard through the Florida Keys, China, Mexico; *Gulf:* Gulf of Mexico, Florida Keys, Central and South America; *Tiger:* Asia

GOOD SIGNS: *All:* meat firm and fills shell; intact body; sweet, lightly briny aroma

BAD SIGNS: *All:* meat doesn't fill shell; shells spotted with black or meat appears discolored, except Tiger shrimp, which have naturally dark shells with black stripes; mangled or ripped bodies; aroma of iodine or ammonia

HEALTH TIPS: A raw, cleaned 7-ounce serving of any variety is approximately 200 calories with high protein, average omega-3 fatty acids, and high cholesterol content.

There are, in fact, brown shrimp, white shrimp, pink shrimp, tiger shrimp, rock shrimp, gulf shrimp, and hundreds of others. It all gets very confusing, and that's without trying to figure out where they all come from. Suffice it to say, waters all around the globe boast their own kind of shrimp. So, let's simplify matters.

The highest-quality shrimp we can buy—unless we're in an area where *fresh* gulf shrimp are sold (whether it's the local catch or flown in)—is the white, or gray, shrimp. Which isn't to say that pink shrimp or brown shrimp are bad, they're fine. They're just not considered the same quality as white. And while you may think you're buying fresh shrimp, you are almost always buying defrosted shrimp. They've been shipped frozen and are defrosted—still in their shells—by the market before they're laid out, or piled, for display. In my local fish market, they sell four different sizes of white shrimp in the shell *and* large shrimp they've peeled and cleaned themselves. You don't even have to go to the trouble of defrosting—a great service and you pay for it!

If you're buying frozen raw shrimp still frozen (be sure to read the guidelines for buying frozen seafood on page 266), they come packed in several forms. IQF packing means "individually quick frozen," and you'll find the shrimp loose in the bag. They may still be in the shell, or they may be peeled, deveined, and ready to cook— the package will tell you. What's good about IQFs is being able to pour out what you need and then shove the rest back into the freezer. If you need a large quantity, you may prefer to choose shrimp packed in a frozen block. With these, to defrost one is to defrost them all!

If you are lucky enough to get truly fresh-caught gulf shrimp, they are slightly different. They're very sweet in flavor but more delicate and softer in texture. And after only one day they begin to deteriorate and turn mushy. But in that one fleeting day they are absolutely glorious, their ephemeral perfection burning bright. So, make that day a feast day!

Tiger shrimp are terrific—similar to white shrimp in flavor and sweetness, but with a slightly different texture. They're crunchier. Their shells are covered in black stripes with gold and pink touches, some of this coloring even reaching the meat. And when they're cooked, the shells turn a beautifully intense orange-red. Use them interchangeably with white or gulf shrimp sautéed, pan-fried, deep-fried, stir-fried, baked, roasted, broiled, grilled, steamed, and boiled. Is there anything you can't do with a shrimp?

When calculating servings of shrimp, it helps to know about how many pieces of raw, shell-on shrimp there are to a pound. I normally buy 1¹/₂ to 2 pounds of large shrimp in the shell for 4 people, depending on how I'm preparing the shrimp, and what I'm serving with them. That can mean 10 to 15 large shrimp per person based on the industry's standards. Here's how to calculate:

1 pound of jumbo shrimp in the shell gives you from 15 to 20 pieces
1 pound of large shrimp in the shell gives you from 26 to 30 pieces
1 pound of medium shrimp in the shell gives you from 31 to 40 pieces

And after cleaning, 1 pound of raw, large shrimp weighs about 13 ounces, good to know if you're buying "individually quick frozen" shrimp that are already clean. If you don't have a scale, count out the shrimp that would be equivalent to the shell-on weight in the recipe. For example, if the recipe calls for 2 pounds of large shell-on raw shrimp, count out about 56 pieces, more or less.

Boiled Shrimp with Ginger-Cilantro Dip

4 servings

PREP AND
COOKING
TIME
30–45
minutes
includes
optional
shrimp
cleaning time

When my daughter, Rachel, was young we often had what we called "shrimp cocktail for dinner." That meant a big platter of boiled shrimp still in their shells—each of us peeling our own as we ate, and scooping up the sauce. Rach had to have cocktail sauce, the familiar kind, with ketchup, lemon, and horseradish. Actually, my husband, Philip, and I loved this meal too, and it was very easy. But here's another sauce for "shrimp dipping": Toss lots of fresh cilantro leaves, garlic, ginger, and soy sauce into the blender and puree—it emerges pungent and fabulous. But if peeling shrimp while you eat isn't going to happen at *your* dinner table, buy fresh or frozen cleaned ones, or peel them yourself before boiling. The sauce obviously works as a dip with chilled or grilled shrimp as an hors d'oeuvre, and it's also good with salmon, grouper, or catfish fillets, scallops, or lobster.

3 quarts water

$^1/_3$ cup distilled white vinegar or other vinegar

4 thin lemon slices

2 bay leaves

Optional: $^1/_2$ teaspoon whole allspice berries

Salt to taste

2 bunches cilantro

3 medium garlic cloves, sliced

3 tablespoons roughly chopped, peeled fresh ginger (see page 214)

$4^1/_2$ tablespoons soy sauce

3 tablespoons vegetable oil

$1^1/_2$ tablespoons fresh squeezed lemon juice

2 pounds large shrimp in the shell, *or* approximately $1^3/_4$ pounds peeled (about 56 pieces)

TO PREPARE: In a large pot set over high heat, bring the water to a boil with the vinegar, lemon, bay leaves, allspice, if using, and salt. Lower the heat and let the liquid simmer for at least 5 minutes, while you prepare the sauce.

Leaving the cilantro in bunches, cut the leaves off by slicing through the bunched stems just below the "head." Don't worry if you have some stems included, they are generally tender. You can quickly pick through and remove any large or tough-looking stems. Pick off any leaves that remain on the cut stems. Place the cilantro leaves in a *large* bowl of cold water and plunge them up and down with your hand to flush out the dirt. If you aren't sure they're clean (cilantro can be sandy—you'll see grit at the bottom of the bowl if it needs another washing), repeat the process in fresh cold water. Lift the cilantro out of the water and dry it thoroughly in a salad spinner or on paper towels. Measure 1¹/₂ cups lightly packed and reserve the remaining leaves for another use.

Place the cilantro, garlic, ginger, soy sauce, vegetable oil, and lemon juice in a blender jar. Puree everything until it is a smooth, green, thickish liquid, 2 to 3 minutes. Set the sauce aside while you cook the shrimp, or cover and refrigerate it for 1 to 2 days, being sure to take it out of the refrigerator an hour before serving.

Bring the water back to a boil and drop in the shrimp. Simmer them for 4 to 6 minutes, stirring from the bottom once or twice, or until just cooked through— they will be solid white throughout. (If you're unsure, pull one out and cut it in half to look.) Pour the contents into a colander and don't bother discarding the lemons or bay leaves, I think they look nice all mixed in.

TO SERVE: Pour the shrimp onto a large platter. Put the sauce into individual dipping bowls with a large bowl on the table for the shrimp shells, and serve right away.

Good Old-Fashioned Cocktail Sauce

¹/₂ cup ketchup or chili sauce

1 tablespoon prepared grated horseradish with a little of its juice, or to
   taste

1¹/₂ tablespoons fresh squeezed lemon juice

Freshly ground black or white pepper to taste

Makes about
¹/₂ cup

PREP TIME
5–10 minutes

   In a small bowl, mix the ketchup or chili sauce with the horseradish and lemon juice. Season the mixture with a generous amount of pepper and serve right away, or cover and refrigerate it for up to 2 weeks.

Stir-Fried Shrimp with
Bok Choy and Eggplant

4 servings

PREP AND
COOKING
TIME
30–50
minutes
includes
optional
shrimp
cleaning time

like to take bites of this with a little piece of everything in one mouthful: crunchy shrimp, crisp—it's loud in your ear—bok choy, and eggplant that's soaked up the flavors of soy, ginger, and hot chili-garlic paste from the sauce. You can also use scallops or pieces of lobster.

3 tablespoons soy sauce

1 tablespoon dry sherry

2 teaspoons finely chopped fresh ginger (see page 214)

1½ teaspoons prepared chili-garlic sauce (supermarket Oriental shelf)

1 teaspoon cornstarch

1¼ pounds large shrimp in the shell, *or* approximately 1 pound frozen, cleaned shrimp, defrosted (about 36 pieces)

1 medium head bok choy

¾ pound Japanese (the long narrow ones) eggplants or baby eggplants, *or* 1 small regular eggplant

3 tablespoons vegetable oil

TO PREPARE: In a small bowl, stir together the soy sauce, sherry, ginger, and chili-garlic sauce. Stir in the cornstarch with a whisk, or use your fingers, to make sure any lumps of starch are broken up. Set the sauce aside.

If using shrimp in the shell, peel them and save the shells for shrimp oil or shrimp broth (see Pantry, to Make), or discard them. Pick up a shrimp and make a shallow slit down the middle of the length of the back to expose the black intestine. Slit all the shrimp and lift out the black intestine with the point of your paring knife or flush it out under cold running water. If using defrosted cleaned shrimp, skip this step. Either way, dry the shrimp *well* with paper towels and set them aside.

Cut the root end off the bok choy and discard it. Separate the head into leaves and wipe each leaf with a damp paper towel if it seems dusty; if the leaves are dirty, you'll have to rinse and dry them. Cut each leaf crosswise into ¾" pieces (if the leaf is very broad, cut it in half lengthwise first) until you have enough to make 4 generous cups. Rinse each eggplant, wipe it dry, and cut off and discard the stem end.

Cut the Japanese or baby eggplants into $1/4"$-thick rounds. If using 1 large eggplant, cut it into quarters, then slice each quarter into $1/4"$-thick pieces. You'll need enough to measure 3 cups. Reserve any extra for another use.

Place a wok over high heat, add the vegetable oil, and, when the oil is smoking, add the shrimp and the vegetables all at once. Stir-fry, making sure everything contacts the hot wok during the cooking, until the shrimp are almost cooked through, 4 to 5 minutes. To check, cut one in half at the thickest part. It should still be *slightly* translucent in the center. Stir the sauce to reamalgamate it, and pour it into the wok. Stir-fry everything for 30 seconds to coat all the ingredients and bring the sauce to a quick boil. Turn off the heat and stir for a few more seconds to make sure all the ingredients are well coated and the shrimp have cooked through and are completely opaque.

TO SERVE: Pour the contents of the wok onto a warm serving platter and serve right away.

Here's the Chinese way of chopping ginger: Peel as much of it as you think you need and cut it into very thin slices across the grain. Lay the slices in a row over one half of a large piece of plastic wrap and fold the other half over the slices. Pound them, don't be afraid—let 'em have it, with the flat side of a cleaver, a meat mallet, or the back of a small skillet. They'll separate into natural fibers. And the thinner you've sliced the ginger in the first place, the finer the pieces will be. Scrape them together, give them one or two quick chops with a large knife or cleaver, and use them whenever chopped ginger is called for.

Grilled Lime Shrimp

*T*oss large shrimp with lots of grated lime zest, hot green chile, cilantro, and garlic, and grill them, threaded on wooden skewers. Make it a light summer dinner, or stuff them into grilled pitas with a spoonful of tomato salsa for lunch or a cook-out on the beach. You can also stir-fry or roast them, and they make perfect hors d'oeuvre. If you have time to marinate the shrimp several hours or overnight, they get even better. Substitute sea scallops or chunks of lobster, if you like.

4 servings

PREP AND COOKING TIME
30–55 minutes includes optional shrimp cleaning time

1^1/$_2$ pounds large shrimp in the shell, *or* approximately 1^1/$_4$ pounds frozen, cleaned shrimp, defrosted (about 42 pieces)

Grated zest of 4 limes (no white pith—see page 133)

1 tablespoon fresh squeezed lime juice

1–2 pickled or fresh jalapeño or serrano peppers, finely chopped (and seeded if you want less heat)

2 large garlic cloves, finely chopped

2^1/$_2$ tablespoons chopped fresh cilantro

Salt and freshly ground black or white pepper to taste

1 tablespoon olive oil

Wooden skewers, soaked in water for at least 30 minutes before using

Lime wedges

TO PREPARE: Start a hot fire in the grill. Fifteen minutes before you're going to grill the shrimp, put the grill grate 4″ to 5″ above the glowing coals if it isn't already there. (I also like to brush the top of the grate with vegetable oil just before grilling to help prevent sticking.)

If using shrimp in the shell, peel them and save the shells for shrimp oil or shrimp broth (see Pantry, to Make), or discard them. Pick up a shrimp and make a shallow slit down the middle of the length of the back to expose the black intestine. Slit all the shrimp and lift out the black intestine with the point of your paring knife or flush it out under cold running water. If using defrosted cleaned shrimp, skip this step. Either way, dry the shrimp *well* with paper towels.

Place the shrimp in a large mixing bowl and toss them with the lime zest and juice. Stir in the jalapeño peppers, garlic, 2 tablespoons of the cilantro, and the salt and pepper. Lastly, stir in the olive oil. (If you add the oil first, it coats the shrimp and prevents some of the lime flavor from penetrating.) Thread the shrimp on the skewers by pushing the skewer through the back at the shrimp's thickest part and then through the tail section. This way the shrimp will lie flat on the grill. (You can transport the shrimp to the picnic already skewered, just be sure the skewers were very well soaked. Or stir-fry or roast the shrimp loose.)

Place the skewers over the coals and grill them for a total of about 5 minutes, turning them once, until the shrimp are golden, firm, and completely opaque when cut open with a knife.

TO SERVE: Place the skewers on a platter with wedges of lime, sprinkle the shrimp with the remaining $1/2$ tablespoon of chopped cilantro, and serve right away, letting everyone take their own skewers.

The easiest and fastest way to peel a garlic clove requires only a large knife, a countertop, and your hands! Place the clove on the countertop and lay the widest part of the knife on top of it. With your palm, press down firmly on the knife to crush the clove lightly. Now you can peel off its skin in a second.

Shrimp with Portobello Mushrooms, Black-Eyed Peas, and Cabbage

4 servings

PREP AND
COOKING
TIME

25–50
minutes
includes
optional
shrimp
cleaning time

*T*his dish is not the flashy sort. It's quietly rich and full—all earthy from the mushrooms, smoky black-eyed peas, and oregano. Even the shrimp fall under the woodsy spell. It's an amalgam of satisfying textures too: firm shrimp, creamy peas, and tender-crisp cabbage. You can substitute crab meat, scallops, or pieces of lobster, if you wish.

One 10-ounce box frozen black-eyed peas, *or* one 11-ounce bag fresh
    black-eyed peas from the produce section, *or* one 15-ounce can
$1^1/_2$ pounds large shrimp in the shell, *or* approximately $1^1/_4$ pounds frozen,
    cleaned shrimp, defrosted (about 42 pieces)
1 small head white cabbage
$^1/_2$ pound Portobello, cremini, or other mushrooms
$^1/_4$ cup olive oil
$1^1/_2$ teaspoons dried oregano
1 large garlic clove, finely chopped
2 tablespoons fresh squeezed lemon juice
Salt and freshly ground black or white pepper to taste
Optional: fresh (flat-leaf or curly) parsley sprigs
Lemon wedges

TO PREPARE: Put the frozen black-eyed peas into $1^1/_2$ cups salted boiling water and simmer them, covered, until tender, 25 to 30 minutes. Drain and set them aside. Or cook the fresh peas according to package directions, drain, measure out $1^1/_2$ cups, and refrigerate the rest for another dish. (Add a little olive oil and vinegar with a touch of chopped garlic for a delicious salad that holds for 3 or 4 days in the refrigerator.) Or briefly rinse the canned black-eyed peas and drain them well.

While the peas are cooking, peel the shrimp and save the shells for shrimp oil or shrimp broth (see Pantry, to Make), or discard them. Pick up a shrimp and make a shallow slit down the middle of the length of the back to expose the black intestine. Slit all the shrimp and lift out the black intestine with the point of your paring knife or flush it out under cold running water. If using defrosted cleaned shrimp skip this step. Either way, dry the shrimp *well* with paper towels and set them aside.

Cut the cabbage in quarters through the core, then cut out the core from each quarter. Thinly slice enough of the cabbage to measure 3 cups and set it aside.

Rinse the mushrooms briefly under cold running water and dry them on paper towels. Trim and discard the dirty end of the stems if you're using Portobellos. Twist or cut off the stems and slice them thinly lengthwise. Cut each cap in half, hold the halves together, turn the cap one-quarter turn, and thinly slice across the cap. (Slice cremini or regular mushrooms thicker without removing the stems or cutting them in half first.) You should have about 4 cups sliced.

Place the mushrooms and cabbage in a large mixing bowl. Sprinkle them with the olive oil, oregano, garlic, and lemon juice. Mix the ingredients thoroughly, and set aside. (The mixture can sit for up to 15 minutes, but not longer, because the salt will begin to leach out the mushroom and cabbage juices.)

Place a very large skillet or wok over high heat. When the pan is hot (test it by dropping in a piece of cabbage, if it's hot you'll hear it sizzle), add the mushroom-cabbage mixture and season it with salt and pepper. Sauté, stirring occasionally, until the cabbage begins to wilt, 3 or 4 minutes. Stir in the shrimp and the black-eyed peas and cook, stirring occasionally, until the shrimp are firm, pink, and just cooked through, 3 to 5 minutes. To check, cut a shrimp in half at the thickest part to see if it's white throughout. If there is liquid in the bottom of the skillet or wok, remove the shrimp and vegetables with a slotted spoon (or pour the mixture through a colander set over a large bowl) and reduce the liquid over high heat for 1 to 2 minutes to thicken slightly and concentrate it. Stir the shrimp mixture back into the concentrated juices and adjust the seasoning with salt and pepper.

TO SERVE: Spoon the shrimp and vegetables onto warm dinner plates and garnish with the parsley sprigs, if desired. Serve right away, with lemon wedges on the side.

Spicy Pan-Roasted Shrimp

4 servings

PREP AND
COOKING
TIME
25–45
minutes
includes
optional
shrimp
cleaning time

*T*he inspiration for this recipe comes from a Southern-style "barbecued shrimp," a dish made in a pan on the top of the stove—a type of barbecue that's altogether different from those that usually come to mind, but with its own charm. The shrimp are started off simmering in butter and chicken broth, then a mixture of Dijon mustard, Worcestershire sauce, cayenne, ground cumin, and chili powder gets stirred in. Some cold butter added at the end emulsifies the broth and creates a spicy, thickened sauce that envelopes the shrimp. It's also good with sea scallops and pieces of lobster.

$1^3/_4$ pounds large shrimp in the shell, *or* approximately $1^1/_2$ pounds frozen,
   cleaned shrimp, defrosted (about 50 pieces)

2 teaspoons Dijon mustard, preferably French

4 teaspoons Worcestershire sauce

3 tablespoons fresh squeezed lemon juice

1 teaspoon cayenne

$^1/_2$ teaspoon ground cumin

1 teaspoon chili powder

1 teaspoon dried thyme leaves

3 tablespoons butter

3 tablespoons chicken broth

Salt and freshly ground black or white pepper to taste

3 tablespoons *cold* butter, cut into small pieces

$^1/_3$ cup thinly sliced scallions, white and green parts

TO PREPARE: Peel the shrimp and save the shells for shrimp oil or shrimp broth (see Pantry, to Make), or discard them. Pick up a shrimp and make a shallow slit down the middle of the length of the back to expose the black intestine. Slit all the shrimp and lift out the black intestine with the point of your paring knife or flush it out under cold running water. If using defrosted, cleaned shrimp, skip this step. Either way, dry the shrimp *well* with paper towels and set them aside.

Put the mustard in a small bowl and gradually stir in the Worcestershire sauce until the mixture is smooth. Stir in the lemon juice, cayenne, cumin, chili powder, and thyme and set the mixture aside, or make it 2 or 3 days ahead, cover, and refrigerate it.

Place a large skillet over a medium-high flame and add the 3 tablespoons of butter. When the butter has almost completely melted, add the chicken broth and the shrimp, seasoning them with salt and pepper. Cook the shrimp, stirring, until they're half cooked, about 2 minutes. Stir in the mustard mixture and cook the shrimp for 2 to 3 minutes more, until they're fully cooked. To check, cut a shrimp in half at the thickest part to see if it's white throughout. Take the skillet off the heat and remove the shrimp with a slotted spoon to a warm bowl or platter while you finish the sauce.

Put the skillet back over medium-high heat to bring it to a strong simmer, and scatter the cold butter over the bubbling liquid. Swirl the pan by the handle until the sauce has absorbed the butter and is nicely thickened. Turn off the heat, grind in a generous amount of fresh black pepper, and salt it if necessary. Stir in the scallions and the shrimp to combine well but not to cook them any further. The scallions should remain bright green and crunchy.

TO SERVE: Spoon the shrimp onto warm dinner plates or a warm serving bowl or platter and serve right away.

Shrimp with
Honey-Ginger-Soy Marinade

4 servings

PREP AND
COOKING
TIME
35–55
minutes
includes
optional
shrimp
cleaning time

*T*he recipe for this marinade has had numerous incarnations. It had its first life in a magazine recipe by Jacques Pépin, the telegenic French chef, for a boneless leg of lamb. I altered it somewhat, and started using it as a 3-day marinade for racks of lamb when I was the chef at the Inn at Pound Ridge—they were the best racks I've ever had. Then I tried it with salmon fillets, grilling them—a terrific combination too, but the fillets had a tendency to stick on the grill. Now, with jumbo shrimp, they get marinated for only 5 minutes. The marinade itself can be made several weeks ahead (yes, weeks) and refrigerated—just give it a good stir before using it. And, of course, you can grill the shrimp (not over too hot a fire) or you can use smaller shrimp, roasting or grilling them a shorter time. Or try marinating sea trout, salmon, or bass fillets half an hour before roasting them.

^{1}/$_4$ cup soy sauce

1 small garlic clove, roughly chopped

1^1/$_2$ tablespoons vegetable oil

1 tablespoon honey

1^1/$_2$ teaspoons dry mustard

1^1/$_2$ teaspoons roughly chopped, peeled fresh ginger (see page 214)

1^1/$_2$ pounds jumbo shrimp in the shell (20–22 pieces), *or* 1^3/$_4$ pounds large shrimp, *or* approximately 1^1/$_2$ pounds frozen, cleaned large shrimp, defrosted (about 50 pieces)

Salt and freshly ground black or white pepper to taste

Optional: thinly sliced scallions, green and white parts

TO PREPARE: Preheat the oven to 550° with the rack at the top.

Place the soy sauce, garlic, oil (if you measure the oil first followed by the honey, the honey slides right out of the spoon), honey, dry mustard, and ginger in the bowl of a food processor or blender and process until finely chopped and well combined, 1 to 2 minutes. Or chop the garlic and ginger very fine by hand and whisk all the ingredients together. Set the marinade aside, or cover and refrigerate it for up to several weeks.

Peel the shrimp and save the shells for shrimp oil or shrimp broth (see Pantry, to Make), or discard them. Pick up a shrimp and make a shallow slit down the middle of the length of the back to expose the black intestine. Slit all the shrimp, and with the tip of your paring knife lift out the black intestine, or flush it out under cold running water. If using defrosted, cleaned shrimp, skip this step. Either way, dry them *well* with paper towels.

Season the shrimp lightly with salt and pepper and place them in a bowl with the honey-ginger marinade, tossing to coat them thoroughly. Let them sit, unrefrigerated, for 5 minutes, stirring them once or twice. At the end of the 5 minutes, remove them from the marinade (discard the marinade plus any additional liquid in the bowl) and place them in one layer on a cookie sheet or in a roasting pan with at least $1/2''$ of space around each shrimp. Put the pan in the oven and roast them until they're cooked through and solid white throughout, 5 to 10 minutes.* To check, cut a shrimp in half at the thickest part to see if it's white throughout.

TO SERVE: Place the shrimp on warm dinner plates, sprinkle them with scallions, if you want, and serve right away.

*The shorter amount of time applies to a thin pan, such as light aluminum; the longer time applies to heavy roasting pans, such as porcelain-coated iron. And, obviously, the smaller the shrimp, the shorter the cooking time in either pan.

Let's talk about frozen fish and seafood for a moment. There are a few points to keep in mind when you buy a product that, in many ways, you're actually buying blind.

1. Buy from a reputable fish dealer (or market that you frequent) who is likely to take very good care of his/her stock and who has a strong enough business to move his/her product rapidly. *And* one to whom you can return something, if you must, without a fight.

2. Inspect the box of frozen seafood carefully. Feel all around it for areas that appear softer or emptier. Either would indicate that the box is in the process of defrosting (or refreezing) or that it has already defrosted once and the contents have shifted to one side, leaving some accumulated liquid in a corner to refreeze. Pass this box up and find another that feels solidly filled and frozen.

3. If frozen in bags, the most carefully handled fillets are individually frozen and shrink-wrapped, then packed in a partially transparent outer bag. The shrink-wrapping makes them airtight and leaves little chance of oxygen reaching, and damaging, the fillets. If the fillets or seafood is unwrapped and moves loosely within the package, inspect it carefully and feel around for defrosting contents. If you can see inside, look at the seafood for ice crystals, discolored spots, and any yellowing or cottony edges. These are signs of freezer burn—oxygen is robbing the seafood of precious bodily juices, which will make it taste about as bad as it looks!

4. Always defrost seafood in the refrigerator overnight (although shrimp can be safely defrosted in a bowl of cold water). It keeps the growth of harmful bacteria to a minimum (bacteria are thrilled when left outside to reproduce to their heart's content) and slows the loss of those famous precious bodily fluids. The greater the natural juice remaining in the seafood, the better the flavor.

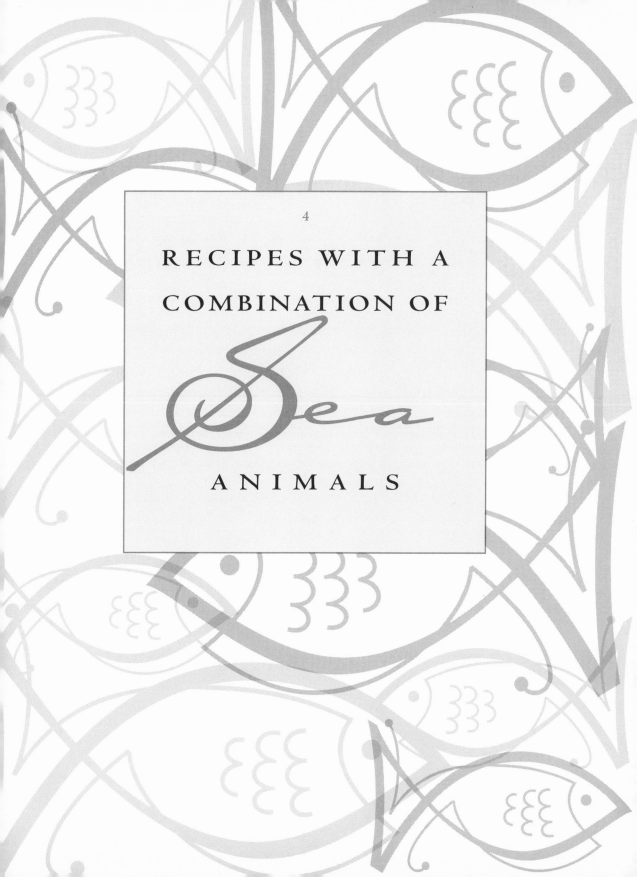

4

RECIPES WITH A COMBINATION OF *Sea* ANIMALS

Scallop and Shrimp Creole

4 servings

PREP AND
COOKING
TIME
45–60
minutes
includes
optional
shrimp
cleaning time

*T*hink Creole sauce, and maybe you can imagine it right now via your "taste-memory bank." A rich tomato sauce comes to mind, with notes of peppers, onions, celery, herbs, and cayenne. This one starts out not so much a sauce, but a thick blanket of vegetables that smothers the scallops and shrimp in richness as they cook. Then the shellfish bestow their juices and turn the dish into a kind of half stew, half soup that's made for a bed of rice or crusty bread for dunking. You could also include shucked oysters, chunks of crab or lobster meat, or pieces of grouper or monkfish fillet.

1 pound large shrimp in the shell, *or* approximately $^3/_4$ pound frozen, cleaned shrimp, defrosted (about 30 pieces)

$1^1/_4$ pounds sea or bay scallops

3 tablespoons bacon fat or vegetable oil

$^1/_2$ cup small diced or chopped onion

$^1/_2$ cup small diced or chopped green bell pepper (see page 271)

$^1/_2$ cup small diced or chopped red bell pepper

$^1/_3$ cup small diced or chopped celery (see page 271)

2 garlic cloves, finely chopped

$^3/_4$ teaspoon dried thyme leaves

$^1/_4$ teaspoon dried oregano leaves

1 bay leaf

$^1/_4$ teaspoon cayenne

2 teaspoons flour

1 cup crushed or chopped drained canned plum tomatoes + $^1/_4$ cup of their juice

Salt and freshly ground black or white pepper to taste

Tabasco sauce to taste

1 tablespoon chopped fresh (flat-leaf or curly) parsley

TO PREPARE: Peel the shrimp and save the shells for shrimp oil or shrimp broth (See Pantry, to Make), or discard them. Pick up a shrimp and make a shallow slit down the middle of the length of the back to expose the black intestine. Slit all the shrimp and lift out the black intestine with the point of your paring knife, or flush it out under cold running water. If using defrosted cleaned shrimp, skip this step. Either way, dry the shrimp *well* with paper towels and set them aside.

Clean the sea scallops by peeling off and discarding the little strip of muscle that is attached to one side. (If your scallops are somewhat old the muscle strip may not be there.) Place the scallops in a colander and wash them well under cold running water—keep an eye open for specks of dark sand. Drain the scallops well and roll them in paper towels to dry them thoroughly. If the scallops are very large, cut them into ¹/₂"- to ³/₄"-thick pieces (it's the thickness that determines the cooking time, not how wide they are). If you're using bay scallops, don't remove the tiny strip of muscle, it's tender. Either way, set the scallops aside while you're preparing the sauce.

Put the bacon fat or vegetable oil into a skillet or stew-type pot that's wide and deep enough to hold all the seafood in about 2 layers with about 2 cups of sauce. Place the skillet over medium-high heat and add the onion, peppers, and celery. Cook the vegetables, adjusting the heat if necessary and stirring frequently, until they have become slightly wilted and a little brown, about 5 minutes. When the vegetables are ready, turn the heat to low and stir in the garlic, thyme, oregano, bay leaf, and cayenne, cooking for about 30 seconds. Add the flour and continue to stir for about 1 minute more to cook away its raw taste. Add the tomatoes and their juice, and simmer the sauce, covered, over very low heat, about 10 minutes, or until the vegetables are almost tender and it's very thick. Stir the sauce once or twice during this period. Season it generously with salt, pepper, and Tabasco, and set it aside. The sauce can be made 3 or 4 days in advance and refrigerated, but be sure to heat it through before continuing with the recipe.

In a separate bowl, mix the scallops and shrimp together and season them well with salt and pepper. (If you're using bay scallops that are *smaller* than ¹/₂" in width, don't mix them in with the shrimp at this point—see Note.) Remove about one half of the sauce to a bowl, spreading the remaining sauce evenly over the bottom of the skillet or pot. Distribute the seafood evenly over the sauce in the skillet and spread the reserved sauce over the top of the seafood—it won't completely cover. Place the skillet over medium-high heat and, without stirring, heat the mixture until you see 3 or 4 bubbles at the surface. Reduce the heat to very low, tightly cover the skillet, and gently simmer the mixture until the shrimp are white throughout and the scallops are still slightly translucent in the center, 8 to 12 minutes, cutting one of each to check, if you're unsure. (If you prefer, you can bake the Creole in a preheated 325° oven once the bubbles have come to the surface.)

The Creole will be much thinner now from the shellfish juices. Taste it for seasoning and adjust it with salt, a generous amount of pepper, and additional Tabasco, if you like.

TO SERVE: Ladle the Creole into warm soup plates or bowls, discarding the bay leaf. Sprinkle each serving with chopped parsley, and serve right away.

NOTE: If you've reserved bay scallops, add them approximately halfway through the cooking (depending on their size), pressing them into the simmering mixture as best as possible. Cover the skillet again and finish cooking.

Cutting bell peppers and celery into small dice is simple. First cut out the stem and core of the peppers and discard them. Cut the pepper in half lengthwise and remove the seeds and ribs. Place the halves on a cutting board, skin side *down,* and cut them into long strips about ¼″ wide (cutting through the pulpy inside is easier, your knife doesn't slip and even a dull knife can cut into its flesh). Now, keeping all the strips parallel to one another, turn them so they are horizontal to you. Doing a small bunch at a time, cut across the strips into ¼″ widths. When you finish cutting all the strips, you've got nice, even ¼″ dice.

To dice celery, first cut the stalks in half crosswise. Then cut them lengthwise into long strips about ¼″ wide. Turn the strips horizontal to you and cut across them into ¼″ pieces, just like the bell pepper.

Chunky Grilled Seafood Salad with Mustard and Horseradish

4 servings

PREP AND
COOKING
TIME
45–55
minutes
includes
optional
shrimp
cleaning
time

*S*erve this warm if you can, right off the grill—the seafood's cut into large pieces so the shrimp still crunch like shrimp, the scallops remain their voluptuous selves, and the swordfish chunks stay meaty and moist. Or, you can grill small, individual, swordfish steaks and pile the other tossed shellfish on top, letting the vinaigrette spill over it all. It's good as an appetizer or a main course, at room temperature for home, and chilled if you take it to the beach or on a picnic. (But add the horseradish just before you serve it, it makes the swordfish mushy.) And, of course, in the winter you can always poach the seafood instead. Mussels and pieces of lobster and salmon fillet make good additions, too.

$^1/_2$ pound sea scallops, $^3/_4''$–1" in height (or bay scallops, see Notes)

$^1/_2$ pound large shrimp in the shell, *or* approximately 7 ounces frozen, cleaned shrimp, defrosted (about 14 pieces)

$^1/_4$ pound cleaned calamari

2 teaspoons red wine or other vinegar

2 tablespoons fresh squeezed lemon juice

2$^1/_2$ teaspoons Dijon mustard, preferably French

$^1/_4$ teaspoon Worcestershire sauce

1 tablespoon prepared grated horseradish with a little of its liquid, or to taste

6$^1/_2$ tablespoons olive oil

2 tablespoons minced shallot or white onion or white of scallion

2 teaspoons capers, preferably the tiny ones called nonpareil

$^1/_3$ cup finely slivered red bell pepper, about 1" long

$^1/_4$ cup finely slivered green bell pepper, about 1" long

Salt and freshly ground black or white pepper to taste

Five or six 8" wooden skewers, soaked in water for at least 30 minutes before using

$^3/_4$ pound swordfish in one piece, $^3/_4''$ thick, *or* four 3-ounce steaks

Optional: 2 cups baby greens or other beautiful lettuces (such as red-tipped), washed and dried

Optional: ¹/₂ cup lump crab meat, picked clean of cartilage (see page 197),
    or king, Dungeness, snow, or Maine crab meat
Optional: 1 tablespoon roughly chopped fresh dill

TO PREPARE: Start a medium-hot fire in the grill. Fifteen minutes before you're going to grill the seafood, put the grill grate 4″ to 5″ above the glowing coals if it isn't already there. (I also like to brush the top of the grate with vegetable oil just before grilling to help prevent sticking.)

Clean the scallops by peeling off and discarding the little strip of muscle that is attached to one side. (If your scallops are somewhat old, the muscle strip may not be there.) Place the scallops in a colander and wash them well under cold running water—keeping an eye open for specks of dark sand. Drain the scallops well and roll them in paper towels to dry them thoroughly. Place them in a bowl large enough to hold them, the shrimp, and the calamari, and refrigerate them.

If using shrimp in the shell, peel them and save the shells for shrimp oil or shrimp broth (see Pantry, to Make), or discard them. Pick up a shrimp and make a shallow slit down the middle of the length of the back to expose the black intestine. Slit all the shrimp and lift out the black intestine with the point of your paring knife or flush it out under cold running water. If using defrosted, cleaned shrimp, skip this step. Either way, dry the shrimp *well* with paper towels and add them to the scallops.

If the calamari bodies are longer than 3″, cut one side of them in half lengthwise to open them up completely; dry them well with paper towels, and add them to the bowl of seafood. Leave smaller calamari and any tentacle sections whole. Refrigerate the bowl of seafood if the kitchen is hot, or set the bowl aside while you prepare the vinaigrette.

Place the red wine vinegar, lemon juice, mustard, and Worcestershire sauce in a medium mixing bowl and whisk the ingredients together until they're smooth. If you're serving the seafood salad warm, whisk in the horseradish (see Notes). Gradually whisk in 5 tablespoons of the olive oil (use the coiled snake towel trick if the bowl isn't steady, see page 153) to make a slightly thick vinaigrette. Stir in the shallot and capers, and add the slivered bell peppers if you're using the vinaigrette within a day. Season the vinaigrette with salt and pepper and set it aside at room temperature while you prepare the seafood. Otherwise, refrigerate the vinaigrette for up to a week, adding the slivered bell peppers the day you use it, and letting it come to room temperature before tossing it with the grilled seafood.

Drizzle 1 tablespoon of the olive oil over the mixed seafood and season it well with salt and pepper. Toss it gently but thoroughly with a rubber spatula.

Remove the wooden skewers from the water. Pick out and thread the scallops onto the skewers through their sides. (If you push the skewer through their ends, there's a good chance they'll split, plus they won't lie flat on the grill.) Leave about $^1/_4''$ space between each scallop (so they cook all around) and at least $^1/_2''$ at each end, so you can handle the skewers. Thread the shrimp on the skewers by pushing the skewer through the back at its thickest part, and then through the tail section. This way they'll all lie flat on the grill. (Scallops and shrimp cook at slightly different rates—skewering them separately lets you control their timing.) Do not skewer the calamari, it goes straight on the grill. Rub the remaining $^1/_2$ tablespoon of olive oil over both sides of the swordfish and season it with salt and pepper.

Before you begin grilling, keep in mind the relative timing: The swordfish cooks in 5 to 6 minutes, the scallops in 4 to 6 minutes, the shrimp in 3 to 5 minutes, and the calamari in about 1 minute. If grilling everything at once seems complicated, do it in separate batches—the scallops and shrimp first, followed by the swordfish, and then finish up with the calamari. This way you can keep a close eye on everything.

Place the scallop skewers over the coals. Grill them on one side for 3 to 4 minutes, or until they're golden brown. Turn the skewers over and grill them for 1 to 2 minutes more, or until they're springy-firm when gently squeezed on their sides and slightly translucent in the center when cut with a knife. For well done, cook another minute or two. Remove the scallop skewers to a platter.

Grill the shrimp skewers for 1 to 3 minutes on one side, turn them over, and grill them until they're firm and completely opaque when cut open, about 2 minutes more. Remove the shrimp skewers to the platter.

Grill the swordfish, turning it once midway to cook through, 5 to 6 minutes total. Place it on the platter.

Grill the calamari for 15 to 30 seconds on each side, just until they turn milky white, and place them on the platter.

Remove the shrimp and scallops from the skewers, cut each piece in half crosswise, and put them in a large mixing bowl. Cut the calamari in half the long way, if it isn't cut already, and then across into thin strips, and add the calamari to the bowl. Remove any skin and dark fat from the swordfish and cut it into $^3/_4''$ to $1''$ chunks. Add the swordfish chunks to the bowl. (Or leave the swordfish whole, if using it as a base.) Discard any liquid on the platter.

If you've cut the swordfish, add all the vinaigrette and gently toss the seafood with a rubber spatula. Taste the salad for seasoning and add salt, pepper, and horseradish to taste, if you haven't added it before. (If you're serving the seafood on top of the swordfish, dress the scallops, shrimp, and calamari with about two thirds of the vinaigrette and reserve the rest.)

TO SERVE: Place the baby greens or red lettuce, if using, on dinner plates and spoon the seafood salad on top of the greens. Garnish with the crab meat and fresh dill, if using, and serve right away. (Or place the individual swordfish steaks on the greens, drizzle each one with the reserved vinaigrette, and spoon the dressed seafood on top, garnishing with the crab meat and dill, if you like.)

NOTES: If sea scallops are unavailable, substitute bay scallops and gently poach them in barely simmering water seasoned with a little salt, bay leaf, and a slice of lemon for 1 to 2 minutes. Drain and add them to the grilled seafood.

The horseradish attacks the texture of the swordfish—it becomes mushy. So prepare the salad, refrigerate it, and stir in the horseradish before serving, or omit it.

Seafood Stew

4 servings

PREP AND
COOKING
TIME
40–55
minutes
includes
optional
shrimp
cleaning time

*I*t's just about all in here: shrimp and scallops and clams and oysters and mussels. And you can add anything else I'm leaving out. This stew is sort of a cross between a chowder and a "stew-stew." It's got lots of sauce whose base is shrimp or lobster broth (from your freezer) or chicken broth, and the abundant flavors the little sea creatures add to the pot. Serve some boiled potatoes and a salad, and you've got it!

³/₄ pound large shrimp in the shell, *or* 8–9 ounces frozen, cleaned shrimp, defrosted (about 21 pieces)

¹/₄ cup bacon fat or butter

1¹/₂ cups small diced onions (see page 161)

2 large garlic cloves, chopped

³/₄ cup red bell pepper, cut into ¹/₂″ dice

1 teaspoon *herbes de Provence* or a mixture of dried herbs such as thyme, basil, rosemary, fennel seed, and marjoram

1 small bay leaf

2¹/₂ tablespoons flour

2 cups *hot* shrimp or lobster broth (see Pantry, to Make) or hot chicken broth

8 littleneck clams in the shell, scrubbed and drained well

1 pound cultivated mussels, scrubbed and drained well

³/₄ pound bay scallops or sea scallops, cut in ¹/₂″–³/₄″-thick pieces, rinsed, and dried on paper towels

¹/₂ cup shucked oysters and their liquor (8–15 medium to large)

¹/₄ cup half and half or milk

Salt and freshly ground black or white pepper to taste

1 tablespoon mixed chopped fresh (flat-leaf or curly) parsley and minced fresh chives

TO PREPARE: If using shrimp in the shell, peel them and save the shells for shrimp oil or toward another round of shrimp broth, or discard them. Pick up a shrimp and make a shallow slit down the middle of the length of the back to expose the black intestine. Slit all the shrimp and lift out the black intestine with the point of your paring knife or flush it out under cold running water. If using defrosted, cleaned shrimp, skip this step. Either way, dry the shrimp *well* with paper towels.

Melt the bacon fat or butter over medium heat in a large stew-type pot and stir in the onions, garlic, red pepper, dried herbs, and bay leaf. Cook the vegetables, stirring occasionally, until the edges of the onions are translucent, about 5 minutes. Turn the heat to low and stir in the flour. Cook the flour, stirring constantly, about 1 minute. Gradually whisk in the *hot* broth. Bring the sauce to a quick boil over high heat, whisking, then immediately reduce the heat so it simmers gently. The mixture will be thick.

Drop the clams into the sauce and simmer them, tightly covered, for 5 to 7 minutes, or until you begin to see a narrow opening slit in most of them. Stir the mussels into the clams and simmer them, covered, about 2 minutes. (The sauce base will still be very thick at this point.) Stir in the shrimp and scallops and simmer them, covered, for 1 or 2 minutes. By this time, the clams and mussels should be opening their shells, adding their juices to the pot, and the shrimp and scallops should be at least half cooked. If not, simmer, covered, for another minute or two (see Note). When the shrimp are firm and white throughout, the scallops slightly translucent in the center, and the various shells have opened about an inch, add the oysters with their liquor, and heat for another 30 to 60 seconds.

TO SERVE: With a slotted spoon or a ladle, transfer the seafood to individual warm bowls or soup plates. In a small saucepan, heat the half and half or milk and stir it into the sauce. Season the sauce with salt and pepper, if necessary. Pour the sauce over the seafood in the bowls, sprinkle each serving with parsley and chives, and serve right away.

NOTE: If the clams aren't open yet and everything else is ready, remove the other seafood with a slotted spoon and continue cooking the clams, covered, until they open. Then drop in the oysters and their liquor and proceed with the recipe.

Appendices

PANTRY, TO MAKE

While the scope of this book doesn't allow for lots of "made-from-scratch" pantry items, there are a few I can't imagine doing without, at least some of the time. All of them have the advantage of being storable, whether as a "preserve," or in the freezer, or just having the precious ability to be refrigerated for practically weeks at a time. So here they are—you'll just have to decide for yourself if any of them mean as much to you as they do to me.

Roasted Garlic

<table>
<tr><td>PREP AND
COOKING
TIME
about 1¹/₄
hours</td><td>The beauty of this stuff, which holds for weeks, covered in its roasting oil, in the refrigerator, is very simple—it just tastes great! Mellow and nutty, soft and sweet, some of us think of it as its own food</td></tr>
</table>

group! Spoon it out, chop it a little—or not—and mix it into sauces, vegetables, grains, or pastas; spread it on bread; and dream about it. Just make it. And don't forget to use the oil it's sitting in.

> 2 heads garlic
> ¹/₂ cup olive oil

TO PREPARE: Preheat the oven to 250°.

Separate the garlic into individual *unpeeled* cloves. Place them in a small, oven-proof pan, and pour the olive oil over them. Place the pan over low heat, just long enough to heat the olive oil gently, 3 or 4 minutes. Cover the pan and place it in the oven. Bake the garlic cloves until they're tender and soft, about 1 hour. Remove the pan from the oven and let the garlic cool in the oil.

When the garlic is cool enough to handle, remove it from the oil and peel—or squeeze—the cloves to release them from their skins (peeling them keeps them more intact). Discard the skins, cover the peeled cloves with their roasting oil (straining it if necessary), and store them, covered, in the refrigerator for up to 3 weeks.

Preserved Lemons

PREP TIME
15 minutes +
3 weeks'
pickling time

*P*reserved lemons are an indispensable part of Moroccan cuisine—they're whole lemons, sliced, quartered, or cut open like petals, lightly coated with coarse salt and allowed to bathe in oil—and sometimes more lemon juice—until the entire lemon, rind and all, becomes mellow and tender, with only an edge of sharpness. *Your* work is done in minutes—the 3-week pickling-in-the-jar process does itself. At the end of it, you have delicate, almost transparent lemons ready to be added to any seafood recipe (or chicken or lamb or vegetable or grain). They keep in the refrigerator for at least 4 months. I learned this method from a young Israeli chef who told me it was his mom's way; he also said she sometimes liked to slip garlic cloves and fresh herbs into the oil before the lemons began their transformation.

3 lemons
Approximately $^1/_4$ cup coarse salt, preferably kosher (it's pure and free of additives)
Approximately $^1/_2$ cup vegetable or olive oil
One 1-pint Mason-type jar or another glass jar with a tight lid
1 wooden skewer

TO PREPARE: Rinse the lemons in cold water and wipe them dry. Slice off both ends of the lemons and discard them. Slice the lemons $^1/_4''$ thick and remove the seeds with the tip of a paring knife.

Place the salt on a small plate and lightly dip one side of each lemon slice into the salt. Place the coated slice in the jar, salt side up. Continue dipping the slices and stacking them in the jar until all the slices are done. If you've reached the top with slices to go, slip the rest around the perimeter of the stack. Pour the oil into the jar to cover the slices by about $^1/_2''$. Screw on the lid securely and turn the jar upside down once or twice to make sure the oil penetrates throughout. Cut a wooden skewer so it's slightly longer than the height of the lemon stack, but shorter than the jar. Remove the lid and push the skewer through from the top of the stack to the bottom. This keeps the lemons from floating out of the oil. Screw the lid back on securely and with a label or marking pen, mark the jar with the date the lemons *will be ready*. Keep the jar on a level surface at room temperature for 3 weeks.

When the lemons are done, store them in the jar, still in the oil, in the refrigerator.

NOTE: Unlike sun-dried tomato oil, I don't use preserved lemon oil for cooking because I feel the salt overpowers its taste.

Shrimp or Lobster Broth

Approximately
2 cups

PREP AND
COOKING
TIME
40–60 minutes

*I*f you freeze your leftover raw shrimp or cooked lobster shells you can make a broth whenever you want (freezing that too) that will add even more flavor to the Seafood Stew on page 276 or Surimi Baked with Red and Green Peppers, page 250. Or use the broth as a base for your own seafood soup. You can double, triple, or quadruple this if you want.

1$^1/_2$ tablespoons butter

$^1/_2$ cup thinly sliced celery

$^1/_4$ cup thinly sliced carrot

$^3/_4$ cup thinly sliced onion

Optional: 5–6 fresh (flat-leaf or curly) parsley sprigs

2 lightly packed cups raw shrimp shells, defrosted if frozen, or chopped cooked lobster shells, or a combination of the two (see Note)

Approximately 2$^1/_2$ cups cold water

2 teaspoons tomato puree, *or* 1 teaspoon tomato paste, *or* $^1/_4$ cup juice from canned tomatoes, if you have an open can

$^1/_4$ teaspoon dried thyme

1 bay leaf

Optional: $^1/_4$ teaspoon whole allspice berries

TO PREPARE: In a medium saucepan, melt the butter over low to medium heat and stir in the celery, carrot, onion, and parsley sprigs, if using. Cover the pan and cook the vegetables, stirring occasionally and regulating the heat so they don't brown, until they're almost half cooked, about 10 minutes. Add the shells, raise the heat to medium, and cook them, stirring occasionally, 1 to 2 minutes. The shrimp shells will begin to turn pink.

Add the cold water just to cover the shells and bring the liquid to a boil over high heat. As soon as the liquid boils, reduce the heat to low and add the tomato puree, paste, or juice. With a ladle or large kitchen spoon, skim any impurities from the surface of the liquid. Add the thyme, bay leaf, and allspice, if using, partially cover the pan, and regulate the heat so the liquid simmers very gently.

Simmer the broth, pressing the shells down into the liquid occasionally, until it has a good, but light, seafood flavor, about 20 minutes for shrimp and 30 minutes for lobster. Strain the broth, pressing on the shells to extract as much flavor as possible, and discard the solids. Cool the broth and use it right away or freeze it for up to 2 months.

NOTE: Break up the leftover shells into small pieces by chopping them with a large knife or cleaver, smashing them with a mallet (kind of fun, but probably not too efficient!), pushing them through a meat grinder, or pulsing them in a food processor, and freeze them. (The bodies of "soft-shell" lobsters are soft enough to partially rip by hand before chopping.) The smaller you chop or grind the lobster shells, the more flavor you'll extract from them, and the more quickly. If you use a food processor, do a small amount at a time. Place the shells into the bowl and *pulse* them into small pieces (they won't come out consistent in size). But don't try to machine-chop any shells that are heavy and thick, like claws. For the machine's sake, do them by hand or discard them.

Shrimp or Lobster Oil

Makes
approximately
½ cup shrimp
oil or ¾ cup
lobster oil

PREP AND
COOKING
TIME
25–30 minutes

*F*reeze your raw shrimp or cooked lobster shells—you can make shrimp or lobster oil to dress up your fillets with a minimum of effort. Simmer the shells with olive oil, on top of the stove or in the oven, to infuse the oil deeply with shellfish flavor. The oil emerges light orange in color, with a flavor that kind of sneaks up on you and then settles in. Strain it, and use the oil like this:

1. Spoon a little of it, simply seasoned with salt and freshly ground pepper, over broiled or baked fillets such as sole, flounder, grouper, bass, red snapper, halibut, or monkfish, or use it on scallops.

2. Sauté seafood in a little of it in a nonstick pan, and drizzle it with more when it's served.

3. Whisk a room-temperature tablespoon or two of it into prepared mayonnaise as a sauce for chilled cooked fish, scallops, lobster, or crab meat; or use it with fried fillets such as catfish or perch, or with fried calamari.

4. Use it, at room temperature, in place of part of the vegetable or olive oil when, and if, you make your own mayonnaise.

It's one of those blessedly ready, have-on-hand ingredients for times when the thought of cooking is not necessarily a welcome one! But lest I suggest that its sole purpose is for use "in a pinch," far from it—it's unexpectedly lovely and elegant enough for a party. And it will hold well, tightly covered, in the refrigerator for several months.

> 2 generous cups lightly packed raw shrimp shells (from approximately
> 1½ pounds shrimp, *or* 2 cups chopped, cooked lobster shells (from 1–2
> whole lobsters) or a combination of the two—see Note)
> 1 cup olive oil

TO PREPARE: Preheat the oven to 325° if you're preparing this in the oven. Either way, put the raw shrimp, or cooked, chopped lobster shells into a small (oven-proof, if using the oven) saucepan deep enough to hold them and the oil comfortably. Add the oil and stir thoroughly. Place the saucepan over medium heat and stir a few times while the oil gets hot, 2 to 3 minutes. Cover the pan tightly and turn the heat as low as possible, or put the pan in the oven. Let the shells simmer for 15 to 20 minutes, stirring them once or twice. Turn off the heat, or remove the pan from the oven, and pour the oil through a strainer into a bowl, pressing on the shells with a wooden spoon. Discard the shells and let the oil cool, then cover and refrigerate it.

NOTE: Chop the shells with a cleaver, or very large knife, into small pieces. Or, if you prefer to do it by machine, start by hand-ripping whatever shells may be soft enough, such as the tails, into pieces. Doing a small amount at a time, place the shells into the bowl of a food processor and *pulse* them to small pieces (they won't come out consistent in size). But don't try to machine-chop any shells that are heavy and thick like claws. For the machine's sake, do them by hand or discard them.

Rosemary-Garlic-Lemon Marinade

Approximately
1 cup

PREP TIME
15 minutes

This is one of the great use-with-everything marinades—it's utterly packed with rosemary and garlic flavor and it holds for weeks. I try to keep a jar of it in my refrigerator at all times because it's good with trout, salmon, cod, snapper, bass, halibut, or grouper fillets; swordfish, tuna, or shark steaks; lobster, and soft-shell crabs. In the non-seafood world, it's perfect for pasta, chicken, veal, and for marinating goat cheese!

2 tablespoons lightly packed fresh rosemary leaves (see Note)
1 large garlic clove, unpeeled
Grated zest of 3 lemons (about 1 1/2 teaspoons), no white pith (see page 133)
1 cup olive oil
Salt and freshly ground black or white pepper to taste

TO PREPARE: Roughly chop the rosemary with a large knife and put it in the food processor—this helps the processor chop it better. Crush the garlic clove with the side of a large knife, peel it, and put it in the food processor with the lemon rind. Process the ingredients for about 1 minute to break them up and combine their flavors. Add the olive oil and process everything until the solids are chopped in tiny pieces, about 2 minutes. Season the oil with salt and pepper.

The oil can be used immediately, at room temperature, or covered and refrigerated for several weeks. (The flavor continues to develop—if at any point it becomes strong for you, add a little more olive oil.) Just be sure to let it come to room temperature before serving.

NOTE: If the rosemary *stems* are *very* young, they're tender and pliable—don't worry about some of them getting into the mix. They'll be chopped up fine as you process everything and are perfectly edible. More mature stems, however, are woody and indigestible.

Great Fish Pantry

This is a list of the storable foodstuffs that appear in the book. You don't need to have all these ingredients, of course, but it can be useful, and fun, to check out the list for basic and intriguing items when setting up your own pantry.

CONDIMENTS:
Anchovy paste or fillets
Capers, preferably the tiny ones called nonpareil
Chinese prepared ingredients:
Oyster-flavored sauce
Black Bean-garlic sauce
Hoisin sauce
Plum sauce
Chili-garlic sauce
Soy sauce
Horseradish, prepared
Mediterranean olives such as:
Amfissa, Atalanti, Sicilian, kalamata, Gaeta, and niçoise
Mirin (Japanese sweet rice seasoning liquid, preferably Eden brand)
Mustard:
Dijon, preferably French
Pommery, whole-grain, preferably French
English-style dry, preferably Colman's
Honeycup, preferably from Canada
Tabasco sauce
Tamari sauce, preferably Eden brand
Worcestershire sauce

OILS:
Hazelnut, preferably French
Hot pepper sesame, preferably Eden brand
Olive:

Pure
Extra-virgin
Toasted sesame, preferably Eden brand
Sesame
Vegetable
Walnut, preferably French

VINEGARS:
Balsamic
Brown rice wine, preferably Eden brand, or rice wine
Cider
Red wine
Aged Sherry
Tarragon

DRIED HERBS AND SPICES:
Basil leaves
Bay leaves
Cayenne
Celery salt
Chili powder
Chinese five-spice powder
Coriander, ground
Cumin, ground and whole
Curry powder
Dill leaves
Fennel seed, whole
Garlic powder
Herbes de Provence
Hot red pepper flakes, crushed
Lemon peel
Marjoram leaves
Orange peel
Oregano leaves
Paprika, preferably Sweet

Hungarian
Peppercorns:
Whole black
Whole white
Rosemary leaves
Sage leaves, rubbed
Savory
Tarragon leaves
Thyme leaves

CANNED AND BOTTLED:
Black beans
Black-eyed peas
Chicken broth
Chick-peas
Chipotle peppers in adobo sauce (Mexican)
Coconut milk (Thai)
Pickled jalapeño or serrano chiles (Mexican)
Plum tomatoes, preferably from Italy
Roasted red peppers
Sun-dried tomatoes in oil
Tahini
Tomatillos (Mexican green tomatolike fruit)

DRIED THINGS:
Ancho chiles (Mexican)
Bread crumbs

PASTA:
Orzo
Soba noodles (Japanese buckwheat)

NUTS:
Pine
Pecans

FROZEN:
Artichoke hearts and/or
  bottoms
Black-eyed peas

CHEESES:
Romano
Parmigiano-Reggiano
Feta
Medium-sharp Cheddar
Mild Cheddar, Colby, or
  Monterey Jack

OTHER:
Cornmeal
Cornstarch
Flour:
  All-purpose
  Whole-wheat
Rice
Salt, preferably kosher or
  sea
Tortillas:
  Corn
  Flour

WINES FOR COOKING:
Marsala, dry
Sherry, dry
Pernod or Ricard
Vermouth, dry (white)
Wine:
  Red
  White

Here's a list of the fresh herbs I've used in recipes throughout the book. While they can't be considered long-term "storable," unless you're growing them in the garden or in a sunny window, they can hold a good week in the refrigerator if they were very fresh when you bought them. The ginger, however, does hold, unpeeled, in the refrigerator for a couple of weeks.

FRESH HERBS AND ONE SPICE!:
Basil
Cilantro
Chives
Dill

Ginger
Mint
Parsley, flat-leaf or curly
Rosemary

Sage
Tarragon
Thyme

About Frozen Fillets

The bottom line is that some frozen fish fillets are very good, some are good, and some are downright terrible. In general, the safest bet is buying them "individually quick frozen," so each piece has been frozen and separately wrapped before being packaged (and they're not naked and flying around in a bag; for more on this see page 266). Packaged this way, pieces can be removed and thawed a few at a time. And be sure always to thaw them in the refrigerator, nice and slow, so no harmful bacteria develop and they lose as little of their precious bodily fluids as possible. And speaking of fluids, they'll need to be thoroughly dried with paper towels before cooking.

However, of the frozen fillets that I've had, two kinds hold up best: One, ocean perch, comes in a frozen rectangular block, at least where I buy it. The other, catfish, is "individually quick frozen." Both the perch and the catfish retain most of their natural sweet flavor and tender juiciness after thawing and cooking them. (The catfish can be baked or grilled while still frozen!) You may find others in your market that you think are worth eating, so perhaps a little experimentation is in order! But that said, here are a few general guidelines based on New York supermarket products.

VERY GOOD

Perch (thawed): Sauté, bake, or broil.

Catfish fillets (thawed): Sauté, grill, bake, or broil.

When grilling, start with a hot fire, and oil the dry fillets well. Place them flat side down first (the side where the skin used to be), and turn them over about midway through their cooking, or as soon as the skin side is golden.

Catfish fillets (still frozen): Roast and grill.

Brush the frozen fillets with olive oil and season them to taste. (Or brush them with the Tamari-Coriander Marinade on page 16.) To roast them, cook them in a 425° oven until opaque. To grill them, slip the seasoned fillets into one of those specially constructed fish grill baskets (that you've oiled first) and place it on the hot grill, turning it once during grilling.

ALL THE FOLLOWING ARE BEST COOKED BY INDIRECT HEAT, LIKE BAKING, TO RETAIN THEIR FLAVOR AND MOISTURE

CAN BE ACCEPTABLE

Halibut when "individually quick frozen": Sauté, broil, bake.

I found different sizes and cuts within one package. Juicy meat, big flakes, but strangely crunchy, then a little mealy, with a slightly "flat" flavor.

Snapper (unnamed from Chile) when "individually quick frozen": Sauté, broil, bake.

Juicy meat, good flakes with faintly natural-sweet flavor. But I found vastly different sizes within one package, and some pieces were tough.

NOT SO GOOD (AND THAT'S BEING POLITE)

Cod: Sauté or bake.

> Big, juicy flakes, but they had a strong, very unpleasant chemical taste. Fillets were very different sizes within the package.

Sole: Don't bother.

> Thin, shredded, ripped fillets that looked, handled, and tasted like shoe leather—or were they more like boiled wool? On top of that, they had a strong chemical taste.

Quickest of the Quick

Recipes—from bass to lobster and simple to elegantly simple—that take 30 minutes or less.
Delicate White Fleshed Fillets:

Bass

Sautéed with Lime Sesame Oil, page 8

Broiled with Garlic-Parsley Bread Crumb Sauce, page 6

Roasted with Herb Pepper Rub, page 10

Broiled with Caper Vinaigrette, Watercress, and Avocado, page 4

Catfish

Grilled in Tamari-Coriander Marinade (without marinating), page 16

Sautéed with Black Pepper, Basil, and Lemon, page 18

Grilled with Spicy Mayonnaise, page 14

Cod

Sautéed with White Wine and Capers, page 24

Grouper

Broiled with Grain Mustard–Pineapple Vinaigrette, page 35

Halibut

Baked with Rosemary and Pre-served Lemon (with already-pre-pared preserved lemon), page 43

Monkfish

Grilled with Rosemary-Garlic-Lemon (without marinating), page 5

Grilled with Walnut-Herb-Olive Oil Sauce, page 56

Sautéed with Lemon-Shrimp (or oyster) Oil (with shellfish oil on hand), page 48

Perch

Sautéed with Buttery-Lemon Pecans, page 62

Baked "Adrienne" with Garlic, Lemon, and Herbs, page 58

Snapper

Sautéed with Rosemary–Brown Butter and Avocado, page 70

Grilled with Tomatillo Salsa, page 72

Sole

Broiled with Olive Oil, Mustard, and Dill, page 88

Sautéed with Tomatoes, Sage, and Lemon, page 84

Sautéed with Balsamic Brown Butter, page 78

Broiled with Red Onion–Herb Vinaigrette, page 82

Darker Fleshed Fillets with Richer Flavor:

Bluefish

Broiled with Mustard-Tarragon Vinaigrette, page 94

Baked with Lemon Pulp and White Wine, page 92

Mahimahi

Simmered in Tamari-Sesame Sauce, page 98

Sautéed with Butter and Lime, page 97

Pompano

Grilled with Mexican Chile Oil and Lime, page 103

Salmon

Poached with Basil Bread Crumbs, page 110

Roasted with Honey Mustard Sauce, page 118

Shad

Broiled Stuffed with Fresh Herbs, page 120

Shark

Sautéed with Fast Tomatoes, Gar-lic, and Hot Pepper Flakes, page 130

Grilled with Cumin Vinaigrette, page 128

Swordfish

Grilled with Sun-Dried Tomato Puree, page 146

Grilled with Chinese Plum–Mus-tard Sauce, page 148

Trout

Sautéed with Mustard-Curry Vinaigrette, page 152

Grilled with Walnut Oil (without marinating), page 156

Tuna

Broiled with Caesar Vinaigrette, page 158

Grilled with Artichokes and Tomatoes (with frozen artichoke hearts or bottoms only), page 170

Grilled with Chinese Oyster-Gin-ger Sauce (without marinating), page 166

Sea Animals with Shells and Armor:

Calamari (Squid)

Stir-Fried with Capers, Red Wine, and Basil, page 178

Recipes for the Grill

Here's a list of recipes that are great for summer grilling—some that call for grilling in the first place, and some that don't—and a short list of sauces and accompaniments (from recipes for less-grillable seafood) that are good for just about anything else that does grill well. Plus five "do-all" marinades that you can make ahead, refrigerate, and pull out to use at the last minute.

Let's talk about grill heat for a moment. Each grill, whether it's charcoal, electric, or gas, performs differently, and its accompanying directions may give you less than ideal instructions. Case in point: My daughter Rachel has a gas grill that tells you (the instructions are printed right on the grill—you have to appreciate that) to grill all fish at low temperature. However, certain thin fillets, like snapper or trout, if cooked at that temperature are likely to be cooked through before they have crisped and browned. In general, I prefer grilling over a medium-hot charcoal fire with a good bed of glowing, ashen coals to get the deep flavor and browning I like (imagining myself to be a mighty woodsman grilling bear over my fire!). But whatever you prefer, you may need to experiment a little with your grill, to find out what you like best. And by the way, has anyone yet made a grill with a nonstick rack?

DELICATE WHITE FLESHED FILLETS:

Catfish
Spicy Mayonnaise, page 14
Tamari-Coriander Marinade, page 16

Grouper
Tropical Fruit Salsa, page 32
Grain Mustard–Pineapple Vinaigrette, page 35
Spicy Black Beans, page 30
Ancho Chile Butter, page 28

Halibut
Curried Veggies, page 39

Monkfish
Lemon-Shrimp (or Lobster) Oil, page 48
Rosemary-Garlic-Lemon Oil, page 52
Walnut–Herb–Olive Oil Sauce, page 56
Roasted Garlic and Sherry Vinegar, page 54

Red Snapper
Black Olive Paste and Orange, page 66
Roasted Tomatoes, page 68
Tomatillo Salsa, page 72
Eggplant and Dill, page 74

DARKER FLESHED FILLETS WITH RICHER FLAVOR:

Mahimahi
Wilted Escarole, Spinach, and Basil, page 100

Pompano
Mexican Chile Oil and Lime, page 103
Indonesian Coconut-Lime Sauce, page 104

Salmon (grilling salmon can be tricky—check the basic instructions in recipe) page 116
Basil Vinaigrette, page 116
Green Hummus, page 114
Purple Cabbage, Mushrooms, and Scallions,

page 108
Spicy Ginger Mushrooms, page 112

Shark
Fast Tomatoes, Garlic, and Hot Pepper Flakes, page 130
Cumin Vinaigrette, page 128
Red Peppers, Red Onions, and Orange, page 132

Swordfish
Sun-Dried Tomato Puree, page 146
Onions and Tomatoes, page 140
Roasted Red Pepper and Mushroom Sauce, page 142
Marinated in Lemon, Rosemary, and Fennel, page 138
Chinese Plum–Mustard Sauce, page 148

Trout
Mustard-Curry Vinaigrette, page 152
Walnut Oil, page 156

Tuna
Deviled Shallot Butter, page 160
Caesar Vinaigrette, page 158
Balsamic Vinegar, Garlic, and Pine Nuts, page 164
Tart-Sweet Red Peppers and Mushrooms, page 168
Artichokes and Tomatoes, page 170
Quickly Braised with Purple Cabbage (cabbage cooked separately), page 162
Chinese Oyster-Ginger Sauce, page 166

SEA ANIMALS WITH SHELLS AND ARMOR:

Calamari (Squid)
Herbs and Greens, page 176

Lobster
Olive Oil, Tarragon, and Pernod, page 219
Ginger-Herb Butter, page 213
Avocado "Whipped Cream," page 217

Oysters in the Shell
Horseradish Butter, page 234

Sea Scallops
Olives in Olive Oil, page 244
In Portobellos with Parsley and Feta Cheese, page 246
Roasted Tomatoes and Garlic, page 238

Shrimp
Lime Shrimp, page 258
Boiled with Ginger-Cilantro Dip, page 254
Honey-Ginger-Soy Marinade, page 264

MIXED SEAFOOD
Chunky Grilled Seafood Salad, with Mustard and Horseradish, page 272

SAUCES OR ACCOMPANIMENTS FOR OTHER GRILLED SEAFOOD: (ADD YOUR OWN CHOICES, TOO)
Garlic-Chipotle Chile Mayonnaise (see calamari Fried Two Ways recipe, page 180)
Lime Sesame Oil (see bass recipe, page 8)
Garlic-Parsley Bread Crumb Sauce (see bass recipe, page 6)
Tomatoes and Basil (see soft-shell crab recipe, page 202)
Caper Vinaigrette, Watercress, and Avocado (see bass recipe, page 4)
Tomatoes, Olives, and Preserved Lemon (see crab

Good for Parties Too

These are dishes that can really perform at a dinner party: as hors d'oeuvre, as a first course, or as dinner! Some are a little elegant and some are fun. I'm sure you'll find others throughout the book you'll want to add to the list.

HORS D'OEUVRE
Swordfish
Tamari-Sesame Sauce as a marinade for cubes skewered individually and grilled (see mahimahi recipe, page 98)
Calamari (Squid)
Fried Two Ways with Garlic-Chipotle Chile Mayonnaise as a dip, page 180
Crab Meat
Chinese Black Bean–Garlic-Ginger Vinaigrette, mixed with a little chilled crab meat and spooned onto croutons, crackers, or cucumber rounds, or in Belgian endive leaves (see soft-shell crab recipe, page 207)
Sea Scallops
Chinese Plum–Mustard Sauce as a dip, scallops individually skewered and grilled (see swordfish recipe, page 148)
Green Hummus, thinned slightly if necessary, as a dip, scallops individually skewered and grilled

(and for vegetables) (see salmon recipe, page 114)
Shrimp, Grilled or Boiled
Ginger-Cilantro Dip, page 254
Basil Vinaigrette as a dip (see salmon recipe, page 116)
Indonesian Coconut-Lime Sauce as a dip (see pompano recipe, page 104)
Garlic-Parsley Bread Crumb Sauce as a dip (see bass recipe, page 6)
Chinese Plum–Mustard Sauce as a dip (see swordfish recipe, page 148)
Green Hummus as a dip (and for vegetables) (see salmon recipe, page 114)
Chinese Black Bean–Garlic Ginger Vinaigrette as a dip (see soft-shell crab recipe, page 207)
Grilled Lime Shrimp, page 258
Tamari-Sesame Sauce as a marinade (see mahimahi recipe, page 98)

Chinese Oyster-Ginger Sauce as a marinade (see tuna recipe, page 166)

FIRST COURSES
Sole
Red Onion–Herb Vinaigrette, page 82
Shark
With Sesame Noodles, page 134
Calamari (Squid)
Two Ways with Garlic-Chipotle Chile Mayonnaise as a dip, page 180
With Herbs and Greens, page 176
Clams
Over Olive Oil–Toasted Bread, page 186
In Red Wine with Tomato, page 190
Crab Meat
Avocado "Whipped Cream" dollop on chilled crab meat (see "Maine" lobster recipe, page 217)
With Fine Spaghetti, Garlic, and Olive Oil, page 194

Do-All Sauces and Accompaniments

While I've matched sauces and accompaniments throughout the book with a particular kind of seafood, many of these accompaniments are tremendously versatile and go equally well with other fillets and shellfish. Here's a list of the most adaptable; use them as you like!

GREAT DO-ALL MARINADES
FOR GRILLING
Tamari-Coriander Mari-
nade (catfish recipe, page
16)
Tamari-Sesame Sauce
(mahimahi recipe, page
98)
Rosemary-Garlic-Lemon
Marinade (Pantry, to Make,
page 286)
Chinese Oyster-Ginger
Sauce (tuna recipe, page
166)
Honey-Ginger-Soy Mari-
nade (shrimp recipe, page
264)

GREAT DO-ALL SAUCES AND
ACCOMPANIMENTS
Delicate White Fleshed
Fillets:
Caper Vinaigrette, Watercress,
and Avocado (bass recipe, page
4)
Fresh Green Herbs (cod recipe,
page 26)
Rosemary and Preserved Lemon
(halibut recipe, page 43)

Roasted Tomato Vinaigrette
(halibut recipe, page 45)
Rosemary-Garlic-Lemon Oil
(monkfish recipe, page 52)
"Adrienne" with Garlic, Lemon,
and Herbs (perch recipe, page
58)
Roasted Tomatoes (snapper
recipe, page 68)
Baked with Slivers of Carrot
and Fennel (snapper recipe, page
64)
Olive Oil, Mustard, and Dill
(sole recipe, page 88)
Balsamic Brown Butter (sole
recipe, page 78)
Red Onion–Herb Vinaigrette
(sole recipe, page 82)
Darker Fleshed Fillets with
Richer Flavor:
Mustard-Tarragon Vinaigrette
(bluefish recipe, page 94)
Lemon Pulp and White Wine
(bluefish recipe, page 92)
Butter and Lime (mahimahi
recipe, page 97)
Tamari-Sesame Sauce
(mahimahi recipe, page 98)

Basil Bread Crumbs (salmon
recipe, page 110)
Spicy Ginger Mushrooms
(salmon recipe, page 112)
Basil Vinaigrette (salmon recipe,
page 116)
Red Peppers, Red Onions, and
Orange (shark recipe, page 132)
Fast Tomatoes, Garlic, and Hot
Pepper Flakes (shark recipe,
page 130)
Roasted Red Pepper and Mush-
room Sauce (swordfish recipe,
page 142)
Sun-Dried Tomato Puree
(swordfish recipe, page 146)
Mustard-Curry Vinaigrette
(trout recipe, page 152)
Garlic and Fresh Herbs (trout
recipe, page 150)
Balsamic Vinegar, Garlic, and
Pine Nuts (tuna recipe, page
164)
Caesar Vinaigrette (tuna recipe,
page 158)
Tart-Sweet Red Peppers and
Mushrooms (tuna recipe, page
168)

Techniques and Tips

Throughout the book you see notes on kitchen hints, food lore, and techniques. I've listed them all here so you can look for the one that interests you and easily find its page.

CLEAN AIR TRICKS

I like my house to smell of good cooking, but I also like to have a choice as to what those smells will be! If you want to purify the air, here are three methods that make a difference. The first is preventative and perhaps the least effective, the other two function after the deed is done, and quite effectively so.

1. Moisten the fillets or seafood with white wine, dry vermouth, lemon juice, or vinegar before cooking, it helps to keep the fishy odor at bay.

2. Sage sticks, made by Southwest Pueblo Indians, are small tied bundles of dried native herbs—predominantly sage, obviously—that are burned to clean rooms of negativity. Not only do they rid the house of bad vibes and bad unseen presences, they sweeten and purify the air of unwanted cooking odors. They burn very slowly, translating their heat, as they do, into herbal wisps of smoke. I like to walk around my house carrying this smoldering torch, like an ambulatory, slightly otherworldly Statue of Liberty! To order them (and they cost between $1 and $2 apiece) write or call the Oke Oweenge Crafts Co-operative, makers of handmade traditional and contemporary Indian crafts, P.O. Box 1095, San Juan Pueblo, NM 87566. Phone: (505) 852-2372. It's best to call them in the morning, New Mexico time.

3. For a quite different aesthetic, there's the Paris-made Lampe Berger. It's a small, decorative, fluid-filled globe that's fitted with a wick and a burner. You light the wick, let it burn for two minutes, and then blow out the flame. The lamp then goes to work, absorbing and destroying unpleasant odors. When I first tried it, I felt my house smelled like someone's grandmother (certainly not mine!) had just scrubbed every surface, leaving me surrounded by that enthralling aroma of "clean"! My lamp is outfitted with "neutral" fluid, but other fragrances are available. For information, call Lampe Berger at 1 (800) 201-8382.

BIBLIOGRAPHY

James Beard Fish Cookery, James Beard, Warner Paperback Library, 1967.

More Classic Italian Cooking, Marcella Hazan, Knopf, 1978.

The Joy of Cooking, Irma S. Rombauer and Marion Rombauer Becker, Bobbs-Merrill, 1975.

The Encyclopedia of Fish Cookery, A. J. McClane, Holt, Rinehart and Winston, 1977.

The Good Cook/Techniques and Recipes, Fish, and Shellfish, Time-Life Books, 1979.

Pacific and Southeast Asian Cooking, Foods of the World Series, Time-Life Books, 1970.

The New World Guide to Beer, Michael Jackson, Courage Books, 1988.

French Country Cooking, Elizabeth David, Penguin Handbook, 1959.

On Food and Cooking, Harold McGee, Charles Scribner's Sons, 1984.

The Cuisines of Mexico, Diana Kennedy, Harper and Row, 1972.

365 Great Barbecue and Grilling Recipes, Lonnie Gandara, Harper Perennial, 1990.

The International Food and Wine Society's Guide to Spanish Cookery, Mary Hillgarth, Drake Publishing, 1971.

The Alaska Seafood *NEWSWATCH,* newsletter from Gault Communications.

The Complete Seafood Handbook, Restaurant Business Magazine, 1995.

In Madeleine's Kitchen, Madeleine Kamman, Atheneum, 1984.

New Cantonese Cooking, Eileen Yin-Fei Lo, Viking, 1988.

An Encyclopedia of Chinese Food and Cooking, Wonona W. and Irving B. Chang, Helene W. and Austin H. Kutscher, Crown, 1970.

The Thousand Recipe Chinese Cookbook, Gloria Bley Miller, Grosset & Dunlap, 1970.

Food, Waverly Root, Simon and Schuster, 1980.

National Fisheries Institute Information Series:

    Blue Water Fishing: Tuna, Mahi-mahi, Shark and Swordfish

    The Chesapeake Bay Industries: Blue Crab and Oyster

    New England Groundfish.

Seafood Savvy, A Consumer's Guide to Seafood Nutrition, Safety, Handling and Preparation, Cornell Cooperative Extension, 1992.

Seafood Nutrition, Joyce Nettleton, Osprey Books, 1985.

The Nutrition Bible, Jean Anderson, M.S. and Barbara Deskins, Ph.D., R.D, William Morrow, 1995.

Index